# Success! Passing the Professional Skills Tests for Teachers

CRITICAL
LEARNING

**You might also like the following books from Critical Publishing**

*Getting into Primary Teaching*
Ed. David Owen and Cathy Burnett
978-1-909682-25-2 In print

*Getting into Secondary Teaching*
Ed. Andy Davies and Mel Norman
978-1-910391-34-1 September 2015

*Primary School Placements: A Critical Guide to Outstanding Teaching*
Catriona Robinson, Branwen Bingle and Colin Howard
978-1-909330-45-0 In print

Our titles are also available in a range of electronic formats. To orderplease go to our website www.criticalpublishing.com or contact our distributor, NBN International, 10 Thornbury Road, Plymouth PL6 7PP, telephone 01752 202301 or email orders@nbninternational.com.

# Success! Passing the Professional Skills Tests for Teachers

Jenny Lawson, Annabel Charles
& Trish Kreft

First published in 2015 by Critical Publishing Ltd

British Library Cataloguing in Publication Data
A CIP record for this book is available from the British Library

ISBN: 978-1-910391-01-3

This book is also available in the following e-book formats:

MOBI ISBN: 978-1-910391-02-0
EPUB ISBN: 978-1-910391-03-7
Adobe e-book ISBN: 978-1-910391-04-4

Cover and text design by Greensplash Limited
Project Management by Out of House Publishing
Printed and bound in Great Britain by Bell & Bain, Glasgow

Critical Publishing
152 Chester Road
Northwich
CW8 4AL
www.criticalpublishing.com

# Contents

# Meet the authors

*Hi, I'm Jenny Lawson.*

*As a long-standing member of the AlphaPlus Consultancy, I have devised many online tests for trainee teachers. Along-side my teaching and examining career, I have authored, and been the series editor for, numerous texts for ICT and mathematics, from Key Stage 1 through to A level and GNVQ. Now retired from full-time teaching, I focus on my own writing and also offer mentoring for writers wanting to be published.*

*I'm Annabel Charles.*

*I have a background in secondary English teaching and test development. I currently work freelance on a range of projects linked to literacy and assessment, including teacher training and item writing.*

*I'm Trish Kreft.*

*I have over 35 years' experience of teaching and managing mathematics and teacher education in a variety of settings, including schools, further education, adult and community learning and university. Since 2006, I have been running my own training company as well as working as an independent consultant in mathematics teacher education, guidance and quality assurance.*

# Introduction

WELCOME TO SUCCESS!

## HOW THE BOOK IS STRUCTURED

After the initial section on 'Preparation and planning: your career path into teaching' and an overview of 'The Professional Skills Tests', this book is then split into two main sections: 'Literacy skills' and 'Numeracy skills'.

The literacy skills section is subdivided according to the skills test structure: spelling, grammar and comprehension. After each of these subsections, there are practice questions – 173 in all.

The numeracy section is presented as a series of topics: number, measure, statistics, presentation of data and algebra. For each topic, the essential knowledge is given, with examples followed by practice questions – 212 in all.

At the end of both the literacy and numeracy sections, there are four practice papers.

At the back of the book, there are answers to all questions and, for the numeracy questions, a 'Show me' section with the working for every question explained.

Finally, there are two glossaries – one each for literacy and numeracy – lists of acronyms and useful websites plus a comprehensive index.

## HOW TO USE THE INFORMATION IN THIS BOOK

Do the online practice tests to identify your strengths and weaknesses.

For your weakest topics, study the notes and examples, and try the practice questions. If you answer a question incorrectly in the numeracy section, read the 'Show me' explanation.

Only when you feel you have grasped the techniques involved for one topic should you move on to the next topic; and so on, until you have revised all necessary topics.

Now try a practice paper or two. For any incorrect answers, work out where you are going wrong. Read back over any relevant theory.

Go back and try another online test.

Repeat until you are confident you will pass the skills tests!

## WHY YOU NEED IT

Ideally, you need to pass first time. If you don't, you may not be offered a place on an initial teacher training (ITT) course.

If you don't pass first time, you can pay for two more attempts. If you fail all three attempts, you have to wait two years before you can have another go and then start your course.

## OVERVIEW OF THE BOOK FEATURES

You'll see a number of icons in the margins of the book and some recurring headings. These might occur anywhere and highlight particular activities or important information.

**KEY POINT:** draws your attention to a really important point within the text.

**GO ONLINE:** directs you to search for online sources of information.

**LOOK IT UP:** directs you to a hard-copy source of information.

**COMMON ERROR:** highlights commonly made mistakes that you should be aware of and seek to avoid.

**FREQUENTLY ASKED QUESTION:** highlights common questions.

**GLOSSARY ITEM:** any words that are defined in the glossary are highlighted in bold on their first appearance in the text, which might sometimes be in a heading, and further signalled by the glossary icon in the margin. The glossaries can be found at the back of the book.

**CALCULATOR ALLOWED:** this shows that you can use a calculator for the next and any subsequent numeracy questions.

**CALCULATOR NOT ALLOWED:** this indicates that you are not allowed to use a calculator for the next and any subsequent numeracy questions.

**TRY THIS:** this heading signals an exercise for you to try that relates specifically to the text you have just read or the section you are working through. The end of the example is also clearly indicated.

**PRACTICE QUESTIONS:** this heading is used before a batch of practice questions, in the same format as test questions, that relate to the section of text you have just read.

**EXAMPLE:** used for worked examples in the numeracy section of the book.

Full **PRACTICE PAPERS** appear at the end of parts three and four of this book and have a tint behind them so you can easily spot them.

A boxed feature identifies the ANSWERS to all the practice questions and the practice papers at the back of the book and the SHOW ME section of the answers gives you the detailed working for all the answers to the numeracy practice questions and practice papers.

# 1 Preparation and planning: your career path into teaching

If you are interested in becoming a teacher, visit the Get Into Teaching website at www.education.gov.uk/get-into-teaching.

Register with Get Into Teaching for personalised support and advice.

## ROUTES INTO TEACHING

To achieve qualified teacher status (QTS), some form of teacher training has to be completed. Initial teacher training (ITT) routes depend on what age range you want to teach, whether you want to specialise in any particular subject(s), any previous experience and your existing qualifications.

| | |
|---|---|
| Assessment only (AO) | For experienced teachers with a degree who have not yet achieved QTS<br>Assessed in a school<br>May not need further training |
| School-centred training (SCITT) | Learn on the job<br>Work as part of a teaching team during training<br>Duration: 1 year<br>End qualification: PGCE and/or master's-level credits |
| University-led training | For graduates and undergraduates<br>Based in a university, but with at least two school placements<br>End qualification: PGCE |
| Teach First | For outstanding graduates<br>Earn while you train<br>Work in a challenging school in a low-income community<br>Duration: 2 years |

| | |
|---|---|
| Researchers in Schools (RIS) | For academics who have completed (or are finishing) a doctorate<br>Salaried programme<br>School-based in non-selective state schools<br>Duration: 2 years |
| School Direct | For graduates who have been working for 3 years<br>Train while working in a school<br>Salaried programme<br>May include PGCE qualification |
| Troops to Teachers | For ex-service personnel |

Whichever route is taken, ITT includes an element of academic study, at least 24 weeks in at least two schools gaining practical classroom experience, and assessment by classroom observation.

## SCHOOL STRUCTURE

| Year | Ages | School | Key Stage | Examinations |
|---|---|---|---|---|
| Nursery | 3–4 | | Early Years Foundation Stage (EYFS) | |
| Reception | 4–5 | Infant or primary | | |
| 1 | 5–6 | | KS1 | |
| 2 | 6–7 | | | SATs |
| 3 | 7–8 | Junior or primary | KS2 | |
| 4 | 8–9 | | | |
| 5 | 9–10 | | | |
| 6 | 10–11 | | | SATs |
| 7 | 11–12 | Secondary | KS3 | |
| 8 | 12–13 | | | |
| 9 | 13–14 | | | SATs |
| 10 | 14–15 | | KS4 | |
| 11 | 15–16 | | | GCSE |
| 12 | 16–17 | Secondary or sixth-form college | KS5 | |
| 13 | 17–18 | | | A level, BTEC, etc |

## WHAT QUALIFICATIONS DO YOU NEED TO ENTER ITT?

Required qualifications depend on the age group you want to teach: primary or secondary.

| Qualification | Primary | Secondary |
| --- | --- | --- |
| Professional Skills Tests (literacy and numeracy) | ✓ | ✓ |
| GCSE grade C or equivalent in mathematics | ✓ | ✓ |
| GCSE grade C or equivalent in English | ✓ | ✓ |
| GCSE grade C or equivalent in science | ✓ | |
| A degree | ✓ | |
| A degree relevant to the subject to be taught OR attendance on an SKE (subject knowledge enhancement) course | | ✓ |

If you don't have a degree and want to teach mathematics, computing, physics, chemistry, languages or design and technology, the ITT provider may offer you a subject knowledge enhancement (SKE) course as part of the selection process.

Bursaries may also be available for these SKE courses, depending on the length of the course.

Find out more about SKE – search for the SKE course directory.

Classroom experience is also recommended and will strengthen your application.

If you hope to teach a secondary subject, the School Experience Programme (SEP), run by the National College for Teaching and Leadership (NCTL), offers placements providing opportunities to observe teaching and pastoral work, to talk to teachers and to plan and deliver part or all of a lesson.

If you are interested in teaching at primary level, one way to gain classroom experience is to organise it yourself though local contacts, or by using the EduBase portal, which lists all educational establishments in England and Wales.

Go to the EduBase portal and identify all schools within a 25-mile radius of your home.

The Get Into Teaching website at www.education.gov.uk/get-into-teaching offers good advice on how to secure classroom experience.

## WHAT QUALITIES DO I NEED?

- ○ A deep understanding of and enthusiasm for your own subject.
- ○ Commitment.
- ○ A positive attitude towards working with children.
- ○ Advanced communication and interpersonal skills.
- ○ Energy, enthusiasm and patience.

# 2 The Professional Skills Tests

Gaining a pass in the Professional Skills Tests is a prerequisite if you want to embark on Initial Teacher Training (ITT); the tests have to be taken – and passed – ahead of the start of ITT.

Details of candidates' bookings, the number of attempts and scores are recorded on a computerised online booking system and this information is made available to ITT providers. ITT providers may then use the results of the tests to inform their decisions as to which applicants are to be offered a place on an ITT course.

Failing to pass first time can adversely affect your prospects of gaining a place on an ITT course.

This is the recommended process:

○   Book a test appointment at a nearby test centre.
○   Submit an ITT application.
○   Prepare for the tests.
○   Take the tests.
○   Attend the ITT interview with test results.

There are a limited number of places on ITT courses so try to pass the Professional Skills Tests first time, and – to avoid disappointment – to schedule them well ahead of the start of your ITT course.

Passing the tests first time is the least expensive and quickest route. So, success is essential, and the key to success is in the preparation for the tests.

## WHO HAS TO TAKE THE TESTS?

All applicants for ITT courses, including early years ITT courses, are required to pass the Professional Skills Tests before commencing their course.

Applicants who haven't passed the tests, even if offered a conditional place, will not be allowed to start their course.

## BOOKING THE TEST

The appointments for the Professional Skills Tests are booked through learndirect. First, you need to register with learndirect. All contact with learndirect is via email, so you need a valid email address.

The information you enter on the registration forms online must match the documents you will present as proof of ID at the test centre. If they don't match, you will not be permitted to take the test on that occasion.

Having registered, you can access your details, book tests, manage your appointments and view any results.

Having booked a test appointment, you may cancel or reschedule, provided you give at least three working days' notice.

If you are unwell, think ahead to your test booking and consider rescheduling.

## WHERE TO TAKE THE TESTS AND WHAT TO EXPECT

Tests are taken at a test centre.

When booking the tests, choose the most convenient test centre for you.

The visit will be for approximately 90 minutes, or longer if you have requested – and been granted – additional test time.

The test centre will have a waiting area with drinking water available, free of charge, plus toilet facilities that you can use before or after the test.

On arrival, you will be given an information sheet to read, which explains the procedure.

A copy of the information sheet is available for download from the Department for Education (DfE) website at www.education.gov.uk/sta/professional.

The next step is validation. Your identity will be checked against the details provided when you registered for the test. Forms of identification and evidence as specified on the registration form must be provided.

If you fail to provide all that is required, you will not be permitted to take the test. The fee for the test is forfeited and another date will need to be booked. Since there is a deadline for the test, this could jeopardise your prospects of starting the ITT course.

If all the necessary paperwork is in order, the test supervisor will allocate a locker key. Everything – apart from your primary form of ID and the locker key – has to be put into the locker for the duration of the test. This includes mobile phones and other electronic devices and personal items such as outdoor clothing, money, food and drink.

Eating and smoking is not permitted in the test room. No paperwork other than the primary ID is allowed in the test room: no pens, dictionaries, revision notes or books.

If you intend to retain any head covering, the test supervisor may ask you to remove the head covering so that you can be searched to ensure you have not secreted a Bluetooth device on your person. This can be done in a private area if you prefer, and this option should be requested during the validation stage.

Only once all your belongings are securely locked away, and the test supervisor is content that you have nothing that could be used to help you in the test, will you be escorted to the test room. Other candidates will already be midway through their tests, so silence must be observed on entering the room, and throughout the test.

Each candidate is allocated a workstation. Your primary ID will be checked again, and the supervisor will ensure the workstation is set up for the test you have booked. You can then start!

When you have completed the test, you should return to the locker to collect your personal belongings and then return the locker key to reception.

You will be asked to complete a short customer satisfaction survey; this is optional but feedback is always appreciated.

The test result is only available during this visit to the test centre, so you will need to wait until it is available. All tests are computer marked and a printed score report is provided.

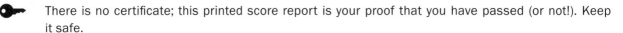 There is no certificate; this printed score report is your proof that you have passed (or not!). Keep it safe.

If you leave the test centre without collecting the score report, you will have to rebook and pay for another test.

Test results are also uploaded to your account on the booking system within 48 hours of the test. If you don't pass the test you will have to wait until the result is uploaded before you can book a re-sit.

## NUMBER OF ATTEMPTS

You are only allowed three attempts, and then have to wait two years (24 months from the date of the second resit) before you are allowed to try again.

## COSTS

The first attempt at each test is free of charge. If the first test is rescheduled, it is still free of charge. The second and any subsequent tests are not free of charge. Currently, the price is £19.25 per test.

Payment is by credit/debit card at the time of booking. Provided sufficient notice is given, fees for cancelled appointments are refunded, and the monies should be received within ten working days.

## FOR HOW LONG ARE THE TESTS VALID?

Test passes remain valid for three years. If you apply for an ITT course which starts after the end of the three-year period you have to re-sit the test(s).

# SPECIAL ARRANGEMENTS

In accordance with the Equalities Act 2010, special arrangements may be requested if you have a documented medical condition or disability that would adversely affect your performance in the test.

o   Extra time may be granted for those with specific learning difficulties such as dyslexia.

o   A modified version of the literacy test may be given to candidates with a hearing impairment. The audio spelling test is replaced by an onscreen multiple-choice format.

o   A modified version of the numeracy test may be given to candidates with a hearing impairment. The audio mental arithmetic test is supplemented by onscreen multiple-choice format questions.

o   Candidates with physical disabilities may be given extra time. They may be allowed to bring specialist equipment with them to the test centre.

o   Candidates with visual impairment may be allocated a larger monitor screen and/or large-print hard copies of the test. They may also be allocated more time.

o   Candidates for whom English is not their first language may request extra time and/or the option to listen to an audio version of the question, to accompany the onscreen instructions.

Full details of what is possible are given on the DfE website.

If you require special arrangements to be made, you have to request these and provide proof of your physical/educational circumstances.

Facilities vary from test centre to test centre. The majority of test centres are fully accessible but if you require special facilities you should check beforehand that the test centre you have requested will be suitable.

Some special arrangements can be made via the online booking system; for some an application form has to be completed. A response should be received within ten working days but more complex applications can take longer.

# PREPARATION FOR THE TEST

Apart from making sure you understand the theory on which you will be tested, before taking the real tests, it's important to take the online practice tests.

Details of the current technical requirements to gain access to the tests are provided on the DfE website. Most operating systems and browsers are supported.

Completing the practice questions and the practice papers provided in this book will reassure you that you can answer the questions correctly and earn marks, but it cannot prepare you fully for the onscreen tests.

The online tests provide essential experience and practice in using the navigational features of the test, including how to:

- enter an answer;
- use the calculator;
- edit an answer;
- flag a question – so you can remember to go back to it, if you have time;
- proceed to the next question;
- end the test, if you have finished before the time runs out.

Entering an answer can be done via the keyboard, by dragging the answer or one or more ticks into place, or clicking on the answer. Full instructions are always given onscreen.

Doing the online tests also familiarises you with other features.

- A clock shows how much time has elapsed.
- A question track shows which questions you have answered so far – clicking on a question number allows you to go back to that question.

Note that there is a 'Help' button in the practice tests, and a 'Pause' button. Neither is available in the real tests!

The onscreen test facility checks your answers, gives a total score and reports on which questions you answered incorrectly, together with the expected answer. In the numeracy tests, there is also an option to work through a question using step-by-step support. The 'Show me' option gives the correct working so you can see where you went wrong.

 Before gaining access to the tests, you will need to complete an initial registration with learndirect. Full details are provided on the DfE website at www.education.gov.uk/sta/professional, with links to the form that has to be completed.

 Copy the activation key so you can paste it into the registration form. It is an easily mistyped combination of letters, for example jhULiqgX.

## THE LITERACY SKILLS TEST

The purpose of the literacy skills test is to ensure that those embarking on the training for a career in teaching have the requisite reading and writing skills. The literacy test does not mirror what is expected of students of GCSE English, nor does it test the ability to teach English. Teachers are, however, to be sufficiently proficient to be able to guide pupils so that the pupils' written work is of as high a standard as possible.

In their day-to-day work, teachers are expected to read and digest large amounts of written information such as school policy documents, government guidance documents and school syllabuses. Teachers are also expected to express themselves well when writing reports on pupils or letters home to parents, or compiling reports for colleagues.

The literacy test focuses on three aspects: spelling, knowledge of grammar and the ability to comprehend a piece of text about 700 words in length. These three aspects are tested in different ways.

| Section | Marks | Rules | Tip |
|---|---|---|---|
| Spelling | 10 | Once this section is left, there is no going back to it. | Limit the amount of time spent on this section. |
| Grammar | 10–12 | One mark per question. | The questions are grouped and apply to one text. Read the whole text to get a better feel for what is required. |
| Comprehension | 10–12 | Marks are awarded according to the number of answers that have to be supplied rather than one mark per question. | Allow enough time to read and digest the text, and to answer the questions. |

## Spelling

The spelling part of the literacy test is worth ten marks. The words are those that a teacher might meet in everyday working situations and must be able to spell correctly. There is no time limit for this section, but once the 'Next Question' button is pressed, there is no going back.

There are only 36 minutes for the whole test, and later sections may be more time-consuming, with much more to read and digest. Try not to spend much more than ten minutes on the spelling section.

The spelling test will look like this.

1. The college makes full use of shared training ◀⟩ [        ] [        ] with its partners.

2. The ◀⟩ [        ] total from Parent Teacher Association fund-raising events is now almost £500.

3. To qualify for the swimming gala, it is ◀⟩ [        ] that we win the next race.

4. Effective ◀⟩ [        ] between school and parents is essential.

5. Peter needs to have more confidence in his own ◀⟩ [        ].

6. In assembly, we celebrate the ◀⟩ [        ] of all our students.

7. Violet was reminded that her continued late arrival was ◀⟩ [        ].

8. One word is ◀⟩ [        ] with another when the two have the same meaning.

9. The student's behaviour was completely ◀⟩ [        ] in the circumstances.

10. The difference in their marks was ◀⟩ [        ].

To listen to a word you click on the audio icon: ◀⟩. You can listen to it as many times as you like.

Type your spelling of the word in the empty box. You can correct your spelling as many times as you like.

If you have a hearing impairment and requested special arrangements when booking the test, you will be presented with the same list of ten sentences, each with one word missing and then offered four alternative spellings for each.

1. The college makes full use of shared _____ with its partners.

> A.  **opportunities**
>
> B.  **oppurtunities**
>
> C.  **oportunities**
>
> D.  **oppertunities**

To answer a question, click on your choice and drag it to the position within the sentence where it belongs.

If you are already confident about your spelling ability, try the spelling part of the online test. If you are not so confident, or score less than ten out of ten, you will need to set aside some time learning how to spell the kinds of words that will appear in the test.

## Grammar

The grammar section of the test is presented as a number of continuous texts, each incorporating some multiple-choice questions. For each multiple-choice question, a piece of text is presented with one part missing and the four options offer alternatives for that missing text.

If it proves difficult to determine what is a question and which are the possible answers, read the whole text through; it may then make more sense!

In most aspects of the grammar test, only one answer is considered to be correct; all other options are incorrect and should be rejected. Sometimes, though, it is necessary to decide which is the best answer; see for example practice questions 125–128, where the correct answer is the most concise option.

## Comprehension

Comprehension is a test of understanding the written word and is assessed using a single piece of complex text (600–700 words).

The comprehension section of the test requires careful reading and understanding of the text, in order to answer the associated questions. The text therefore requires reading at least once, and time needs to be allowed for this, on top of answering the questions.

Questions are set, lettered A, B, C, ..., requiring you to read and understand the text and to demonstrate the skills coded C1–C9.

| Code | Skill |
|------|-------|
| C1 | Attributing statements to categories |
| C2 | Completing a bulleted list |
| C3 | Sequencing information |
| C4 | Presenting main points |
| C5 | Matching texts to summaries |
| C6 | Identifying the meanings of words and phrases |
| C7 | Evaluating statements about the text |
| C8 | Selecting headings and subheadings |
| C9 | Identifying possible readership or audience for a text |

In the comprehension section, some question types are more time-consuming than others but then marks are awarded according to the number of answers rather than one per question, so it can prove advantageous to allocate more time to certain types of question.

After trying some questions, you may realise that you are better at one type than another. The questions can be answered in any order, so choose what you consider to be 'easy' questions, and do them first.

## Top tips for the literacy skills test

In the spelling section, click the audio button as many times as you like, to hear a word. Don't leave this section until you are happy with your answer – or you have decided you cannot spend more time on it. You cannot return to the section once you've moved ahead.

In the grammar section, read the whole text through before starting to make choices.

In the comprehension section, read the whole text through twice before you start answering questions. Read through the first time quickly to get the gist of the piece. Read through the second time more slowly to understand it better.

Do the easiest questions first.

# THE NUMERACY SKILLS TEST

In the numeracy test, unless special arrangements have been made, you have 48 minutes to answer 28 questions, and these are split into two sections:

- ○ 12 mental arithmetic questions;
- ○ 16 written questions for which an onscreen calculator is provided.

During the first mental arithmetic section, each question is presented via headphones and is individually timed. You can make notes and work out your answer on paper before entering it onscreen.

Then, in the calculator section, the 16 questions test two aspects of numeracy:

- ○ 7 questions test three aspects of 'interpreting and using written data';
- ○ 9 questions require the solution of a 'written arithmetic problem'.

The first 12 (mental) questions and the final 9 (calculator) questions test the topics listed in the table on page 14.

The numeracy skills test does not test your knowledge of the mathematics national curriculum, nor your ability to teach mathematics.

The middle 7 questions can also test skills from throughout the topic list but are primarily designed to test your ability to interpret and use written data to:

- ○ identify trends;
- ○ make comparisons in order to draw conclusions;
- ○ interpret information.

| Topics tested in the first 12 and final 9 questions | Mental arithmetic | Arithmetic problems | Page numbers |
|---|:---:|:---:|---|
| Time | ✓ | ✓ | 126 |
| Amounts of money | ✓ | ✓ | 123 |
| Proportion involving fractions | ✓ | ✓ | 110, 120 |
| Proportion involving percentages | ✓ | ✓ | 116, 120 |
| Proportion involving decimals | ✓ | ✓ | 113, 120 |
| Ratios | | ✓ | 121 |
| Percentages in various contexts | ✓ | ✓ | 116 |
| Fractions | ✓ | ✓ | 110 |
| Decimals | ✓ | ✓ | 113 |
| Measurements involving distance | ✓ | ✓ | 128 |
| Measurements involving area | ✓ | ✓ | 129 |
| Measurements involving other measures eg volume | ✓ | | 131 |
| Conversions from one currency to another | ✓ | ✓ | 125 |
| Conversions from fractions to decimals | ✓ | ✓ | 115 |
| Conversions from decimals to fractions | ✓ | ✓ | 114 |
| Conversions involving other measures | | ✓ | 132 |
| Averages: mean | | ✓ | 135 |
| Averages: median | | ✓ | 137 |
| Averages: mode | | ✓ | 139 |
| Range | | ✓ | 140 |
| Combinations of measures of average | | ✓ | 142 |
| Using simple formulae | | ✓ | 183 |

All 28 questions carry one mark regardless of the number of responses required.

## ❓ FAQS

Q: In the numeracy test, if all questions carry one mark regardless of the number of required responses, surely some tests will be harder to pass than others?

A: No two tests can ever be the same. However, to ensure candidates are treated equally, regardless of which test they take, the numeracy skills tests have been calibrated statistically against a benchmark test. Then, a test with slightly harder questions is given a slightly lower pass mark and a test with slightly easier questions is given a slightly higher pass mark.

## Types of response

In the audio/mental section, an answer box appears into which to enter the answer.

For the onscreen section, there are several different types of response.

o  With the multiple-choice questions, a range of answers is presented, only one of which is the correct answer.

o  With a single-response answer, as with the audio section, you will see an answer box into which you enter the answer.

o  With the multiple-response type, there is only one mark but you have to give several answers. These may be statements that you have to classify as true or not true.

o  For some questions you need to select answers and place them in the correct position.

o  For some, you point and click on the correct answer.

Do the online practice tests to become familiar with the different types of response strategy.

> The textual nature of this book offers no opportunity for such technological variety, so the practice questions, and the questions in the practice papers, are worded as if they were onscreen, with additional numbering/lettering applied for ease of cross referencing with the answers.

## Top tips for the numeracy skills test

Answers, when entered using the keyboard, are as a number, not in words.

Units are always provided (eg eggs, %) so only the number has to be entered.

Only digits are allowed, with a decimal point if needed. No additional spaces or characters should be entered, just the number.

If you enter 2cm instead of 2, you will not earn the mark.

No leading zeroes should be entered.

If you enter 0125 instead of 125, you will not earn the mark.

### Tips for the audio section

Each question is read aloud twice, so you have time to understand what is required.

The first time you hear a question, jot down the numbers involved. Listen also for key words which tell you what operation is needed: add, subtract, multiply or divide.

Start working out the answer as soon as you have enough information.

During the second reading of the question, listen for special instructions such as the level of **accuracy**, or the format to be used for questions involving time.

A fixed time is allowed and it should be long enough for you to do the calculation, before the next question is read to you. However, be aware of strategies that save you time:

5 × £1.99 = 5 × (£2 − 1p) = £10 − 5p = £9.95.

Note that fractions must be entered in the lowest terms.

If you run out of time, guess an answer; that's better than not putting anything.

## Tips for the onscreen section

The numeracy syllabus includes many topics. Some you might find easy, others not so. To maximise your score in the test, don't waste time on a question that looks difficult to you. Answer the easiest questions first. You can always go back, if you have time, and fill in the gaps.

All the information needed to work out an answer is given in a question. Read the question twice before starting to answer it, to locate the essential data.

Check the stem of the question carefully. You won't need to spend time – and risk making a mistake – in counting the number of data items, or points on a scatter graph, if that information is already provided in the stem.

Remember that you don't have to get every question right to pass. Just do your best!

# 3　Literacy skills

Literacy skills are tested in three ways: through spelling, through grammar and through comprehension. This section considers each of these aspects of literacy, with exercises and practice questions, followed by four complete practice papers.

Sample online tests are provided at sta.education.gov.uk; try one and see how you fare. The feedback tells you which questions were answered incorrectly, so this will provide an indication of your strengths and weaknesses.

Then, work through the relevant section within this book, do some exercises, try some practice questions, and when you feel ready, try a practice text before trying another online test. Hopefully, you will see an improvement! Success!

## 3.1　Spelling

Four approaches are offered in this book.

○ **Phonics** – spelling through sound. Starting on page 18, the skill of spelling is explored through an examination of the sounds that together form a word, and how these sounds are represented using letters of the alphabet. English words are notoriously difficult to spell, but an understanding of phonics may help you to spell more accurately.

○ On page 23, word-building and deconstruction – spelling one syllable at a time – is offered as one way of trying to make sense of how words are formed and therefore how they are spelt.

○ On page 26, the challenge of **homophones** is addressed. One solution is learning by rote – using the Look/Say/Cover/Write/Check method.

○ On page 30, spelling strategies for common mistakes are examined– looking for and identifying patterns and exceptions that break the rule.

After each section, there is a set of practice questions. Your aim is to score higher in each of these 'tests'.

Knowing how to spell a word sometimes depends on the role the word is playing in the sentence: this is called the **word class**. In particular, you need to be able to recognise a word as a **noun**, an **adjective**, a **verb** or an **adverb**. The Literacy Glossary on page 278 explains all these and other relevant terms in detail.

Practise writing words that you find difficult to spell. Writing a word ten times can help you to remember how to spell it.

>  **Try this**
>
> You can improve your spelling by reading more and noticing words around you, on billboards, news headlines and adverts. Look for patterns and create your own spelling dictionary, with words that you will need to use in your professional role as a teacher.

## PHONICS

When trying to spell a word, it is essential to listen to how it sounds.

> **Try this**
>
> Say aloud each of these 40 words, all of which appear in the online practice tests, and then write out each one five times.
>
> | | | | |
> |---|---|---|---|
> | accomplishments | achievable | acknowledge | administrative |
> | anxiety | capabilities | commemorative | communication |
> | complimentary | crucial | cumulative | detrimental |
> | disapproving | exaggerated | exhaustive | existence |
> | formally | grammatically | illuminating | inappropriate |
> | independently | ineffective | implementation | justifiably |
> | mathematical | meticulous | negligible | omitted |
> | opportunities | particularly | perpetrator | predecessor |
> | preference | preferred | procedural | relieved |
> | subsequently | synonymous | unacceptable | unnecessary |

The words you will be tested on are all words which you might reasonably expect to meet in official documents that you need to read, and might need to include in reports or letters home to parents. Notice that they are all long words!

Some words, called compound words, are simply shorter words joined together to match the meaning:

breakfast    fingerprint    handbag    newspaper    toothpaste    whiteboard

Some words can be split into smaller words, and this may help in remembering how to spell them:

together    to-get-her

For other words, seeing a small word within it might help you to remember how to spell it:

re**hear**sal    au**die**nce    env**iron**ment

> **✎ Try this**
>
> Watch out for small words within longer words, on noticeboards or in the newspaper, and make a list of them.

All long words, though, can be broken into **syllable**s, even antidisestablishmentarianism!

A syllable can be:

○  a single **vowel** sound, such as 'ah';

○  a combination of a vowel and a **consonant**, such as 'go';

○  a combination of a vowel and more than one consonant, such as 'cat' and 'stop'.

What about 'y'? Is it a consonant or a vowel? In words like 'hymn' it is a vowel; in words like 'player' it is a consonant. So 'y' is a part-time vowel.

A vowel sound can be short or long, and may sound like its name (see Table 3.1).

**Table 3.1** Vowel sounds

| Vowel | Sounds like its name | Short |
|---|---|---|
| a | paper | fat |
| e | methane | met, said, thread, bury |
| i | side, shy, **eye**, **high**, **height** | sip, busy, hymn, w**o**men |
| o | low, b**o**ne, d**ough**, road, foe | hot |
| u | **u**nion, f**ew**, f**eu**d, c**u**cumber, barbec**ue** | but, l**o**ve |

Much depends on the type of syllable and what vowels are used.

○  An **open syllable** ends on a vowel and the vowel sound is long, and says its name.

   pa/per        me/thane      bi/cycle      show          union

○  A **closed syllable** ends on a consonant and the vowel sound is short.

   fat           met           sip           hot           but

○  Two vowels together make a long vowel sound.

   pleat         free          shout         boot

○  A vowel and a consonant can make a long vowel sound.

   charm         worse         flower

Single vowels and combinations of vowels make long sounds too. Table 3.2 lists the vowel phonemes.

All words have at least one syllable and each syllable has a vowel, so listen carefully and try to decide what vowel(s) are used.

**Table 3.2** Long vowel sounds

| Vowel sound | Possible combinations of letters |
|---|---|
| ae | s**ay**, p**a**le, p**ai**l, r**ei**n |
| ee | f**ee**t, m**ea**t, m**e**tre, ch**ie**f, s**ei**ze |
| ie | m**i**nd, m**y**, f**i**ne |
| oe | r**oa**d, bl**ow**, c**o**ne, b**o**ld |
| ue | sp**oo**n, tr**ue**, fl**ew**, d**u**ne |
| oo | l**oo**k, sh**ou**ld, p**u**t, f**u**ll |
| ar | h**ar**m, gr**a**ss, p**a**th, h**ea**rt, cl**er**k |
| ur | h**er**, b**ir**d, h**ear**d, abs**ur**d |
| or | b**or**n, fl**oo**r, w**ar**n |
| au | p**aw**, m**o**re, **au**dit, t**augh**t, f**ough**t, f**a**ll |
| er | wood**en**, c**ir**c**u**s, sist**er** |
| ow | h**ow**, m**ou**nt |
| oi | b**oy**, s**oi**l |
| air | f**air**, p**ear**, sh**are**, wh**ere**, h**ei**r |
| ear | h**ear**, h**ere**, t**ier**, qu**ery** |

How a word is pronounced should help in deciding which vowel (or combination of vowels) to use, but many words are said nowadays with the 'uh' sound.

grammar     cert**ai**n     desperate     admir**a**tion

quality     pen**ci**l     devel**o**p     hol**o**gram

> ## ✍ Try this
>
> List ten words that include a silent letter or the 'uh' sound. Decide how best to pronounce them and practice writing them.

Although there are 19 consonants in the alphabet, there are many more different sounds or **phonemes** that can be made by one, two or three consonants grouped together. Some examples are shown in Table 3.3.

For each of the phonemes, there are one or more combinations of letters that make the sound, so it's not surprising that many words are difficult to spell, even when you listen carefully.

**Table 3.3** Phonemes

| Sound | Examples | Notes |
|-------|----------|-------|
| b | **b**ake, stu**bb**le | Used single or doubly |
| d | **d**art, mu**ddl**e | Used single or doubly |
| f | **f**ix, pu**ff**, **ph**oto, enou**gh** | The 'f' is soft |
| g | **g**olf, **gh**astly | The 'g' is hard |
| h | **h**appy | |
| j | **j**ealous, **ge**neral, **gi**ant, sol**di**er | The 'j' is soft |
| k | **c**ollapse, **ch**aos, **k**een | The 'k' is hard |
| l | **l**ump, co**ll**ar | Used single or doubly |
| m | **m**eat, su**mm**er | Used single or doubly |
| n | **n**otice, di**nn**er, **kn**ow, **gn**arled, **pn**eumonia, **mn**emonic | |
| p | **p**ig, a**pp**le | Used single or doubly |
| r | **r**eligion, **rh**ythm | |
| s | **s**ilent, **c**eiling, **sc**issors, ne**ce**ssary, defi**c**it, adole**sce**nt, di**sci**pline | 'c'; 'sc' sounds |
| t | **t**rue, **th**yme, **pt**erodactyl | |
| w | **w**ord | |
| y | **y**es | |
| z | **z**enith, **x**ylophone, **cz**ar, plea**se** | |
| ch | **ch**ip, mu**ch**, ma**tch** | |
| kw | **qu**estion | |
| ng | stri**ng**, pi**nk** | |
| sh | **sh**ield, **sch**edule, **ch**ateau | |
| sk | **sk**ill, **sch**ool, **sc**are, de**scr**ibe, di**scu**ssion | |
| th | **th**en | |
| th | **th**ink | |
| wh | **wh**en | |

For some consonants, what follows determines how the consonant is pronounced:

o  The 'c' sound can be 'hard' – as in cat – or sound like an 's' when followed by an 'e' or an 'i' – in cinema.

o  The combination 'sc' sounds like 'sk' if followed by 'a', 'i', 'o', 'r' or 'u'; but like 's' if followed by 'e'.

Some words even include silent letters that are not pronounced!

| plum**b**er | We**d**nesday | di**s**cipline | twel**f**th | **g**nat | **h**onour | **k**nife |

| autum**n** | choco**l**ate | cu**p**board | surprise | mor**t**gage | guess | answer | **w**rite |

To help you to remember the spelling, try pronouncing the words with the silent letter emphasised.

## Practice questions

**1**   Please accept this as the only _____ of your application.

   *acknowledgment*        *acknowlegment*        *acknowlegement*        *acknowledgement*

**2**   Regular attendance at school will increase the _____ of your child doing well in his or her exams.

   *likelyhood*              *likelihood*              *liklihood*              *likeliehood*

**3**   The PE team has been ably _____ by Mrs Suzanne Williams for the last four years.

   *lead*                    *led*                    *lede*                    *leid*

**4**   Sahira has really _____ from the one-to-one tuition she has had this term.

   *benefited*              *beneffited*              *bennefitted*              *beneffitted*

**5**   The proposed reorganisation of the pastoral system may be _____.

   *contravercial*          *contraversial*          *controvercial*          *controversial*

**6**   The new assessment policy will _____ all previous versions.

   *supersede*              *supercede*              *superseed*              *superceed*

**7**   In this school, we celebrate _____, wherever it is demonstrated.

   *excelance*              *excelance*              *excellence*              *excelence*

**8**   Your interpretation of the set topic was both _____ and moving.

   *humourous*              *humorous*              *humorus*              *humourrus*

**9**   Once they reach Year 11, students have the _____ of leaving the college at lunchtime.

   *privilege*              *priviledge*              *privilegge*              *privillege*

**10**  This is a good subject to take at GCSE for anyone wishing to pursue _____ studies later on.

   *bussiness*              *busyness*              *business*              *businness*

# WORD BUILDING AND DECONSTRUCTION

Long words become easier to spell if you can break them down into smaller parts. To do this, you need to work out how they are built.

A stem word can be added to with a **prefix** and or a **suffix**, and every word, however long, can be broken into smaller parts in this way.

| PREFIX | PREFIX | PREFIX | STEM | SUFFIX | SUFFIX | SUFFIX | SUFFIX |
|--------|--------|--------|------|--------|--------|--------|--------|
| anti | dis | e | **stabl(e)** | ish | ment | arian | ism |

## Adding a prefix

A prefix is used to alter the meaning of the stem word. Examples are given in Table 3.4.

**Table 3.4** Prefixes

| Prefix | Meaning/effect | Example |
|--------|----------------|---------|
| dis | not/apart | **dis**agree |
| in | not/into | **in**efficient, **in**vade |
| un | not | **un**necessary |

In most cases, adding the prefix has no effect on the word, apart from changing its meaning.

However, the prefixes il-, im- in- and ir-, when used with a word that starts with the same letter, result in a double letter, which is unheard. Care is needed in spelling these words.

| **il**legible | **il**logical | **il**licit | **il**legal |
|---|---|---|---|
| **imm**oral | **imm**obile | **imm**ature | **imm**ortal |
| **inn**umerate | **inn**ocuous | **inn**umerable | **inn**oxious |
| **irr**elevant | **irr**eligious | **irr**econcilable | **irr**ational |

Notice also that for the prefix meaning all, only one 'l' appears in the full word:

already altogether always

'All right' is two words.

## Adding a suffix

There are many suffixes, each one changing the meaning, or part of speech, of the word:

○ creating a plural of a noun – book/books;
○ changing the tense of a verb – walk/walked/walking;
○ turning a verb into a noun – maintain/maintenance;
○ turning a verb into an adjective – excel/excellent;
○ turning an adjective into an adverb – slow/slowly.

Whenever a suffix is added to a word, the spelling of the stem may be altered in the process. For example, for words ending in -our or -ous, the vowel 'u' may be dropped or altered:

humo**u**r/humor<u>ous</u>        genero**us**/generos<u>ity</u>

But this is not always the case. A different suffix has a different effect.

honour/honour<u>able</u>        maint**ai**n/maint<u>e</u>nance

For most nouns, to create the plural from the singular form of the word, you simply add an 's': book/books.

For other groups of words, there are some simple rules as listed in Table 3.5.

**Table 3.5** Rules for creating plurals

| Ending in | Method | Singular | Plural |
|---|---|---|---|
| -ch sounding 'k' | Add an 's' | stomach | stomachs |
| -ch sounding 'ch' | Add 'es' | bench | benches |
| -s, -sh, -x; -z | Add 'es' | bus, bush, box, buzz | buses, bushes, boxes, buzzes |
| -ife | Change to 'ives' | knife | knives |
| -is | Change to 'es' | analysis | analyses |
| -y | Change to 'ies' | country | countries |

Adding a suffix can be straightforward, or it might involve changing the spelling of the base of the word too. However, there are general rules, which depend on which letter is at the end of the root and which letter is at the beginning of the suffix; see Table 3.6.

**Table 3.6** Rules for adding a suffix

| Stem ends in | Rule | Examples |
|---|---|---|
| a single silent 'e' | Delete the 'e' if the suffix starts with a vowel | care/cared/ caring dance/dancer inflate/inflation gentle/gently |
| 'c' | Include a 'k' | picnic/picnicking |
| double 'l' | Drop one of the 'l's | skill/skilful |
| a consonant and -y | Change the -y to an -i unless the suffix starts with an 'i' | ready/readily try/tried/trying |
| a consonant | The consonant may be doubled; this depends on how many syllables there are and how the word is stressed. See page 34 for more details. Even so, there are exceptions: benefit/benefited | fit/fitted/fitting |

Where a verb allows both version of a suffix, but they have different meanings, the context will determine which is correct:

○   dependant = noun describing a person who depends on another;

○   dependent = adjective describing the dependence of one thing/person on another.

British or American spelling? Some words can end in -ise or -ize; either is acceptable in the test, but in your own writing, just be consistent.

Some words can be used as nouns or as verbs and change their spelling – and how they are pronounced – according to context.

| Noun | Verb |
| --- | --- |
| the advice | to advise |
| the licence | to license |
| the practice | to practise |
| the prophecy | to prophesy |

Some words are based on the same concept – they share a basic meaning – but as they change, the way they are pronounced changes, even though the spelling of the syllables does not!

○   photo: longer final 'o';

○   photograph: equal emphasis on the two 'o's and more emphasis on final syllable;

○   photographic: the 'a' becomes shorter;

○   photographer: the second 'o' becomes shorter.

It may help you to learn some spellings by thinking through how the different forms are created and how they are pronounced. For some words, the syllable on which the most emphasis is given indicates the spelling:

○   decent/descent;

○   desert/dessert.

If you think you know how to spell a word but lack confidence in a choice of one letter, think about how the word is said and how it is formed.

| Verb | To prefer | The first 'e' is sounded as 'ee'; the second 'e' is sounded as 'er' |
| --- | --- | --- |
| Past tense | preferred | To make the past tense, the suffix -ed is added, but to retain the sound of 'prefer' an extra 'r' is needed |
| Noun | preference | To make a noun, the suffix -ence is used. The 'r' is not doubled, and the sound of the first 'e' is shortened |

## Practice questions

**11**   Aim to teach students a range of _____ for tackling unfamiliar spellings.

*strategys*                *strategies*                *strategeys*                *strategis*

**12**    There are three new _____ available from different awarding organisations.

    *syllabuses*           *syllabuss*           *syllabus*           *syllabusi*

**13**    Some _____ have been noticed in the way examination entries have been completed.

    *irregulariteys*        *irregularitys*        *irregularities*        *irregularitties*

**14**    The relevant graphs are included in the _____ at the end of the report.

    *appendixs*         *appendixes*        *appendices*        *appendicies*

**15**    I would like us to reach a _____ on how to proceed in this matter.

    *consensus*         *concensus*        *consencus*        *concensuss*

**16**    Please make sure you attend every _____ session between now and half term.

    *practise*          *practice*          *practiss*         *pracctice*

**17**    Once pupils' cursive handwriting is sufficiently well formed, they will be given a pen _____.

    *lisence*           *license*           *licence*          *lisense*

**18**    If you need help with your project, your class teacher can _____ you.

    *advice*           *advise*          *addvice*         *addvise*

**19**    The threat of a detention usually has an immediate _____ on pupil behaviour.

    *effect*           *affect*           *efect*          *afect*

**20**    Please complete the _____ paperwork and return it to me tomorrow.

    *relavent*          *relavant*         *relevent*         *relevant*

## LEARNING BY ROTE: WORDS THAT SOUND THE SAME

For many words, you will know how to spell them without having to think about them too much. For other words, you might struggle.

For the trickier words, to ensure you don't lose marks in the test, you will need to develop strategies. Here is one way of learning new words: the Look/Say/Cover/Write/Check method.

- Look at the word and decide how it was constructed. Look for words within, prefixes and suffixes.
- Say the word aloud, slowly, emphasising any silent letters and breaking the word into smaller parts.
- Cover the word and try to imagine the spelling while saying the words to yourself.
- Write the word using joined-up writing.
- Check it against the original spelling, letter by letter.
- Repeat until you can spell it correctly.

Attempt to learn a few new words at a time, and check you have not forgotten them a week later.

> ### ✐ **Try this**
>
> Scan back and forward through the pages of this spelling section and identify ten words that you know you cannot spell with confidence.
>
> Use the Look/Say/Cover/Write/Check method for these words. Then identify ten more words that you need to learn. And so on ...

Another 'trick' is to create a **mnemonic** to help you to remember how to spell the word. Usually the first letter of each word is a letter of the word you want to spell.

> BECAUSE: big elephants can always understand small elephants.
>
> RHYTHM: rhythm helps your two hips move.

There are others though that echo one or more letters.

> Stationary is parked cars. Stationery is envelopes and pens.
>
> I can exaggerate the sound g by doubling it.
>
> Algebra is a mathematical discipline.
>
> The pet rat was the perpetrator.

In this section, groups of words are identified which share some common attribute, and one that makes them easy to misspell.

If you are not sure what a word means, look it up in a dictionary and create your own 'spelling bee', listing the words you are learning and their definitions.

## Sounds the same

Some groups of letters sound the same but are spelt differently. For example, the 'er' sound can be spelt using each of the five vowels.

> separate    persuade    sir    worth    pursue

For words that sound the same but are spelt differently – these are called homophones – only the context can be used to determine which spelling is correct.

> ### ✐ **Try this**
>
> Check that you understand the difference between the 94 homophones listed below. If you are not sure, look the words up in a dictionary and make notes of their meaning and usage.
>
> Here are two examples.
>
> *aloud/allowed*
>
> aloud = adverb meaning audibly or loudly
>
> allowed = past tense of verb to allow, to let (someone) have or do something

*to/too/two*

to = proposition expressing direction of motion (to the school) or infinitive marker (to teach)

too = adverb meaning also, or to a higher degree than necessary (talking too loudly)

two = cardinal number

| | | | |
|---|---|---|---|
| altar/alter | cygnet/signet | meter/metre | stake/steak |
| ascent/assent | draft/draught | might/mite | stile/style |
| augur/auger | discreet/discrete | muscle/mussel | storey/story |
| bail/bale | draw/drawer | naval/navel | strait/straight |
| balmy/barmy | dual/duel | no/know | team/teem |
| bare/bear | faint/feint | pail/pale | their/there/they're |
| bated/baited | fare/fair | pain/pane | theirs/there's |
| berth/birth | fate/fete | passed/past | threw/through |
| bizarre/bazaar | faun/fawn | peace/piece | throes/throws |
| bored/board | flair/flare | peal/peel | tide/tied |
| born/borne | forth/fourth | plain/plane | tire/tyre |
| border/boarder | gilt/guilt | pray/prey | toe/tow |
| bough/bow | grate/great | principal/principle | vain/vane |
| brake/break | heroin/heroine | prise/prize | waist/waste |
| breach/breech | hoard/horde | program/programme | wait/weight |
| buy/by | hole/whole | right/write | waive/wave |
| canvas/canvass | idle/idol | ring/wring | wear/where |
| cereal/serial | knew/new | role/roll | weather/whether |
| check/cheque | leant/lent | scene/seen | wet/whet |
| coarse/course | led/lead | seam/seem | which/witch |
| cord/chord | licence/license | shear/sheer | who's/whose |
| cue/queue | mail/male | shore/sure | you're/your |
| curb/kerb | manner/manor | sight/site | |
| currant/current | medal/meddle | sleight/slight | |

Some pairs of words have almost the same letters, but not quite, and how to spell each word depends on the context.

> ### ✍ Try this
>
> Check that you understand the difference between these 36 pairs of words.
>
> If you are not sure, look the words up in a dictionary and make notes of their meaning and usage. Here are two examples:
>
> accept = agree to receive or do something    except = apart from
>
> affect = make a difference to                 effect = a result (noun), or to bring about (verb)
>
> | | | |
> |---|---|---|
> | adverse/averse | elusive/illusive | loath/loathe |
> | aural/oral | emigrant/immigrant | lose/loose |
> | censor/censure | eminent/imminent | palate/pallet |
> | complement/compliment | ensure/insure | passed/past |
> | confidant/confident | enquire/inquire | personal/personnel |
> | council/counsel | envelop/envelope | poor/pour |
> | dairy/diary | exercise/exorcise | practice/practise |
> | defer/differ | final/finale | precede/proceed |
> | defuse/diffuse | flounder/founder | quiet/quite |
> | desert/dessert | foreword/forward | stationary/stationery |
> | dual/duel | formally/formerly | swat/swot |
> | elicit/illicit | lightening/lightning | waist/waste |

## Practice questions

**21**  This schedule for completing reports should be _____ for everyone.

    *manageable*        *managable*        *manageble*        *managible*

**22**  The pupils _____ when faced with a test format that they had not encountered before.

    *paniced*        *panicced*        *panicked*        *panickd*

**23**  Please supply the relevant details as _____ as possible.

    *consisely*        *concicely*        *concisely*        *consicely*

**24**  Grammar is taught in three _____ sessions each week.

    *discreet*        *discret*        *disscrete*        *discrete*

**25** The most important _____ to bear in mind when carrying out research is 'do no harm'.

    *principal*                  *principple*                *principle*                *principale*

**26** Please make sure that the school hamster has _____ cage covered each evening.

    *its*                  *it's*                *i'ts*                *its'*

**27** The trip will only go ahead if the _____ is fine and suitable for outdoor pursuits.

    *whether*                  *weather*                *wether*                *wheather*

**28** Jan was _____ unaware that he should have been in the hall with the rest of the class.

    *apparently*             *apperently*            *apparantly*           *apperantly*

**29** Some children are becoming too _____ on the support of a teaching assistant.

    *dependent*             *dependant*            *depandant*           *dapandent*

**30** Ali Khan, the educational _____, will be in school on Friday.

    *psycologist*           *phsychologist*          *psychollogist*         *psychologist*

## SPELLING STRATEGIES FOR COMMON MISTAKES

Some words can be misheard (or mis-said) and, as a result, might be incorrectly spelt.

o The contraction could've (short for could have) is often written <u>incorrectly</u> as 'could of'. Ditto for should've, would've.

o The word 'of' should be pronounced 'ov' but some say the 'f' and then might spell it <u>incorrectly</u> as 'off'.

The word 'of' is never part of a verb form.

## One or two?

An easy mistake is to use a double consonant when there should only be one, or vice versa.

Of the 40 words used in the online tests, these all have a double consonant:

|  |  |  |  |
|---|---|---|---|
| a**cc**o**m**plishments | co**mm**emorative | co**mm**unication | disa**pp**roving |
| exa**gg**erated | forma**ll**y | gra**mm**atically | i**ll**uminating |
| ina**pp**ropriate | ine**ff**ective | omi**tt**ed | o**pp**ortunities |
| predece**ss**or | prefe**rr**ed | una**cc**eptable | u**nn**ece**ss**ary |

These words might sound as if they have a double consonant but they don't:

    cumulative            preference

To help you to decide which words need a double consonant and which don't, consider how the word is constructed; see page 23. However, the general rule for one-syllable words is to double the final consonant if the word ends consonant-vowel-consonant (CVC):

- clap/clapped
- stop/stopping

For two-syllable words, it depends on which syllable is stressed. Only double the consonant if the stress is on the second syllable:

- begin/beginning
- enter/entered

The double rule only applies to words that end in CVC!

- clean (VVC)/cleaning
- see (VCC)/seeing
- sight (CCC)/sighted
- settle (CCV)/settled
- blue (CVV)/bluest
- ride (VCV)/rider

The English language is notoriously difficult because there are many rules, but also exceptions. These, you will have to learn!

## 'a' versus 'i'

How a word ends can involve choosing between two vowels.

- Use -able when the stem is a complete word: adaptable, bearable, acceptable.
- Use -able when the stem ends in a hard 'c' or a hard 'g': amicable, navigable.
- Use -ible when the stem is not a word: audible, credible.

Exceptions: accessible, collapsible.

> ### ✐ Try this
>
> Make a list of ten words that end in -able, and ten more that end in -ible.

## '-ly' versus '-ally'

definite/definitely    immediate/immediately

For words that end in -ic, -ally is needed instead:

basic/basically    tragic/tragically

Only one exception: publicly!

## 'ie' or 'ei'?

The saying goes 'i before e, except after c, whenever the sound you are making is ee'.

| i before e | except after 'c' | Exceptions! |
|---|---|---|
| whenever the sound you are making is 'ee' | | |
| believe<br>grievance<br>hygiene<br>mischief<br>niece<br>yield | conceive<br>deceive<br>perceive<br>receive | caffeine<br>either<br>neither<br>protein<br>seize |

What about when the sound is not 'ee'?

| i before e | NOT i before e |
|---|---|
| friend<br>view | forfeit<br>weight<br>species<br>weird |

## Practice questions

**31**  Students will need to demonstrate considerable _____ if they wish to take part in this dance project.

   *comitment*          *commitment*          *committment*          *comittment*

**32**  Offering both courses will _____ all members of the department teaching Year 10.

   *necessitate*          *necesitate*          *neccessitate*          *neccesitate*

**33**  Please check through the _____ for the Christmas concert by tomorrow.

   *program*          *programme*          *programe*          *proggramme*

**34**  The school's anti-bullying policy covers sexual and racial _____.

   *harasment*          *harrassment*          *harassment*          *harrasment*

**35**  You will _____ receive a reminder when your library book is due back.

   *automaticaly*          *automaticcally*          *automatically*          *automaticly*

**36**  The incident that _____ in the playground has been dealt with by Mr Thomas.

   *ocured*          *occured*          *ocurred*          *occurred*

**37**   Winning the silver cup was a huge _____ for the netball team.

    *achievement*           *achievment*           *acheivement*           *acheivement*

**38**   We hope that students will _____ this opportunity to take part in an exciting local event.

    *seeze*           *sieze*           *seize*    ·           *seaze*

**39**   Your stories should be imaginative and engaging for the reader but also _____!

    *beleievable*           *believable*           *beleiveable*           *believeable*

**40**   Please find enclosed a _____ for the money you kindly donated to the school fund.

    *receipt*           *receit*           *reciept*           *reciet*

# 3.2    Grammar

Before starting to examine the grammatical rules, it's important to understand the terminology associated with grammar.

If you encounter a word you don't fully understand, refer to the Literacy glossary on page 278.

## CONSISTENCY WITH STANDARD WRITTEN ENGLISH

Teachers (and their pupils) are expected to write using Standard English. The literacy test cannot test your ability to write well. Instead, it aims to test your ability to identify the correct ways of expressing yourself. This is achieved by offering four options to complete a sentence or section of text, one of which is correct, and three of which are grammatically incorrect.

In the test, you will be presented with two or three short pieces of text, within each of which several questions are asked. For example, there might be a letter home to parents, or an internal document about school uniform. If you choose all the correct options for each piece of text, you will have addressed a range of grammatical challenges.

To introduce the various grammatical challenges, and to give practice in answering these types of questions, what follows is a description of the 'theory' for each grammatical challenge, and a series of short isolated questions that focus entirely on that aspect of grammar.

### Failure to observe sentence boundaries; abandoned or faulty constructions and sentence fragments

The most common **sentence boundaries** are the capital letter (at the start) and the full stop (at the end).

> *A sentence is marked by a capital letter at the start and a full stop at the end.*

Sentences can also end with a question mark to show it is a question, ie an interrogative sentence.

> *What date is it?*

Sentences can also end with an exclamation mark, if it is an **exclamative** sentence or an **imperative** sentence.

> *Happy birthday!  Smile!*

Any option that includes a full stop, a question mark or an exclamation mark followed by a lower-case letter is an incorrect option.

Longer sentences require additional **punctuation** to indicate where the reader might pause and breathe, and to make the meaning clear. To decide where these should be – or ought not to be so as to eliminate options presented in a question – it helps to identify sections of a sentence that provide additional meaning: who is it about, what happened, when did it happen, where did it happen, why/how did it happen.

Three punctuation marks are available, and each has its own particular uses: the comma, the colon and the semicolon.

## Uses of the comma (,)

A comma is used to separate the opening word or phrase from the subject of the sentence.

> *Alternatively, we could …*    *However, I …*    *Instead, you might …*    *Next, they …*
> *On the other hand, she …*    *Suddenly, he …*    *Unfortunately, we …*

The comma can be used to separate a phrase from the main part of the sentence. These adverbial examples all address the question 'when?'.

> *In the morning, the children have three separate lessons.*
> *After break, there is a double period of a core subject.*
> *In the afternoon, there are usually three more separate lessons.*

Commas can be used to separate cause and effect clauses of a sentence.

> *If the alarm bell rings, everyone must evacuate the building.*
> *Because a mathematics qualification is so important for your future, it is essential that …*

The comma may also be used to separate items in a list.

> *On Mondays, Wednesdays and Fridays, the whole afternoon is allocated to sport, or science, or design and technology.*

Note that the first comma is replacing 'and': On Mondays and Wednesday and …

It is not necessary to place a comma before the final 'and' in a list of things. So, there is no comma after 'Wednesday'.

Note that the final three commas help to make it clear that 'design and technology' is a single subject.

Commas are also used in dialogue to separate what is said from the speech tag. Notice the position of the speech marks, in relation to the comma.

> *'I hate maths,' moaned George. Mary said, 'I know an easy way to do fractions.'*

Any option which includes a comma followed by a capital indicating a new sentence is an incorrect option. Commas cannot be used to end a sentence.

Pairs of commas may be used to mark parenthesis.

> *Joan Howard, the girl who came top in both mathematics and English, is to be awarded this year's Achievement Prize.*

## Uses of the colon (:)

The colon is most often used to introduce a list.

> *The Autumn term will be busy for all staff: induction of the new intake, preparations for the harvest festival, and the run-up to Christmas events.*

The colon may also be used to separate two sentences where the first leads on to the second.

> *The school has much to commend it: the Ofsted report was complimentary and staff retention is at an all-time high.*

## Uses of the semicolon (;)

The semicolon is used to separate two (or more) equal-weight word classes.

If the two parts could be sentences, then using a semicolon stresses that while they stand alone, they are closely related.

> *Use of the semicolon is rare; its appearance is unusual, even in textbooks.*

More commonly, the semicolon is used to separate items in a list that have been introduced using the colon, and avoids presenting the sentence as a stem followed by bulleted list.

> *According to the timetable, there is much to do on Thursday: timekeeping at the swimming gala; organising the table tennis match; and patrolling the changing rooms.*

> *According to the timetable, there is much to do on Thursday:*
>
> o   *timekeeping at the swimming gala;*
> o   *organising the table tennis match; and*
> o   *patrolling the changing rooms.*

Note that a comma can serve the same purpose, but if one or more of the list items is long and/or they include commas themselves, the semicolon is necessary.

Questions that test the failure to observe sentence boundaries usually comprise identical wording with alternative punctuation/capitalisation.

Eliminate the options that are clearly wrong; this reduces the number of options you might need to choose between.

Using a full stop before the sentence has ended creates a fragment. For a sentence to be complete, it needs at least one finite verb.

o   The finite verb can be a present participle with auxiliary verb 'to be'.

o   The finite verb can be a past participle with auxiliary verb 'to have'.

o   The finite verb must be linked to a subject.

Examine each 'sentence', starting at the capital letter and ending with a full stop, and discount any options that break the one-finite-verb rule.

# Practice questions

**41**   School opens at 8:30 _____ or to go straight into their classrooms.

    A. in the morning pupils are welcome to use the library from then

    B. in the morning, pupils are welcome to use the library from then

    C. in the morning. pupils are welcome to use the library from then

    D. in the morning; pupils are welcome to use the library from then

**42**   For book week, we ask that children _____ or other accessory.

    A. come to school dressed as a character from a book they don't need a complicated costume – just a hat

    B. come to school dressed as a character from a book, they don't need a complicated costume, just a hat

    C. come to school dressed as a character from a book. They don't need a complicated costume – just a hat

    D. come to school dressed as a character from a book; they don't need a complicated costume. Just a hat

**43**   Yasmin has worked well this year in physics: she has demonstrated _____ willing to participate fully in lessons.

    A. a secure grasp of the topics covered and has completed all assignments to a high standard, she is always

    B. a secure grasp of the topics covered, and has completed all assignments to a high standard, she is always

    C. a secure grasp of the topics covered, and has completed all assignments to a high standard; she is always

    D. a secure grasp of the topics covered and has completed all assignments to a high standard; she is always

**44**   For the school trip, _____ boots, sleeping bag and wash bag.

    A. pupils should bring the following, warm clothes, a waterproof coat and

    B. pupils should bring the following: warm clothes, a waterproof coat and

    C. pupils should bring the following. Warm clothes, a waterproof coat, and

    D. pupils should bring the following warm clothes: a waterproof coat and

**45**   The school fair will be held in the hall _____ wet and windy.

    A. and adjoining classrooms. If the weather is

    B. and adjoining classrooms. Should the weather be

    C. and adjoining classrooms, if the weather is

    D. and adjoining classrooms; if the weather is

**46**  With the support of the PTA, we are planning _____ by all year groups.

    A. to build a brand new play area at the back of the school. This will be used

    B. to build a brand new play area at the back of the school. Which will be used

    C. to build a brand new play area at the back of the school. Used

    D. to build a brand new play area at the back of the school. To be used

**47**  _____ the main entrance. Please ensure that you remind them they should be entering the college by the west door only.

    A. Students using

    B. For students using

    C. Some students are using

    D. To students when using

**48**  Ambitious to do well in their exams, _____ too soon and become stale.

    A. so some students start revising

    B. and some students start revising

    C. while some students start revising

    D. some students start revising

## Lack of cohesion

Cohesion is necessary if a reader is to follow a train of thought successfully.

The opening sentence in a paragraph might have, as its subject, the **noun phrase** 'newly qualified teachers'. Rather than repeat this noun phrase, in a subsequent sentence, a **personal pronoun** might be substituted. The personal pronoun options are I/me, you, he/him, she/her, it, we/us, they/them.

For cohesion, every pronoun must 'agree' with the noun phrase it replaces.

The noun phrase 'newly qualified teachers' is third-person plural, so the personal pronoun must also be third-person plural. Using 'they' as a subject and/or 'them' as an object, would be correct; any other personal pronoun would confuse the reader.

Identify the noun or noun phrase to which the pronoun relates, and make sure they 'agree'.

## Practice questions

**49**  Effective teachers have high expectations for students' learning and behaviour. _____ and challenge them to reach their potential.

    A. They know their capabilities, encourage all to participate

    B. They know their learners' capabilities, encourage all to participate

    C. You know their capabilities, encourage all to participate

    D. He knows their learners' capabilities, encourage all to participate

**50**    Unfortunately, only a small number of pupils have expressed interest in taking part in the Outdoor Pursuits Weekend. _____ go ahead and book the youth hostel anyway.

    A.  So we have decided to

    B.  However, we have decided to

    C.  Moreover, we have decided to

    D.  And we have decided to

**51**    Pupils who forget to bring the correct money for the trip should go to the bursar. _____ bring it in as soon as possible.

    A.  They should make sure they

    B.  He should make sure they

    C.  You should make sure you

    D.  You should make sure they

**52**    The Year 4 children were extremely loud on Friday afternoon. _____.

    A.  A class disturbed the Year 6 children who were taking an exam

    B.  This lesson disturbed the Year 6 children who were taking an exam

    C.  This noise disturbed the Year 6 children who were taking an exam

    D.  The class disturbed the Year 6 children who were taking an exam

## Lack of agreement between subject and verb

Every sentence needs a finite verb and a subject for this verb. For the grammar to be correct, the subject and verb have to 'agree'.

The subject will be a noun or noun phrase, or a pronoun. It can be categorised by its **person** (first, second or third) and by its **number** (as singular or plural). The form of the verb has to match this categorisation.

With short sentences, it is relatively straightforward to identify the subject of the verb.

> *The school day starts with an assembly in the main hall.*
>
> Subject = the school day: third-person singular.
>
> Verb = starts: third-person singular of the verb to start – I start, you start, he/she/it starts, we start, you start they start.

Longer sentences can be trickier to unravel.

> *Making time for revision of both mathematics and science are important.*

Seeing 'mathematics and science' so close to the verb 'are' might suggest that 'mathematics and science' is the subject, and being plural, this would agree with the verb. However, the subject is 'making time for revision (of both mathematics and science)' and this is singular. So, the verb should be singular too; third-person singular 'is' would be correct.

**Determiners** might serve as the subject. These can be singular or plural, and need to agree with the verb that follows.

| Singular | Plural |
|----------|--------|
| This     | These  |
| That     | Those  |

Some nouns look singular, because of the absence of a final 's', but are actually plural. For example, 'criteria' is the plural of 'criterion'.

These are always singular: anything, each, everyone, nobody, something, the government.

## Practice questions

**53**   The range of GCSE courses offered at this school _____ to meet the needs of all students.

    A. are designed    B. is designed    C. designed    D. being designed

**54**   Every Tuesday this term, the doctor or the nurse _____.

    A. are available in school to see children with their parents

    B. are being available to see children with their parents

    C. is been available to see children with their parents

    D. is available in school to see children with their parents

**55**   Each of the senior teachers _____ responsible for one or more of the faculties in the college.

    A. is    B. are    C. were    D. been

**56**   Candle Hill Primary School was one of the schools which _____ highly commended by the inspectors.

    A. was    B. was being    C. were    D. were been

## Should have/of, might have/of

In speech, the tendency is to contract words. *I will* becomes *I'll*; *they will* becomes *they'll*. When 'have' is shortened to 've', *should have* becomes *should've* and *might have* becomes *might've*. Unfortunately, the 've' sounds very like 'of'. Consequently, it is a common error to write 'of' instead of 'have'. This is grammatically incorrect!

## Practice questions

**57**   Exam entries _____ given to the examination officer by the end of last week.

    A.  should have been

    B.  could have been

    C.  should of been

    D.  could of been

**58**  By next Tuesday at the latest, you _____ finished your end-of-term assignment on this topic.

A. will of          B. must have          C. could of          D. can have

**59**  Your essay on *Macbeth* _____ included more quotations to support your ideas.

A. will have          B. might of          C. could have          D. should of

**60**  It _____ better if you had asked permission before leaving the school premises.

A. might of been          B. should have been          C. must of been          D. might have been

## Inappropriate or incomplete verb forms

The **finite verb** in a sentence can be one, two or three words, depending on the tense being used: past, present, future, past progressive, present progressive, past perfect, present perfect, and so on!

The single-word verb form may be preceded by the auxiliary verb(s) based on 'to be' or 'to have', depending again on the tense being expressed.

For grammatical correctness, the single-word verb form must comply with the conjugation of the verb, and be in **agreement** with the subject.

The English language has many irregular verbs, with lots of different spelling to apply in the appropriate tense/subject situation. For example, the verb forms of 'to lay' and 'to lie' are a challenge.

○  To lay: this is a **transitive verb** – it needs an object.

*Hens lay eggs. Mother is laying the table. The plates are laid on the table.*

○  To lie: this is an **intransitive verb** – it has no object. It has two meanings: to tell an untruth, or to recline. The past tense of 'to lie' is 'lied' (told an untruth) or 'lay'.

*The ailing pupil lies on the sickroom bed. He lay still and had lain there for an hour.*

The word 'of' is never part of a finite verb.

## Practice questions

**61**  If we _____ the coach would arrive back so late, we would have contacted parents in advance.

A. had of known          B. had known          C. had have known          D. have known

**62**  The pupils _____ by reception waiting for the school bus for 25 minutes.

A. were stood          B. was standing          C. were standing          D. was stood

**63**  A new climbing frame _____ in the infants' playground, thanks to the generosity of the PTA.

A. has been built          B. has been builded          C. has been build          D. has been building

**64**  We try to ensure that every afternoon, children _____ and rest for an hour.

A. lay down          B. laid down          C. lie down          D. lies down

## Wrong or missing preposition, eg different from/than/to

A **preposition** (think of it as pre-position) usually comes before a noun or pronoun and 'governs' that noun/pronoun, indicating its relation to some other word in the sentence.

Examples of prepositions are: *about, above, across, after, at, between, by, for, from, in, near, of, on, than, through, to, towards, under, with.*

When given after a verb, the phrase starting with the preposition gives more information, often 'where?' or 'when?'.

> *The book is on the table. Katie sits between James and Clare. The mathematics lesson was after science.*

Sometimes the preposition follows an adjective and a comparison is needed.

> *Brian is older than Alf. This year's results are different from last year's.*

## Practice questions

**65**  When children become _____ one activity, they should be encouraged to move on to another.

A. bored of          B. bored on          C. bored with          D. bored at

**66**  We want this end-of-term show to be _____ the ones we have put on in previous years.

A. different than        B. different of          C. different to          D. different from

**67**  The new registration system is superior _____.

A. than the one before              B. to the one before

C. of the one before                D. as the one before

**68**  The sports hall is located _____.

A. to left of the main building behind the playing field

B. left of the main building behind the playing field

C. to the left of the main building behind the playing field

D. at the left of the main building behind the playing field

## Noun/pronoun agreement error

Lack of cohesion is often caused by noun/pronoun agreement errors; see page 42. This occurs when a pronoun in a follow-on sentence, doesn't agree with the subject introduced earlier.

Within a single sentence, however, it is also possible to have a noun/pronoun agreement error. In the same way that subjects and verbs need to agree, nouns and possessive pronouns must both be singular or both be plural.

Pronouns serve many purposes, so where they appear in a sentence also determines which pronoun to use.

| Subject | Object | Possessive noun phrase | Reflexive pronoun |
|---------|--------|------------------------|-------------------|
| I | me | mine | myself |
| you | you | yours | yourself |
| he | him | his | himself |
| she | her | hers | herself |
| it | it | its | itself |
| we | us | ours | ourselves |
| they | them | theirs | themselves |

Identify the noun or noun phrase to which the pronoun relates, and make sure they 'agree'.

## Practice questions

**69**  It would be helpful if all members of staff parked _____ in the allocated spaces.

  A. their cars          B. its car              C. there cars          D. his/her car

**70**  It is important that children learn to put their books and pens away _____.

  A. theirselves         B. themselves           C. theirselfs          D. themselfs

**71**  In Year 7, each pupil chooses mathematical tasks at _____ ability level.

  A. her                 B. their                C. they                D. his/her

**72**  The girls put on a fantastic concert; every musician, singer, dancer and backstage helper did _____ utmost to make it a success.

  A. his                 B. her                  C. their               D. they

## Determiner/noun agreement error; inappropriate or missing determiner

A determiner, like an adjective, gives more information about a noun. There are several different types of determiner.

| Type | Determiner |
|------|------------|
| Demonstrative | this (book) |
| Indefinite | some (pupils) |
| Interrogative | which (classroom) |
| Personal | we (teachers) |
| Possessive | our (policy) |

A possessive determiner indicates ownership.

> I *own that book. It belongs to* <u>me</u>. *It is* <u>mine</u>. *It is* <u>my</u> *book*.

| Subject | Object | Pronoun | Determiner |
|---|---|---|---|
| I | me | mine | my |
| you | you | yours | your |
| he | him | his | his |
| she | her | hers | her |
| it | it | its | its |
| we | us | ours | our |
| they | them | theirs | their |

 If the determiner is omitted altogether, the sentence will not be grammatically correct.

## Practice questions

**73** There are _____ mistakes in this piece of work than the last one, which is excellent!

   A. less        B. lesser        C. few        D. fewer

**74** A large _____ of students still need to hand their forms in to the school bursar.

   A. amount        B. number        C. quantity        D. total

**75** The caretaker has taken down _____ decorations in the hall, in preparation for parents' evening.

   A. them        B. this        C. those        D. that

**76** The amount of funding allocated to each school will depend on how _____ students opt to stay on to complete sixth-form studies.

   A. many        B. much        C. many of        D. much of

**77** Nadia has tried hard in all lessons to do _____.

   A. the best and gain highest marks possible

   B. her best and gain a highest marks possible

   C. the best and gain these highest marks possible

   D. her best and gain the highest marks possible

**78** Staff should ensure that _____ after use.

   A. all them laptops are returned to the computer suite

   B. all those laptops are returned to that computer suite

   C. all laptops are returned to the computer suite

   D. all laptops are returned to computer suite

**79** While there is no one right way to conceptualise teaching and learning, _____.

    A. there is high level of agreement at Carlton College about centrality of relationships

    B. there is a high level of agreement at Carlton College about the centrality of relationships

    C. there is some high level of agreement at Carlton College about a centrality of relationships

    D. there is the high level of agreement at Carlton College about a centrality of relationships

**80** The Principal, Ms Janowski, told the parents _____ in its next Ofsted inspection.

    A. that the school was aiming to gain the highest grade

    B. that school was aiming to gain a highest grade

    C. that a school was aiming to gain an highest grade

    D. that her school was aiming to gain highest grade

## Problems with comparatives and superlatives

When comparing two, or more than two, people or things, adding the ending (-er, -est) to the adjective indicates how many.

> *Jim is* <u>cleverer</u> *than Harry. Tommy is the* <u>cleverest</u> *in the class.*

When adding the suffix (-er or –est) seems clumsy, more/most can also be used to show the number involved in the comparison.

> *Roast potatoes are* <u>more</u> *popular than boiled potatoes. Chips are the* <u>most</u> *popular choice.*

Avoid using -est or 'most' when only two are being compared.

## Practice questions

**81** The new whiteboard is _____ than the last one we had in this classroom.

    A. more better        B. best        C. more good        D. better

**82** The final goal was the _____ moment for the Year 9 football team!

    A. happiest        B. most happiest    C. most happy        D. most happier

**83** Mr Brown's lessons are noisier than _____.

    A. Miss Jones        B. Miss Jones's    C. Miss Jones is    D. Miss Jone's

**84** Of the two options the school leadership team is considering, the second is the _____ for the school.

    A. most cost-effective    B. better cost-effective

    C. more cost-effective    D. more better cost-effective

## Problems with relative pronouns in subordinate clauses

A **relative pronoun** refers back to a previously mentioned noun and starts a subordinate **clause** which adds information about the noun.

Simple sentences comprising one clause like 'Term starts on 7 September 2015.' can be made more complex by including a subordinate clause with additional information.

> Term starts on 7 September 2015, <u>which is the first Monday of the month</u>.

The pronoun 'which' has to be in agreement with the noun to which it refers '7 September 2015'.

These are the relative pronouns:

○ who (used for a subject noun) and whom (used for an object noun) when referring to people;

○ which and that (for inanimate things); and

○ whose (for possession).

Also, 'of whom' and 'of which' might be used to introduce a subordinate clause.

> Mary, the new pupil of whom little is known, will be assessed when she arrives on Tuesday.

> The playground, the surface of which is crumbling, will be out of bounds while it is repaired.

## Practice questions

**85**  The mock GCSE exam timetable _____ we operated last year worked very well.

A. what                 B. who                 C. thus                 D. that

**86**  Could the person _____is blocking the school entrance, please move it now.

A. who's car            B. whoses car          C. whose car            D. whom car

**87**  Janek was one of the students _____nominated for a school prize.

A. who was              B. which were          C. who were             D. which was

**88**  _____ of the school, has won a place at Cambridge.

A. Jenna Jones, who is head girl              B. Jenna Jones who is head girl

C. Jenna Jones, whom is head girl             D. Jenna Jones that is head girl

## Inappropriate or missing adverbial forms

Adverbs 'add' to a verb, providing more information. They can also modify adjectives and other adverbs.

Many adverbs are formed by adding -ly to the end of an adjective, but not all.

The word 'fast' works both as an adjective and as an adverb:

> He ran fast; she was a fast runner.

The word 'quick' can only be used as an adjective giving more information about the noun (runner):

>    *She was a quick runner.*

For an adverb form of 'quick', add -ly.

>    *She ran quickly.*

To give emphasis, 'very' or 'much' might also be used; these can modify adverbs and adjectives.

>    *The teacher spoke very loudly. The classroom was much colder.*

## Practice questions

**89**  Make sure the children walk back to the coach _____ so they do not get cold after swimming.

    A. quick              B. quicker              C. more quicker        D. quickly

**90**  Despite being shy and quite reserved, Tamsin always behaves _____ with the other children.

    A. friendly           B. in a friendly way       C. as a friend          D. friendily

**91**  _____ such an appalling mess in the sixth-form common room!

    A. Never I have seen      B. I have seen never

    C. Never have I seen      D. Have never I seen

**92**  Elouise is extremely musical and plays the violin and flute _____.

    A. very good           B. very well            C. very better          D. very best

## SENSE, CLARITY AND FREEDOM FROM AMBIGUITY

Writing that is grammatically correct can still mislead the reader. Sentences that are too long to follow or that lack clarity are not acceptable. Clumsily constructed sentences which lead to **ambiguity** are also unacceptable.

In this section, rather than identifying the one correct option from four possible options, the challenge is to select the best option: the one which makes most sense, is most clear and contains no ambiguities.

## Wrong tense or tense inconsistency

Within one simple sentence, the **tense** needs to be consistent so that the information given makes sense.

The tense is given by the form of the verb and this can relate to one of three basic time frames: the past, the present or the future. There are also additional verb forms to indicate whether the action continues, or happened just once in the past, or will happen just once in the future.

>    *Mr Jones <u>was working</u> at the High School in 2010.*

*The playground* is being resurfaced.

*The Autumn term* will start *on the first Monday of September.*

A more complex sentence, that is one with more than one clause, can tell of some progression, so it might refer to an event in the past and also look forward to some event in the future.

*Jane* did not get *the grades she wanted so she* will be resitting *her exams in February.*

Aiming for a sense of passing time and/or the progression of events, using the correct tenses, provides the greatest clarity of expression.

In choosing the 'correct' option (and to earn a mark in the test), the challenge is to choose the option that makes most sense, is most clear and exhibits no ambiguity.

## Practice questions

**93**   Parents' evening for new Year 7 pupils will be held on 15 September and _____.

   A.  we are meeting you then

   B.  we will have been meeting you then

   C.  we will be meeting you then

   D.  we will have met you then

**94**   When school places are allocated by us, only one school place _____ the admission criteria for more than one school.

   A.  was offered, even if your child fulfils

   B.  has been offered, even if your child is fulfilling

   C.  offered, even if your child fulfil

   D.  will be offered, even if your child fulfils

**95**   Joni completed all her homework last year, took part in group activities and _____ well in class.

   A.  concentrated          B.  concentrates    C.  was concentrating    D.  had concentrated

**96**   After the internal moderator _____, the marks were submitted to the awarding organisation.

   A.  confirmed that all marking judgements were accurate and consistent

   B.  has confirmed that all marking judgements were accurate and consistent

   C.  had confirmed that all marking judgements were accurate and consistent

   D.  having confirmed that all marking judgements were accurate and consistent

## Unrelated participles

Present **participles** end in -ing and this verb form is often used to start a clause. In what follows, there will be a noun to which the participle relates.

In these two examples, who 'knows' about the approaching exams?

*Knowing the exams were approaching, the teacher provided extra lessons for revision.*

*Knowing the exams were approaching, pupils are provided with extra lessons for revision.*

On first reading, both could be correct! In the first, the teacher knows the exams are approaching and decides to put on extra revision sessions. In the second, although some pupils may know the exams are approaching, this is not related to the fact that the teacher is putting on extra revision sessions.

In choosing the 'correct' option (and to earn a mark in the test), the challenge is to choose the option that makes most sense, is most clear and exhibits no ambiguity.

## Practice questions

**97**   Appreciating the importance of formative assessment in the classroom, _____.

   A. it is important to incorporate peer assessment activities into every lesson

   B. teachers should incorporate peer assessment activities into every lesson

   C. children should be given peer assessment activities in every lesson

   D. peer assessment activities should be incorporated into every lesson

**98**   Being young, _____.

   A. it is difficult for children to understand the importance of school rules

   B. children's understanding of the importance of school rules is limited

   C. understanding the importance of school rules is limited for children

   D. children find it difficult to understand the importance of school rules

**99**   Reading the report, _____ to ensure the safety of the children.

   A. it was clear that every precaution was taken

   B. we are confident that every precaution was taken

   C. every precaution was obviously taken

   D. there was evidence that every precaution was taken

**100**   Having been asked to supply additional evidence for moderation, _____.

   A. Mr Jones is submitting some more Year 6 written work to the local authority

   B. submitting some more Year 6 written work by Mr Jones to the local authority

   C. the local authority will be submitted some additional Year 6 written work by Mr Jones

   D. some additional Year 6 written work will be submitted by Mr Jones to the authority

## Attachment ambiguities

The order in which words are arranged within a sentence can cause ambiguity.

Compare these sentences, and consider the effect of the positioning of 'on Friday'.

> *On Friday, Class 6B were excited to hear about the trip to the seaside.*
>
> *Class 6B were excited, on Friday, to hear about the trip to the seaside.*
>
> *Class 6B were excited to hear, on Friday, about the trip to the seaside.*
>
> *Class 6B were excited to hear about the trip to the seaside on Friday.*

When were Class 6B excited? When did they hear about the trip? When is the trip?

For clarity of writing, there should be no ambiguity.

 In choosing the 'correct' option (and to earn a mark in the test), the challenge is to choose the option that makes most sense, is most clear and exhibits no ambiguity.

## Practice questions

**101**  The Head of Drama informed the class _____.

    A.  about the theatre visit on Thursday

    B.  on the Thursday theatre visit

    C.  about the theatre visit due to take place on Thursday

    D.  Thursday about the theatre visit

**102**  There were lots of children running around, but as far as I could tell, _____.

    A.  the girl hit the boy with the tennis racquet

    B.  the girl hit the boy who had the tennis racquet

    C.  the boy hit the girl with the tennis racquet

    D.  the boy hit the girl and the tennis racquet

**103**  Brunsworth Academy is looking for _____ for the autumn term.

    A.  teachers of French, German and Mandarin Chinese

    B.  teachers who can teach French, German and Mandarin Chinese

    C.  teachers of French, German or Mandarin Chinese

    D.  teachers who can teach one or more of French, German and Mandarin Chinese

**104**  Many books on the topic _____.

    A.  are in the library which can be easily found

    B.  can easily be found in the library

    C.  are in the library easily found

    D.  can be in the library easily found

## Vague or ambiguous pronoun reference

The need for careful use and placement of pronouns has already been addressed. See the issue of lack of cohesion (page 38), the requirement for agreement between a subject pronoun and a verb (page 39), and the need for noun/pronoun agreement (page 42; page 46).

In longer sentences, with many clauses and phrases, it becomes more difficult to trace the noun, or more likely the noun phrase, to which the pronoun relates.

First, identify the pronoun and then any noun(s) to which it might relate.

> *At the end of each day, the cleaners are to stack the chairs and sweep the hall.* <u>*They*</u> *won't be needed until next week.*

To what, or whom, does 'They' refer? The pronoun 'They' is plural, so that limits the options to 'cleaners' and 'chairs'. Either might be true! The text lacks clarity and that makes it unacceptable.

In choosing the 'correct' option (and to earn a mark in the test), the challenge is to choose the option that makes most sense, is most clear and exhibits no ambiguity.

## Practice questions

**105** _____ in *A Midsummer Night's Dream* was praised by the local paper.

    A. When Tia Powell was in Year 9, her performance

    B. When she was in Year 9, Tia Powell's performance

    C. When she was in Year 9, her performance

    D. When Tia Powell was in Year 9, Tia Powell's performance

**106** Mrs Jones, Head of PE, has invested in a German trampoline _____.

    A. because she thinks they make the best one

    B. because she thinks Germany makes the best one

    C. because she thinks he makes the best one

    D. because she thinks it makes the best one

**107** Jonas's friend has asked if _____ with refreshments tomorrow night.

    A. he can help

    B. he and his friend can help

    C. they can help

    D. he and Jonas can help

**108** Throwing the ball at the fence, James saw _____.

    A. it fall to the ground

    B. the fence fall to the ground

    C. them fall to the ground

    D. those fall to the ground

## Confusion of words, eg imply/infer

The English language includes many words that look and/or sound similar to other words. The meanings differ but may not be well known and can easily be confused.

This causes problems for spelling, and the challenge of homophones is addressed on page 30. For the grammar section of the test, the meanings and uses of the following groups of words might be tested.

> ### ✐ Try this
>
> Look up these terms using a dictionary and commit their meanings to memory.
>
> accept/except                   different/differing
>
> affect/effect                   discreet/discrete
>
> allusion/illusion               disinterested/uninterested
>
> continual/continuous            infer/imply
>
> deny/rebut/refute               stationary/stationery

## Practice questions

**109** All Year 8 students, _____, will take part in swimming today.

    A. accept those who have brought a letter from home

    B. those who have brought a letter from home accepted

    C. those who have brought a letter from home expected

    D. except those who have brought a letter from home

**110** This _____ that schools are responsible for checking that individual students have submitted their forms correctly.

    A. infers          B. implies          C. imply          D. infer

**111** Many of the students seem to be _____ of financial awareness sessions with someone from the local bank.

    A. disinterested in taking up the offer

    B. uninterested in taking up the offer

    C. not uninterested in taking up the offer

    D. not disinterested in taking up the offer

**112** Showing the film to Year 5 and Year 6 _____ is a good idea.

    A. all together in the school hall

    B. altogether in the school hall

    C. all together in one place in the school hall

    D. altogether in one place in the school hall

# PROFESSIONAL SUITABILITY AND STYLE

Even when a piece of writing is grammatically correct and contains no ambiguities, it can still fall short of might be expected of a professional such as a qualified teacher.

This section of the test focuses on the more subtle skills that should be evident in a polished piece of writing.

## Non-parallelism in lists

A list presents numerous things or concepts or events, one after another. The accepted way of doing this is to adopt the same word class for each item on the list.

*Harry is taking five subjects: English, mathematics, science, art and sport.*

*Kate has hope of <u>becoming</u> a teacher and <u>teaching</u> at secondary level.*

*Les has problems: <u>his attitude</u> to work, <u>his punctuality</u> and <u>his failure</u> to meet acceptable standards of behaviour.*

It may seem to echo, but a well-constructed list is a repetitive structure, and words (like 'his') or verb forms (like -ing) should appear more than once.

## Practice questions

**113** _____, children should enjoy their experience of reading.

    A. Whether at school or when at home

    B. When they are at school or if they are at home

    C. Whether they are at school or at home

    D. When at school or whether at home

**114** This is not only poorly written _____.

    A. but it is badly punctuated as well

    B. but also badly punctuated

    C. and it is badly punctuated as well

    D. and also badly punctuated

**115** If your child is unwell, the school secretary will either telephone you or _____.

    A. an email will be sent out

    B. send you an email

    C. they will email you

    D. there will be an email

**116** The objectives of this course are to: _____.

    A. exploring new aspects of the curriculum, learn about the new format tests and sharing teaching ideas

    B. explore new aspects of the curriculum, learning about the new format tests and sharing teaching ideas

    C. exploring new aspects of the curriculum, learning about the new format tests and share teaching ideas

    D. explore new aspects of the curriculum, learn about the new format tests and share teaching ideas

## Inconsistent register and tone, eg you/one; active/passive; colloquialisms; appropriateness for audience

The register is conveyed by the choice of words and how these are used to form sentences and paragraphs. Long words and long sentences require the reader to have great literacy skills. Short sentences, using everyday language and keeping jargon to a minimum, should be more easily understood by the majority of readers. The choice of words, and decisions about the structure of the writing, should therefore take into account the target audience.

When speaking, the tone of voice indicates the formality or otherwise of the communication, and should take into account the relationship between the speaker and the listener. Writing can also have a **tone**. Deciding what tone to use, again, is a case of identifying the audience and meeting their requirements.

There are lots of pitfalls.

○ Choose between formal and informal according to the content and audience. Use 'one' consistently or 'you' for a less formal approach.

○ Slang or colloquialisms are not acceptable in formal writing, and should be avoided.

○ Choose between active and passive in the construction of any one sentence. Passive is best avoided if the style is to be clear and straightforward, but is useful for an impersonal style.

○ It is acceptable to intersperse the occasional active construction, especially if it means a short sentence after several long ones, or provides a short and snappy command.

    *Lesson preparation can be time-consuming but will reap rewards in the longer term. Do it now!*

○ Be consistent. Whatever register or tone you decide to adopt, use it throughout.

In deciding which option to choose, look for the most appropriately expressed: the one showing consistency and a regard for the target audience.

# Practice questions

**117** Zachary has been an enthusiastic participant in all sports offered as part of the curriculum and as captain of the football team, _____.

    A. the boy done great

    B. he has been top notch

    C. he has been excellent

    D. the lad has given it his all

**118** Many students have started working towards their exam portfolios, looking carefully at the set topics and _____.

    A. planning their major topic

    B. their major topic is being planned

    C. having planned their major topic

    D. were planning their major topic

**119** Staff have engaged enthusiastically with the proposals for the new curriculum and now they are _____.

    A. on a roll

    B. making good progress

    C. going great guns

    D. getting stuck in

**120** Check your child's school bag regularly for letters home; _____!

    A. one will be surprised at what you find in there

    B. you will be surprised at what you find in there

    C. they will be surprised at what people find in there

    D. it's surprising what people find in there

## Shift in person within sentences or across sentences

The need for agreement between 'person' within and across sentences has already been noted. The need for careful use and placement of pronouns has also been addressed. See the issue of lack of cohesion (page 38), the requirement for agreement between a subject pronoun and a verb (page 39) and the need for noun/pronoun agreement (page 42; page 46).

In longer sentences, with many clauses and phrases, or multiple sentences, it becomes more difficult to trace the noun, or more likely the noun phrase, to which a pronoun relates. In policy documents, for example, written by teachers for teachers, it needs to be clear who 'you' and 'they' are!

## Practice questions

**121** Staff will accompany the children to the zoo. _____ to continue work on this term's project on animals in captivity.

    A. They will take this opportunity

    B. We will take this opportunity

    C. You will take this opportunity

    D. He will take this opportunity

**122** You are welcome to wait for your child in the playground, but _____ car in local streets and not in the school drive.

    A. parents should park their

    B. we must park our

    C. one should park one's

    D. you must park your

**123** Your child is very important to us and we do our utmost to ensure _____ happy and thriving at all times.

    A. they are

    B. he or she is

    C. we are

    D. you are

**124** Staff should be on time for early morning briefing: it is important that _____.

    A. all teachers are there

    B. you are all there

    C. they are all there

    D. we are all there

## Excessive length and rambling sentences; redundancy/tautology

Even when a piece of writing is grammatically correct, there may still be room for improvement.

If the length of time it takes to read proves overly long, the reader might lose interest. It is therefore essential to be brief and to the point.

- ○ Any word – or phrase – that is not needed is called redundant and should be deleted.
- ○ The reader only needs to be told once. Any repetition amounts to **tautology**.

To identify the correct option, choose the one that conveys the message in as few words as possible.

## Practice questions

**125**  Thank you to the PTA _____.

    A.  and to those people, who are parents of first year children have donated prizes for the raffle at the school fair which is to be held on next Saturday

    B.  and to those people, who are parents of first year children and who have donated prizes for the raffle at the school fair to be held on next Saturday

    C.  and to those parents of first year children who have donated prizes which are for the raffle at the school fair which is to be held on next Saturday

    D.  and to those parents of first year children who have donated prizes for the raffle at the school fair next Saturday

**126**  The consensus among governors was that _____.

    A.  advance planning was completely essential

    B.  planning was essential

    C.  planning was completely essential

    D.  advance planning was essential

**127**  Wearing the correct kit is _____ for all students taking part in PE lessons.

    A.  a necessary requirement

    B.  a compulsory requirement

    C.  a needed requirement

    D.  an important requirement

**128**  Keeping your marking up to date is _____ preparing your lessons thoroughly.

    A.  as equally important as

    B.  as important as

    C.  equally as important as

    D.  important as

## Inappropriate conjunctions (also known as connectives), eg 'The reason is because'

**Conjunctions** (also called **connectives**) can be used to join sentences to form a single sentence.

| although | and | as | because | but | for | if | in case |
|----------|-----|-----|---------|-----|-----|-----|---------|
| or | since | so that | though | unless | while | yet | |

Conjunctions are also used to join other parts of speech, for example the items in a list.

Conjunctions, used appropriately, create a more readable narrative. Instead of many short sentences, each one describing some event, conjunctions can be used to present longer, more interesting sentences, holding the attention of the reader for longer. Conjunctions can show the relationship between events and ideas.

However, conjunctions used inappropriately will result in disjointed or confusing writing.

To identify the correct option, choose the one that conveys the message as smoothly as possible.

## Practice questions

**129** _____, you will fail this exam.

    A. Unless you don't try harder

    B. So you don't try harder

    C. Unless you try harder

    D. So you try harder

**130** No sooner had the coach arrived _____ we got out and started to explore the town!

    A. when        B. than        C. but        D. and

**131** The last applicant did not get the job _____ first-rate qualifications and relevant experience.

    A. in spite having

    B. because of having

    C. although having

    D. despite having

**132** As the voting is now closed, _____ of the prefects will be announced shortly.

    A. the names      B. so the names      C. and the names      D. because the names

# 3.3    Comprehension

To demonstrate the various skills and how these might be tested, 41 practice questions have been devised, set against a total of six different texts. For each of the six texts, questions are lettered alphabetically, A, B, C, ... See page 12 for an explanation of the coding C1–C9.

| Title | Page | Skill | | | | | | | | |
|---|---|---|---|---|---|---|---|---|---|---|
| | | C1 | C2 | C3 | C4 | C5 | C6 | C7 | C8 | C9 |
| 1: Children missing education | 63 | E | A | F | D | | C | | B | G |
| 2: RoSPA school visits guide | 66 | A | | B | E | | C | D | F | G |
| 3: Careers guidance | 69 | | D | | | F | C | G | A, B | E |
| 4: Travel and transport needs | 73 | B | D | A | | C | | E | | F |
| 5: Punctuation and spelling policy | 76 | E | B | A | | F | G | | C | D |
| 6: Discipline in schools | 79 | A | F | B | C | E | D | G | | |

Each text is approximately the same length as the texts in the real test. To be able to answer the questions, you will need to read the whole text through at least twice.

Read through once quickly, to get the gist of the piece, and then read through more slowly, checking that each paragraph has been understood. After the first read, sum up the whole text in one sentence. After the second read, sum up each paragraph in one phrase.

The length of time it takes you depends not only on your speed of reading but also the complexity of the material. Reading quickly might mean you miss important information. Reading too slowly might result in your running out of time.

> ###  Try this
>
> Time yourself in the reading of text 6 on page 79. It is the shortest text and approximately 600 words long. From this, work out how long it takes you to read 100 words. Text 3 on page 69 is the longest text, at around 700 words. Time yourself reading this text. What is your pace?

Each question type is now considered in turn. Many of them require skimming the whole text again, rather than focusing on one section.

## ATTRIBUTING STATEMENTS TO CATEGORIES

The rubric for this type of question starts with the presentation of a short list of audience types.

- ○ Text 1, practice question 137 (page 66): Local authorities (LA); Schools (S); Parents (P);
- ○ Text 2, practice question 140 (page 68): RoSPA (R); Schools (S); Health and Safety Executive (HSE);
- ○ Text 4, practice question 155 (page 74): Audit of the infrastructure (AI); Strategy for developing infrastructure (SI); Sustainable school travel (SST);
- ○ Text 5, practice question 164 (page 78): Grammar (G); Spelling (S); Writing (W);
- ○ Text 6, practice question 167 (page 80): Schools (S); Headteachers (H); Teachers (T).

Notice that each option is a stakeholder who is quite different from all of the others. Notice also the coding to one, two or three letters, which reduces the amount of text to be entered onscreen.

This coded list is then followed by a longer list of extracts taken from the text. The challenge is to decide which extracts relate to which target audience. There is one mark per extract correctly categorised.

It is important to have read all of the text at least once. To find these extracts a further scan will be needed, and maybe reading a bit before and after to decide on the category.

This type of question may also be found in practice paper 3, question A (page 101) and practice paper 4, question C (page 108).

## COMPLETING A BULLETED LIST

Three phrases have to be selected from a list of many. The three correct options fit with a stem of a bullet list given at the end of the question, the last item of which has been provided.

Read the stem carefully; it indicates the subject of the sentence that has to be completed by the four bullet points.

- ○ Text 1, practice question 133 (page 64): Local authorities must ensure that they
- ○ Text 3, practice question 150 (page 71): Effective careers guidance happens when
- ○ Text 4, practice question 157 (page 75): Local authorities should ensure that they
- ○ Text 5, practice question 161 (page 77): At Bold Hill Primary School, the teaching of writing
- ○ Text 6, practice question 172 (page 81): Punishments

Notice also the final bullet point that has been provided. Non-parallelism in lists is unacceptable (see page 53). If options are similar and seemingly correct, choose the one that matches the style of the fourth bullet point.

This type of question may also be found in practice paper 2, question C (page 95) and practice paper 4, question D (page 108 ).

## SEQUENCING INFORMATION

Sequencing the statements means finding them in the text and numbering them 1, 2, 3, and so on.

In the practice questions and test papers, taking into account that this book is on paper, as opposed to onscreen, the five or six statements are already numbered, so the task is to identify the order in which these statements appear in the text.

See practice questions 138 (page 66), 141 (page 68), 154 (page 74) and 160 (page 77).

As a strategy, it may help first to number the paragraphs and then note in which paragraph a statement appears. Once they are all found, these paragraph numbers can be turned into ordinal numbers.

Time yourself doing this type of question. How quickly can you find all the statements, by scanning through the text?

This type of question may also be found in practice paper 3, question B (page 101) and practice paper 4, question E (page 109).

## PRESENTING MAIN POINTS

This type of question offers eight or nine points, only three of which accurately convey information given in the text and are important enough to be 'main' points.

See practice questions 144 (page 69) and 169 (page 81).

Read the stem of the question carefully as it provides important information that should help you to eliminate some of the options and identify the three main points.

This type of question may also be found in practice paper 1, questions C (page 88) and E (page 89).

## MATCHING TEXTS TO SUMMARIES

For this type of question, four summaries are given that relate to particular paragraphs within the text. They are not given in the order they appear in the text.

See practice questions 152 (page 72), 156 (page 75), 165 (page 78) and 171 (page 81).

This type of question may also be found in practice paper 3, question E (page 102) and practice paper 4, question B (page 108).

## IDENTIFYING THE MEANINGS OF WORDS AND PHRASES

One phrase that appears within the text is presented, together with a list of six possible meanings of the phrase. Working out which is the correct option usually hinges on understanding the precise meaning of a few words.

The answer may require one correct option, or identifying the two closest options. Read the rubric carefully!

There is often repetition of the text, in the original selected phrase and the six options, so focus on what is different.

See practice questions 135 (page 65), 142 (page 68), 149 (page 71), 166 (page 79) and 170 (page 81).

This type of question may also be found in practice paper 1, question D (page 88), practice paper 2, questions A (page 94) and B (page 95) and practice paper 3, question F (page 102).

## EVALUATING STATEMENTS ABOUT THE TEXT

Four statements, made about information given in the text, are to be assigned to one of five categories:

- The statement is supported by the text (S).
- The statement is implied to be the case or is implicitly supported by the text (I).
- The text provides no evidence or information concerning the statement (NE).
- The statement is implicitly contradicted or implicitly refuted by the text (IC).
- The statement is contradicted by the text (C).

Notice the coding, which reduces the amount of text to be entered onscreen.

It is important to locate the relevant information in the text, and to read enough of the text carefully, before making a decision for each of the statements.

See practice questions 143 (page 68), 153 (page 72), 158 (page 75) and 173 (page 82).

This type of question may also be found in practice paper 2, question D (page 95) and practice paper 3, question D (page 102).

## SELECTING HEADINGS AND SUBHEADINGS

The stem of this type of question specifies whether a heading or a subheading is to be selected from the four options offered. For a subheading, the relevant paragraphs are given.

Notice that the question asks for the 'best', so while more than one of the options might suit the text, only one is considered to be the best.

Careful reading of the whole document (for a title) or the selected paragraphs (for a subheading) is essential.

It is possible to have two C8 questions in the comprehension section of a test, one asking for the heading, and one for a subheading.

See practice questions 134 (page 65), 145 (page 69), 147 (page 71), 148 (page 71) and 162 (page 78).

This type of question may also be found in practice paper 1, questions A and B (page 88).

## IDENTIFYING POSSIBLE READERSHIP OR AUDIENCE FOR A TEXT

For this type of question, a range of audiences for the document is offered and two groups are to be identified:

- the readership group that would find it the most relevant (M);
- the readership group that would find it the least relevant (L).

Notice the coding to one letter, M or L, which reduces the amount of text to be entered onscreen.

The range of possible audiences includes a cross section of those who might read the document: HM Government, HSE, Ofsted inspectors, KS2 moderators, local authorities, school governors, headteachers, assistant headteachers, staff responsible for careers guidance in school, teachers responsible for health and safety in school, literacy co-ordinators, secondary heads of year, secondary teachers, teachers leading school visits, specific subject teachers, parents, police, bus drivers, and so on.

For each of these 'stakeholders', the job role or position in society impacts on what should or need not be of relevance. For the M option, while more than one group maybe ought to read the text, the correct answer will be the group for whom it is 'most' relevant. Similarly, for the L option, several groups might not be interested, but the correct answer is the group for whom it has the least relevance.

See practice questions 139 (page 66), 146 (page 69), 151 (page 72), 159 (page 76) and 163 (page 78).

This type of question may also be found in practice paper 3, question C (page 102) and practice paper 4, question A (page 108).

# 1: CHILDREN MISSING EDUCATION

All children, regardless of their circumstances, are entitled to a full-time education which is suitable to their age, ability, aptitude and any special educational needs they may have. Children missing education (CME) are at significant risk of underachieving, being victims of abuse and becoming NEET (not in education, employment or training) later on in life. Local authorities should have robust procedures and policies in place to enable them to meet their duty in relation to these children, including appointing a named person to whom schools and other agencies can make referrals. Local authorities should undertake regular reviews and evaluate their processes to ensure that these continue to be fit for purpose in identifying and dealing with CMEs in their area.

The purpose of section 436A of the Education Act 1996 is to ensure that local authorities' arrangements enable them to establish the identities of children in their area who are not registered pupils at a school, and are not receiving suitable education otherwise than at a school. The LA should consult the parents of the child when establishing whether the child is receiving suitable education. Local authorities should have procedures in place to prevent children at risk of becoming CME. Those children identified as not receiving suitable education should be returned to full-time education either at school or in alternative provision. This duty only relates to children of compulsory school age.

From June 2013, Ofsted has been implementing a new joint inspection for multi-agency arrangements for the protection of children which will include CMEs.

Parents have a duty to ensure that their children of compulsory school age are receiving efficient full-time education. Some parents may elect to educate their children at home and may withdraw them from school at any time to do so, unless they are subject to a School Attendance Order. Where a parent notifies the school in writing of their intention to home educate, the school must delete the child from its admission register and then inform the local authority.

Children with special educational needs statements can be home educated. Where the statement sets out special educational provision that the child should receive at home, the local authority is under a duty to arrange that provision. Where the statement names a school as the place where the child should receive his or her education but the parent chooses to home educate their child, the local authority must assure itself that the provision being made by the parent is suitable to the child's special educational needs. In such cases the authority must review the statement annually.

Schools, including Academies and Free Schools, must monitor pupils' attendance through their daily register. Schools should agree with their local authority the intervals at which they will inform local authorities of the details of pupils who are regularly absent from school or have missed ten school days or more without permission. Schools must also notify the authority if a pupil is to be deleted from an admission register in certain circumstances. Pupils who remain on a school roll are not necessarily missing education but schools should monitor attendance and address it when it is poor. It is also important that pupils' irregular attendance is reported to the authority.

Schools also have safeguarding duties under section 175 of the Education Act 2002 in respect of their pupils, and as part of this should investigate any unexplained absences. Academies and independent schools have a similar safeguarding duty for their pupils.

Schools must also arrange full-time education for excluded pupils from the sixth school day of a fixed period exclusion. This information can be found in the school attendance and exclusions advice.

Based on Statutory guidance November 2013 www.gov.uk/government/uploads/system/uploads/attachment_data/file/350737/CME_guidance__final_template___CB_.pdf.

## Practice questions for Comprehension 1

**133** Select three phrases from the list below to complete the bulleted list.

The last bullet point has been completed for you.

1. have a specific person to whom schools and other organisations can refer CMEs
2. bring in a joint inspection for multi-agency arrangements for the protection of children
3. clarify which children in their area are not registered at a school
4. guarantee that children of compulsory school age are receiving full-time education
5. are confident that a child with a special educational needs statement who is home educated, is receiving adequate provision
6. monitor attendance and refer irregular attendance to parents
7. investigate any unexplained absences as part of their safeguarding duties
8. arrange full-time education for excluded pupils from the sixth school day of exclusion

Local authorities must ensure that they:

- 
- 
- 
- have robust procedures and policies in place to meet their duty in relation to CMEs.

**134** Select the best subheading to cover paragraphs 4 and 5.

    **1.** Meeting the needs of home-educated children

    **2.** Full-time education for children of compulsory education age

    **3.** Children with special educational needs statements

    **4.** Local authority provision for children who are home educated

**135** From the list select the option closest to the meaning of the phrase as it appears in the context of the passage.

'Schools should agree with their local authorities the intervals at which they will inform local authorities' (paragraph 6)

    **1.** Schools should agree with their local authorities the dates when they will inform local authorities

    **2.** Schools should agree with their local authorities the days when at which they will inform local authorities

    **3.** Schools should agree with their local authorities the times when at which they will inform local authorities

    **4.** Schools should agree with their local authorities how quickly they will inform local authorities

    **5.** Schools should agree with their local authorities how often they will inform local authorities

    **6.** Schools should agree with their local authorities how efficiently they will inform local authorities

**136** From the list below select three points that accurately convey information about children missing education (CMEs) given in the text.

    **1.** CMEs are at significant risk of becoming subject to a School Attendance Order.

    **2.** Local authorities should regularly evaluate their procedures to ensure they are appropriate for addressing issues with CMEs.

    **3.** The aim of section 436A of the Education Act 1996 is to ensure schools' arrangements enable them to identify pupils who are not registered.

    **4.** Schools should have processes established to prevent children becoming CMEs.

    **5.** Children of all ages who are not receiving an appropriate education should be returned to school or alternative provision made.

    **6.** Schools must remove a child's name from its admission register once informed by parents that the child will be educated at home.

    **7.** Where the statement of a home-educated child with special educational needs specifies particular education provision, the parents are responsible for arranging that provision.

    **8.** Schools, including Academies and Free Schools, must record pupils' attendance and report irregular attendance to the authority.

    **9.** Under section 175 of the Education Act 2002, local authorities and schools have safeguarding duties in respect of their pupils.

**137**  Read the statements below and based on the evidence provided by the passage decide which refer to:

Local authorities (LA)

Schools (S)

Parents (P)

**1.** They have safeguarding duties which includes investigating unexplained absences.

**2.** They may withdraw their children from school at any time to home educate them.

**3.** They should discuss with parents whether a child is receiving a suitable education.

**4.** They must provide information if a child misses ten days of school or more without permission.

**5.** They should clarify which children in their area are not receiving a suitable alternative education.

**138**  Identify the order in which these statements appear in the text.

**1.** Schools, including Academies and Free Schools, have safeguarding duties under Section 175 of the Education Act 2002.

**2.** Underachievement is a serious risk for children missing education.

**3.** Information about education for excluded pupils can be found in the school attendance and exclusions advice.

**4.** Children may be withdrawn from school by parents to be home educated unless they are subject to a School Attendance Order.

**5.** Parents should be consulted by the LA when establishing whether a child is receiving a suitable education.

**6.** Local authorities must be notified if a pupil is to be deleted from an admission register under certain circumstances.

**139**  The following groups might all be potential audiences or readers of this document, although some would find it more useful than others. Which group would find it the most relevant and which group the least relevant?

- Headteachers
- Local authorities
- Parents
- Secondary teachers
- Governors
- Ofsted inspectors

## 2: RoSPA SCHOOL VISITS GUIDE

As well as being a welcome break from the school routine, school visits enable pupils to learn new skills, gain fresh understanding and to develop positive attitudes to their environment, their peers and their teachers. School visits can be part of the curriculum (eg theatre visits or field trips); supplement the curriculum (for example Forest School); they can enhance the curriculum (such as visits to historic cities) and can promote personal development (eg adventurous activities). Some visits may be regular opportunities for learning outside the classroom (eg swimming) or take place in other schools (eg sports fixtures). In some cases visits may be for purely leisure purposes. A visit may be part of the school day or take place over a week or longer. Whatever the intended purpose or duration, the gains can be educational and personal; and are often remembered long after the educational reason for the visit has been forgotten.

RoSPA believes children and young people benefit from being challenged to visit new places and try out new and exciting activities. Through these experiences they can develop self-knowledge and understanding which can be of great value. If we always keep children as safe as possible, they may never experience the challenges involved in school visits, nor gain the associated benefits. Our aim in this guide and in our policy overall, is to help you to plan to keep children and young people as safe as necessary, while providing them with the opportunity for new experiences and challenges.

HM Government estimates that, in the UK, school age children undertake 7–10 million days of activity outside the classroom each year, with all the potential benefits described above. This is likely to be a conservative estimate. In general school visits are low-risk activities – but this is because a lot of thought and planning has gone into assessing and managing any risks to the health and well-being of pupils and staff as well as recognising the many potential benefits. We tend to remember examples of school visits where a child or member of staff was seriously injured or killed because, rightly, these events receive a lot of attention in the national and local press, but these are rare occurrences. Even rarer, are examples of serious incidents on school visits where a teacher or member of staff was found to be legally negligent.

Aside from liability for negligence, schools and their governors or senior managers can face criminal liability for breaches of health and safety law. However, in the period 2005–2010, there were only two HSE (Health and Safety Executive) prosecutions relating to school trips in the UK.

With any school visit, the focus should be on how real risks arising from such visits are to be managed, and not on trivial, hypothetical risks, or on burdensome paperwork. Where sensible and proportionate measures have been taken by those with responsibility for planning and organising school visits, and these can be demonstrated, the HSE state that it is highly unlikely that there would be a breach of health and safety law or that it would be in the public interest to bring a prosecution. Accidents can happen, and health and safety law reflects this fact.

Prosecutions invariably result from incidents where there has been recklessness or a clear failure to consider and adopt sensible measures. An accident happening does not necessarily mean there has been a breach of health and safety law. Despite the benefits, those planning school visits often focus on preparing for the hazards and associated risks, with the result that any intended benefits may be overlooked or given insufficient attention.

Injuries from leisure activities show that children are far more likely to get injured playing football or rugby at school than going on a school walking trip. Children and young people are most at risk of injury at school between the ages of 10 and 14. However this is related to the fact that they spend more time at school rather than school being a more risky venue than home or elsewhere.

Based on RoSPA School Visits Guide www.rospa.com/schoolandcollegesafety/
teachingsafely/info/school-visits-guide.pdf.

## Practice questions for Comprehension 2

**140** Read the statements below and based on the evidence provided by the passage, decide which refer to:

RoSPA (R)

Schools (S)

Health and Safety Executive (HSE)

1. Their policy is to keep children and young people safe while ensuring they are offered new and challenging experiences.
2. They enable children and young people to experience 7 to 10 million days of activity outside the classroom each year.
3. They may focus too much on the potential dangers of school visits and not enough on the positive outcomes.
4. They believe that if appropriate care in planning for school visits can be demonstrated, it is unlikely that health and safety law would be breached.
5. Their view is that visiting new places and trying out new activities is beneficial to young people.

**141** Identify the order in which these statements appear in the text.

1. Examples of school visits when a child or member of staff was killed are rare.
2. If children are always kept as safe as possible, they may never experience the challenges and benefits of school visits.
3. Between 2005 and 2010, there were only two HSE prosecutions linked to school trips in the UK.
4. School visits can be part of the curriculum, supplement the curriculum, enhance the curriculum and can promote personal development.
5. There is a greater risk of injury for children and young people when they play sports such as rugby than when on a school walking trip.

**142** From the list select the two options closest to the meaning of the phrase as it appears in the context of the passage.

'trivial, hypothetical risks' (paragraph 5)

1. troublesome, possible and likely risks
2. small, potential but unlikely risks
3. significant, speculative and possible risks
4. irritating, plausible but improbable risks
5. insignificant, theoretical and relatively improbable risks
6. laughable, realistic but mostly impossible risks

**143** Read the statements below and decide whether

- the statement is supported by the text (S)
- the statement is implied to be the case or is implicitly supported by the text (I)

- the text provides no evidence or information concerning the statement (NE)
- the statement is implicitly contradicted or implicitly refuted by the text (IC)
- the statement is contradicted by the text (C)

1. School visits offer children worthwhile and enriching experiences.
2. If an accident happens on a school visit, health and safety law has been breached.
3. Teachers should consider the risks and benefits when they are planning school visits.
4. School visits should be planned, organised and led by experienced teachers.

**144** From the list below select the four main points that most accurately describe school visits.

1. School visits by their nature are often high-risk activities.
2. School visits may be remembered by pupils some time after the reason has been forgotten.
3. Schools are always prosecuted where accidents happen in the course of a school visit.
4. Schools and their governors can be liable for negligence.
5. It is important to keep children as safe as possible, eliminating all risks.
6. The benefits of school visits should be primarily educational.
7. School visits where a child or member of staff was injured or killed receive a lot of press attention.
8. Those planning school visits should focus on managing real risks, not simply completing excessive paperwork.
9. It is between the ages of 11 and 14 that children and young people are at greatest risk of injury at school.

**145** Select the best subheading for paragraph 3.

1. HM Government's policy on school visits
2. The benefits of school visits
3. Serious incidents on school visits
4. The low risk of school visits

**146** The following groups might all be potential audiences or readers of the article, although some would find it more useful than others. Which group would find it the least relevant and which group the most relevant?

- The HSE
- Teachers responsible for health and safety in school
- Headteachers
- HM Government
- Teachers leading school visits

## 3: CAREERS GUIDANCE

One of your senior leaders, such as an Assistant Headteacher, should have responsibility for overseeing arrangements for careers education. This might include taking the lead on procuring external services and monitoring their impact, or line managing an internal careers adviser. They might also take responsibility for organising work experience placements. This member of staff should receive appropriate CPD (continuing professional development) to ensure they are able to carry out their role effectively.

It is the school's responsibility to budget for the provision of Careers Education and Guidance. It is important to ensure that adequate provision for this has been made within your school's budget. It is up to the school to decide on resources. The governors' key role is to ensure that value for money is being achieved. For this to happen you need to be happy that all the key questions about quality, professional expertise and competence, and impact measurement are being addressed.

Ensuring that schools are providing good quality and achieving value for money is one of the most important jobs for governors. In the provision of careers guidance companies have been working hard to ensure that the quality of their provision is easy for schools to measure. Senior leaders should be reporting back to governors regularly on this. How can you achieve this in your school?

Is the guidance provided by qualified staff? This is especially important if you are using independent careers companies. If your school is providing its own staff, what training have they had? Having a careers professional on the staff is not necessarily sufficient to meet the requirements of ensuring access to independent and impartial guidance. This is because schools need to demonstrate that the source of the guidance is independent of any school set targets with regard to destinations.

In terms of qualifications, the Careers Development Institute insists that anyone registering as a careers professional should either be qualified to NVQ level 6 or be working towards achieving this level within two years.

How is the impact of the provision measured? This is one of the most challenging areas. How is the impact of the guidance being reported, firstly to the school? Secondly, how is this being communicated to governors? If nothing else, this is an important value for money indicator. For example, you should know how many interviews are being provided. Has provision been made for everyone and, if not, how are pupils being selected for advice and guidance sessions? Effective guidance provision can influence many other aspects of the life of a school; for example guidance which motivates and inspires pupils can have positive effects on areas like attendance, behaviour, college and university applications. If these measures remain stubbornly immoveable could the provision of guidance help to improve them? Governors can also find out about the impact of careers guidance by talking to the pupils themselves, for example by holding focus groups or consulting the student council.

What happens to your pupils when they leave school? Is there free movement from school to both education and employment? Are those pupils seeking employment finding apprenticeships that carry with them the guarantee of further training and qualifications? Governors should ensure that they receive reports on destinations from the local authority or from the school depending on who takes responsibility for the provision of the information. At present, local authorities are responsible for the collection of destination data from local schools and colleges. Information is published on this website: https://www.gov.uk/government/collections/statistics-destinations.

Given the extensive work this requires, however, there is a time delay of around a year prior to publication. The information for leavers in the academic year 2011–2012 is published in June 2014 and is currently the most up to date information available from the Department for Education. Work is being done to reduce the delay from collection to publication.

How can we evidence our good practice? Schools with well-established good practice in the provision of careers education and guidance can have their provision assessed against a nationally established standard. The advantages of having a quality kite mark are many. Firstly, it is the best way to ensure the quality of the careers education and guidance provide in your school. Most importantly, it is the best way of advertising to children, parents and inspectors that your school takes its responsibilities very seriously.

Based on 'What careers guidance is currently provided in our school?' from National Governors Association www.gov.uk/government/publications/careers-education-and-guidance-school-governors-and-trustees-briefing.

## Practice questions for Comprehension 3

**147**  Select the best heading for this document.

   **1.** The roles of Senior Leaders in your school

   **2.** Careers Education and Guidance in your school

   **3.** Destinations of School Leavers at your school

   **4.** The Careers Development Institute and your school

**148**  Select the best subheading to cover paragraphs 7 and 8.

   **1.** The importance of destination data for school leavers

   **2.** Free movement from school to education and employment

   **3.** Reducing the delay from collection to publication

   **4.** Local authorities' responsibility for destination data

**149**  From the list select the two options closest to the meaning of the phrase as it appears in the context of the passage.
   'If these measures remain stubbornly immoveable' (paragraph 6)

   **1.** If these rules remain severely entrenched

   **2.** If these targets remain inordinately unattainable

   **3.** If these indicators remain obstinately unchangeable

   **4.** If these steps remain inflexibly unchanged

   **5.** If these outcomes remain intractably unalterable

   **6.** If these processes remain disturbingly inflexible

**150**  Select three phrases from the list below (continues overleaf) to complete the bulleted list. The last bullet point has been completed for you.

   **1.** guidance is provided solely or primarily by external services

   **2.** the headteacher has responsibility for overseeing arrangements

   **3.** the person in charge of guidance receives appropriate CPD

   **4.** the impact of provision is reported to the school and to the governors

   **5.** governors talk to the pupils about careers by holding focus groups

**6.** guidance has a positive impact on many aspects of school life

**7.** all pupils are receiving the same level of advice and guidance

**8.** guidance is linked to school set targets with regard to destinations

**9.** there is minimal delay between collection and publication of destination data

Effective careers guidance happens when:

- 
- 
- 
- guidance is provided by qualified professionals.

**151** The following groups might all be potential audiences or readers of the article, although some would find it more useful than others. Which group would find it the least relevant and which group the most relevant?

- Head teachers of junior schools
- Local authorities
- Assistant headteachers
- Staff responsible for careers guidance in school
- School governors
- Parents of secondary-age students

**152** Match each of the summaries below to the relevant paragraph of the text: paragraphs 1, 4, 6 and 9.

**1.** Monitoring the effectiveness of careers provision within a school

**2.** Ensuring there is a designated senior member of staff responsible for careers education

**3.** Checking the qualifications of staff, internal and external, who are involved in careers education

**4.** Having a quality kite mark for careers education has many advantages

**153** Read the statements below and decide whether

- the statement is supported by the text (S)
- the statement is implied to be the case or is implicitly supported by the text (I)
- the text provides no evidence or information concerning the statement (NE)
- the statement is implicitly contradicted or implicitly refuted by the text (IC)
- the statement is contradicted by the text (C)

**1.** One of the main roles of governors is to quality assure what happens in a school and deliver value for money.

**2.** Careers guidance needs to align with school set targets for students' destinations.

**3.** Schools should carefully monitor the quality of externally provided careers guidance.

**4.** Effective careers guidance is delivered throughout the school to all year groups.

# 4: TRAVEL AND TRANSPORT NEEDS

Local authorities should, in large part, base their assessment of children and young people's travel and transport needs on the data provided by schools or colleges, often contained within school travel plans. Effective school travel plans, updated as necessary, put forward a package of measures to improve safety and reduce car use, backed by a partnership involving the school, education, health and transport officers from the local authority, and the police. These seek to secure benefits for both the school and the children by improving their health through active travel and reducing congestion caused by school runs, which in turn helps to improve local air quality. Many travel plans are produced as a result of planning conditions placed on new developments by local authority planning departments. This highlights the need for all relevant departments (eg highways departments, planning departments, transport departments, children's services, environment departments, and public health) to be fully engaged when addressing this duty.

Local authorities already collect much of the information required for the audit of the infrastructure supporting sustainable school travel. Local authorities should audit infrastructure in accordance with any relevant guidance and the requirements of any infrastructure implemented. Specific school routes audits are considered good practice. The specifics of the audit and how often it should be reviewed are for a local authority to decide on as appropriate. However, the audit should include a mapping exercise to show how schools are served by:

o   bus and other public transport routes (including school transport provided by the local authority);

o   footpaths, cycle ways, roads and associated features (including crossing points and patrols, traffic calming measures, speed limits, 20mph zones); and

o   any other arrangements made to support sustainable school transport that may be in operation (including the provision of cycle training, road safety training and independent travel training; the provision of walking promotion and barrier removal schemes, car sharing schemes, park and stride/ride schemes, cycle parking).

The audit should also consider data relating to personal safety and security, and other factors that influence travel choices, such as poor behaviour on school buses and/or the incidence of bullying on the journey to school. School travel plans will help local authorities to understand any specific local issues, including perceptions of pupils and parents. The arrangements or requirements for children with special educational needs (SEN) or disabilities should also be considered and whether, for example, some might benefit from independent travel training which can result in a skill for life.

Following the assessment of pupil needs, and audit of the sustainable transport infrastructure that supports travel to school, local authorities must establish a strategy for developing that infrastructure so that it better meets the needs of children and young people in their area. These improvements should address a range of objectives, including environmental improvements, health benefits and enhanced child safety and security. The strategy should be a statement of the authority's overall vision, objectives and work programme for improving accessibility to schools and will be an important source of information to parents on the travel options available to them when expressing their preferences for particular schools in the admissions round.

The strategy should be evidence-based, including an assessment of the accessibility needs and problems of the local authority's area. Local authorities must monitor the implementation of their strategy and revise these as they feel necessary.

Local walking, cycling and bus strategies should inform the local authority's duty to promote sustainable school travel. In line with the physical Olympic and Paralympic legacy, as set out in HM Government's document 'Moving More, Living More', promotion of walking and cycling to school can be an effective way to increase physical activity in children.

The sustainable school travel duty should have a broad impact, including providing health benefits for children, and their families, through active journeys, such as walking and cycling. It can also bring significant environmental improvements, through reduced levels of congestion and improvements in air quality to which children are particularly vulnerable.

Based on 'New home to school travel and transport guidance' www.gov.uk/government/uploads/ system/uploads/attachment_data/file/295189/Home_to_School_Transport_Consultation_ Document.pdf.

# Practice questions for Comprehension 4

**154**  Identify the order in which these statements appear in the text.

   **1.** Audits of specific school routes are considered good practice.

   **2.** The physical Olympic and Paralympic legacy is set out in 'Moving More, Living More', produced by HM Government.

   **3.** Effective school travel plans are backed by a partnership including representatives from education, health, transport and the police.

   **4.** The data provided by schools and colleges should form the basis of local authorities' assessment of pupils' transport needs.

   **5.** The strategy for developing infrastructure should be a reflection of the local authority's overall vision.

   **6.** The infrastructure audit should consider the needs and requirements of children with special educational needs.

**155**  Read the statements below and decide which refers to

   • Audit of the infrastructure (AI)

   • Strategy for developing infrastructure (SI)

   • Sustainable school travel (SST)

   **1.** This should be delivered in line with relevant guidance.

   **2.** This will be invaluable for parents when selecting a school for their children.

   **3.** The details of this process and how frequently it should be carried out is at the discretion of a local authority.

   **4.** This should result in important benefits for the environment and the health of children and their families.

   **5.** This should include taking account of factors that impact on travel option choice.

**156** Match each of the summaries below to the relevant paragraph of the text: paragraphs 2, 5, 6 or 7.

   **1.** The monitoring and evaluation of the strategy for developing the infrastructure

   **2.** The effect of sustainable school travel

   **3.** The mapping exercise involved in an audit of the infrastructure

   **4.** The importance of promoting sustainable school travel

**157** Select three phrases from the list below to complete the bulleted list.
The last bullet point has been completed for you.

   **1.** base their evaluation of pupils' travel needs on the information provided by schools and colleges

   **2.** put forward a raft of measures to improve safety and reduce car use

   **3.** produce travel plans as an outcome of planning conditions placed on new developments

   **4.** carry out specific school routes audits as part of their brief

   **5.** support sustainable school transport, including the provision of road safety training for pupils

   **6.** understand any specific local issues, including the views and perspectives of pupils and parents

   **7.** provide advice to parents on the travel options available to their children when selecting a school

   **8.** offer independent travel training for any pupils for whom it would be beneficial

   Local authorities should ensure that they:

   •

   •

   •

   • monitor and revise their strategy for developing infrastructure as necessary.

**158** Read the statements below and decide whether:

   • the statement is supported by the text (S)

   • the statement is implied to be the case or is implicitly supported by the text (I)

   • the text provides no evidence or information concerning the statement (NE)

   • the statement is implicitly contradicted by the text (IC)

   • the statement is contradicted by the text (C)

   **1.** Travel plans involve a number of different departments working together.

   **2.** Transport is an important consideration for parents when selecting schools for their children.

   **3.** The local authority should ensure that car sharing schemes are set up to reduce congestion.

   **4.** Effective school travel plans benefit the whole community, not just children and young people.

**159** The following groups might all be potential audiences or readers of this document, although some would find it more useful than others. Which group would find it least relevant and which group the most relevant?

- Local authorities
- Headteachers
- Transport departments
- Police
- Parents
- Bus drivers

# 5: PUNCTUATION AND SPELLING POLICY

## Bold Hill Primary School Grammar, Punctuation and Spelling Policy

This document sets out the policy for teaching grammar, punctuation and spelling at Bold Hill Primary School. The aim of this policy is to ensure that there is a consistent approach to teaching grammar, punctuation and spelling across the school. It will contribute to the school's wider aims of improving the quality of learning and raising standards of achievement for all pupils. It should be read in conjunction with other school policies, including *The Curriculum Aims*, *The Guide to Teaching English* and *The Assessment Policy*.

The more children enjoy writing and see the purpose of it in the wider world, the better writers they will become. Writing at Bold Hill is underpinned by a focus on speaking and listening, including listening to and telling stories, working in groups and sustained, dialogic interaction between staff and children. It incorporates an understanding of the relationship between thinking and writing – children need to think in order to write but should also use writing as a way of developing and exploring their thinking.

Grammar, punctuation and spelling are an integral part of the writing process. Pupils who can use these tools with ease are able to concentrate on the content of their writing. Being able to construct and punctuate sentences accurately and spell with confidence has a significant effect on a child's ability to write fluently and accurately.

Grammar is a way of describing language in spoken and written English. It includes terms such as nouns and verbs to describe how words function in sentences. Grammar is learnt naturally through interaction with other people and reading. Explicit knowledge of grammar can help children to understand how sentences are constructed and the choices they can make when writing.

Punctuation is the way phrases, clauses and sentences are indicated so that they are clear and communicate meaning for readers. Spelling is the correct transcription of words on a page.

Standard English is the form of English which is common to everyone in Britain and is a global language; it is not linked to a particular region or dialect. It is the language of public documents, dictionaries and thesauruses. Children are taught to speak and write Standard English at Bold Hill, as required by the national curriculum, so that they can use it confidently when appropriate.

Grammar, punctuation and spelling are taught explicitly in discrete sessions each week. Understanding of grammatical concepts is reinforced within English activities, including reading, writing and spoken English. The curriculum is planned to cover all the statutory content in the Primary English Curriculum, including the grammatical concepts and terminology, designated punctuation and spelling word lists. A range of approaches is adopted to match the needs of different learners, and staff deliberately deploy creative and exciting ways to engage all pupils and ensure every child has the opportunity to fulfil and exceed expectations. Parents can support their children by helping them to learn their weekly spellings and giving them opportunities to write at home.

Children's understanding of different features of writing is reinforced through a consistent approach to defining terms and by providing formative feedback both orally and as part of written comments on work (see *The Assessment Policy*). Children will set their own targets, in discussion with their teachers, and their progress will be carefully and regularly monitored. Summative assessment of writing is through termly moderated teacher assessment.

There is a statutory end of key stage test in grammar, punctuation and spelling for pupils in Year 6. A revised version of this test, aligned to the new curriculum, will be introduced in 2016. Results from these tests are passed to Bold Hill Academy and other secondary schools our pupils transfer to. From 2016, there will also be a statutory test for Year 2 pupils. To provide appropriate preparation for these tests, children will be given the opportunity to practise test-style questions in different contexts to build their confidence. For example, children will be given weekly spelling tests with certificates awarded to recognise progress. A formal grammar, punctuation and spelling test will be set once a year to provide feedback to parents and monitor progress across the school.

Based on the punctuation and spelling policy of a fictitious school.

## Practice questions for Comprehension 5

**160** Identify the order in which these statements appear in the text.

1. Children who can construct and punctuate sentences and spell confidently are able to write more fluently.

2. Speaking and listening includes stories, group work and dialogic interaction.

3. A new version of the Key Stage 2 grammar, punctuation and spelling test will come on stream in 2016.

4. Standard English is not associated with a particular area of the country or dialect.

5. The policy contributes to the wider aims of the school in improving the quality of learning for all.

6. Grammar, spelling and punctuation are taught in discrete lessons each week.

**161** Select three phrases from the list below (continues overleaf) to complete the bulleted list. The last bullet point has been done for you.

1. is underpinned by a focus on speaking and listening

2. incorporates a way of describing language in different modes

3. recognises that writing is the correct transcription of words on the page

4. encompasses an understanding of the relationship between thinking and writing

5. is reinforced through a range of literacy activities

6. recognises that explicit knowledge about grammar helps children to make choices as they write

7. is assessed through formal weekly tests which are teacher-marked

8. recognises that writing is learnt naturally through interaction with other people and reading

At Bold Hill Primary School, the teaching of writing:

- 
- 
- 
- includes a focus on Standard English as required by the national curriculum.

162 Select the best subheading to cover paragraphs 4, 5 and 6.

1. The importance of grammar, spelling, punctuation and Standard English
2. Definitions of grammar, spelling, punctuation and Standard English
3. How children learn grammar, spelling, punctuation and Standard English
4. Grammar, spelling, punctuation and Standard English in the national curriculum

163 The following groups might all be potential audiences or readers of this document. Which group would find it least relevant and which group the most relevant?

- The governors at Bold Hill Primary School
- The headteacher at Bold Hill Academy
- The staff at Bold Hill Primary School
- Parents at Bold Hill Primary School
- English staff at Bold Hill Academy
- Ofsted inspectors visiting Bold Hill Primary School

164 Read the statements below and based on the evidence provided by the passage decide which refers to

- Grammar (G)
- Spelling (S)
- Writing (W)

1. The more pupils enjoy this, the better writers they will become.
2. It includes terms such as nouns and verbs to describe how words function in sentences.
3. Certificates are awarded to recognise progress in this aspect of the curriculum.
4. Understanding is reinforced through a range of English activities.
5. This is assessed termly through moderated teacher assessment.

165 Match each of the summaries below to the relevant paragraph of the text: paragraphs 1, 2, 7 and 9.

1. The role of grammar, punctuation and spelling
2. Approaches to teaching
3. The overall aims of the policy
4. Compulsory national testing of grammar, punctuation and spelling

**166** From the list select the two options closest to the meaning of the phrase as it appears in the context of the passage.

'sustained dialogic interaction' (paragraph 2)

    **1.** repeated opportunities for discussion among children, monitored by the teacher

    **2.** regular transmission teaching by the teacher, with questions for the children

    **3.** continuous discussion involving dialogue between teacher and children

    **4.** occasional class debates led by the teacher and involving the children

    **5.** dynamic whole-class oral work initiated by the children, observed by the teacher

    **6.** uninterrupted learning conversations in class between teacher and children

# 6: DISCIPLINE IN SCHOOLS

## Discipline in schools: teachers' powers

Teachers have statutory authority to discipline pupils whose behaviour is unacceptable, who break school rules or who fail to follow a reasonable instruction (Section 90 and 91 of the Education and Inspections Act 2006).

- The power also applies to all paid staff (unless the headteacher says otherwise) with responsibility for pupils, such as teaching assistants.
- Teachers can discipline pupils at any time the pupil is in school or elsewhere under the charge of a teacher, including on school visits.
- Teachers can also discipline pupils in certain circumstances when a pupil's misbehaviour occurs outside of school.
- Teachers have a power to impose detention outside school hours.
- Teachers can confiscate pupils' property.

What the law allows: teachers can discipline pupils whose conduct falls below the standard which could reasonably be expected of them. This means that if a pupil misbehaves, breaks a school rule or fails to follow a reasonable instruction the teacher can impose a punishment on that pupil. To be lawful, the punishment (including detention) must satisfy the following three conditions:

- The decision to punish a pupil must be made by a paid member of school staff or a member of staff authorised by the headteacher.
- The decision to punish the pupil and the punishment itself must be made on the school premises or while the pupil is under the charge of a member of staff; and
- It must not breach any other legislation (for example in respect of disability, special educational needs, race and other equalities and human rights) and it must be reasonable in all the circumstances.

A punishment must be proportionate. In determining whether a punishment is reasonable, section 91 of the Education and Inspections Act 2006 says the penalty must be reasonable in all the circumstances and that account must be taken of the pupil's age, any special educational needs or disability they may have, and any religious requirements affecting them.

The headteacher may limit the power to apply particular punishments to certain staff and/or extend the power to discipline to adult volunteers, for example to parents who have volunteered to help on a school trip. Corporal punishment is illegal in all circumstances.

Schools should consider whether the behaviour under review gives cause to suspect that a child is suffering, or is likely to suffer, significant harm. Where this may be the case, school staff should follow the school's safeguarding policy. They should also consider whether continuing disruptive behaviour might be the result of unmet educational or other needs. At this point, the school should consider whether a multi-agency assessment is necessary.

A clear school behaviour policy, consistently and fairly applied, underpins effective education. School staff, pupils and parents should all be clear of the high standards of behaviour expected of all pupils at all times. The behaviour policy should be supported and backed-up by senior staff and the headteacher. Good schools encourage good behaviour through a mixture of high expectations, clear policy and an ethos which fosters discipline and mutual respect between pupils, and between staff and pupils.

Schools should have in place a range of options and rewards to reinforce and praise good behaviour, and clear sanctions for those who do not comply with the school's behaviour policy. These sanctions will be proportionate and fair responses that may vary according to the age of the pupils, and any other special circumstances that affect the pupil. When poor behaviour is identified, sanctions should be implemented consistently and fairly in line with the behaviour policy. Good schools will have a range of disciplinary measures clearly communicated to school staff, pupils and parents.

Based on www.gov.uk/government/uploads/system/uploads/attachment_data/file/353921/
Behaviour_and_Discipline_in_Schools_-_A_guide_for_headteachers_and_school_staff.pdf.

## Practice questions for Comprehension 6

**167** Read the statements below and based on the evidence provided by the passage decide which refer to

- Schools (S)
- Headteachers (H)
- Teachers (T)
- **1.** They should establish a range of rewards and punishments.
- **2.** They may extend the power to discipline to adult volunteers, for example parents helping on a school visit.
- **3.** They should support and back up the behaviour policy.
- **4.** They are permitted to give detentions outside school hours and confiscate pupils' property.

**168** Identify the order in which these statements appear in the text.

- **1.** Punishments must not breach any other aspect of legislation.
- **2.** In certain circumstances, pupils can be disciplined when they misbehave outside school.
- **3.** Schools must consider whether repeated bad behaviour is a result of pupils' needs not being met.
- **4.** The law allows teachers to discipline pupils whose behaviour falls below the standard that could reasonably be expected of them.

**5.** Punishments may vary according to the age of the pupil and any other relevant circumstances.

**6.** Pupils can only be punished by a paid member of staff or a member of staff given such authority by the headteacher.

**169** From the list below select three points that accurately convey the rules governing discipline in schools.

**1.** Headteachers must authorise all punishments administered in schools.

**2.** Corporal punishment is legal under certain, limited circumstances.

**3.** All paid staff (unless otherwise directed by the headteacher) have statutory authority to discipline pupils.

**4.** Section 91 of the Educations and Inspections Act 2006 says that punishment should take into account pupils' ability and socio-economic background.

**5.** Teachers can discipline pupils at any time pupils are in their charge.

**6.** Punishments must ensure that pupils do not suffer any significant harm.

**7.** Schools must review punishments in the light of continuing disruptive behaviour to see whether they need to be revised.

**8.** In the event of a severe breach of school rules, schools must implement a multi-agency assessment.

**9.** All punishments must be fair and in all the circumstances appropriate to the severity of the misdemeanour.

**170** From the list select the two options closest to the meaning of the phrase
'clear sanctions for those who do not comply with the school's behaviour policy' (paragraph 7)

**1.** clear rules for those who do not respect the school's behaviour policy

**2.** clear principles for those who do not acknowledge the school's behaviour policy

**3.** clear punishments for those who do not conform to the school's behaviour policy

**4.** clear practices for those who do not comport with the school's behaviour policy

**5.** clear consequences for those who do not compete for the school's behaviour policy

**6.** clear penalties for those who do not abide by the school's behaviour policy

**171** Match each of the summaries below to the relevant paragraph of text: paragraphs 2, 5, 6 and 7.

**1.** The importance of a clear school policy

**2.** When safeguarding issues are suspected

**3.** The legal position on the disciplining of pupils

**4.** Range of rewards and sanctions

**172** Select three phrases from the list below (continues overleaf) to complete the bulleted list about punishments.
The last bullet point has been done for you.

**1.** can only be given while pupils are on school premises

**2.** may involve detention outside school hours

**3.** should be implemented consistently and fairly

**4.** can only be given by members of the teaching staff

**5.** must be communicated to parents before they are carried out

**6.** may vary according to the age of the pupil

**7.** should be notified to the headteacher before they are implemented

**8.** should not be given to pupils while on a school visit

Punishments:

- 
- 
- 
- should be reasonable in all the circumstances.

**173** Read the statements below and decide whether

- the statement is supported by the text (S)
- the statement is implied to be the case or is implicitly supported by the text (I)
- the text provides no evidence or information concerning the statement (NE)
- the statement is implicitly contradicted by the text (IC)
- the statement is contradicted by the text (C)

**1.** A clear school policy on behaviour which is followed by all staff is fundamental to effective education.

**2.** Headteachers and other senior teachers are the staff who have most responsibility for discipline.

**3.** A positive atmosphere and good relationships are important ways of promoting good behaviour.

**4.** Sound discipline and good behaviour is a crucial aspect of effective education.

# 3.4    Literacy practice papers

The answers to these questions appear on page 217.

Aim to complete each of these four papers under examination conditions.

## Literacy Practice Paper 1

### Spelling

For questions 1–10, select the correctly spelt word from the list of alternatives.

1.  Worksheets should be _____ to all pupils in the class.

    *accessible*            *accesible*            *acesible*            *acesible*

2.  Students who are _____ late should be sent to their head of year.

    *persistantly*          *persistently*         *persistentley*       *persistantley*

3.  Children _____ play outside during the lunch break.

    *normaly*               *normly*               *normerly*            *normally*

4.  The new benches for the hall are more _____ than the seating we had before.

    *manoevreable*          *manoeuvrible*         *manouvrable*         *manoeuvrable*

5.  The clash of dates presents the leadership team with a _____.

    *dilema*                *dilemma*              *dilemna*             *dillemma*

6.  You can ask your form teacher to provide a _____ for you.

    *referance*             *refarence*            *refarance*           *reference*

7.  The audience was visibly _____ by the children's performance.

    *affected*              *effected*             *afected*             *efected*

8.  The _____ for next year is now on the notice board in the staffroom.

    *calender*              *callender*            *calendar*            *callendar*

9.  There has been an _____ response to my request for help at parents' evening.

    *extraordinary*         *extrordinary*         *extrardinary*        *extraordinry*

**10.** Children were _____ drawn to the puppet show at the school summer fair.

*irresistably*          *irresistibly*          *irresistibily*          *irresistabley*

# Grammar

**A**  *Complete the following passage. Select the best of the given alternatives at the points at which there are blank lines.*

*You will need to check that you have made the best overall set of choices for completing the passage.*

**This is an extract from a letter to parents and carers of prospective Year 7 pupils from the headteacher.**

Dear Parents and Carers

On behalf of the governors and staff, I would like to congratulate your son or daughter on

A.  having secured a place at Chalk Hill Academy.

B.  being secured a place at Chalk Hill Academy.

C.  they're having secured a place at Chalk Hill Academy.

D.  you're having secured a place at Chalk Hill Academy.

We very much hope your children will enjoy their time with us. Please be assured that our

A.  first priority is their well-being.

B.  main concern is there well-being.

C.  first priority is there well-being.

D.  main concern is their well-being.

The induction evening for parents and pupils is on 6 July and this is when I

A.  will explaining the philosophy of the school and the curriculum for Year 7.

B.  am explaining the philosophy of the school and the curriculum for Year 7.

C.  will be explaining the philosophy of the school and the curriculum for Year 7.

D.  are going to be explaining the philosophy of the school and the curriculum for Year 7.

During the evening, there will be an opportunity to see round the school, buy uniform and

A.  meeting other Year 7 pupils and their parents.

B.  meet other Year 7 pupils and their parents.

C.  a meeting of other Year 7 pupils and their parents.

D.  to meet up other Year 7 pupils and their parents.

The staff and I

A.  am looking forward to meeting you and your child then.

B.  will be looking forward to meeting you and your child then.

C. are looking forward to meeting you and your child then.

D. is looking forward to meeting you and your child then.

In the meantime, if you have any queries do not hesitate to get in touch and we

A. will provide as prompt a response as possible.

B. will be providing a prompt response as possible.

C. will provide as prompt response as possible.

D. will be providing prompt a response as possible.

Yours sincerely

Amanda Beale

Headteacher

Chalk Hill Academy

**B**  *Complete the following passage. Select the best of the given alternatives at the points at which there are blank lines.*

*You will need to check that you have made the best overall set of choices for completing the passage.*

**This extract is taken from a discussion paper about the marking policy in a school.**

Our assessment policy is due to be reviewed this year. As part of this review, we will be looking at our marking policy. We need to review how staff are marking at the moment and, in particular, ask:

- what is the purpose of marking?
- who is the audience for our marking?
- how important is it to keep to the same protocols?

Finally, we need to decide

A. how to make marking manageable for staff?

B. how must we make marking manageable for staff?

C. how can we make marking manageable for staff?

D. how are we make marking manageable for staff?

Marking takes up a good deal of teacher time and needs to yield concomitant benefits for learning. A review will provide an opportunity:

A. for clarifying the purposes and principles and consider existing practice.

B. to clarify the purposes and principles and consider existing practice.

C. for clarification the purposes and principles and considering existing practice.

D. to clarify the purposes and principles and considering existing practice.

A successful marking policy will:

A. enhance pupils' learning and may lead to an improvement in standards of achievement.

B. enhancing pupils' learning and is leading to an improvement in standards of achievement.

C. enhance pupils' learning and leading to an improvement in standards of achievement.

D. enhancing pupils' learning and lead to an improvement in standards of achievement.

C *Complete the following passage. Select the best of the given alternatives at the points at which there are blank lines.*

*You will need to check that you have made the best overall set of choices for completing the passage.*

**This is an extract from a staff circular about a local arts festival.**

For the third consecutive year, the school is preparing to take part in Carledge Arts Festival. This festival is sponsored by a local department store and was established to promote the arts in schools. If you are new to the school, you

A. could have heard about Carledge Arts Festival or might of been involved in previous years.

B. might of heard about Carledge Arts Festival or could have been involved in previous years.

C. might have heard about Carledge Arts Festival or might have been involved in previous years.

D. could of heard about the arts festival or could have been involved in previous years.

Pupils from all the schools in the town and surrounding villages take part in the festival, which is hugely popular with everyone. Last year, 2000 pupils:

A. have took part in the festival in one way or another.

B. taken part in the festival in one way or another.

C. have taken part in the festival in one way or another.

D. took part the festival in one way or another.

Carledge Arts Festival is well worth being involved in because:

A. these kinds of festivals present so many unique learning opportunities.

B. these kind of festival presents so many unique learning opportunities.

C. these kinds of festival present so many unique learning opportunities.

D. these kinds of festivals presents so many unique learning opportunities.

# Comprehension

*Read the following extract and answer the questions that follow it.*

Nearly twice as many girls as boys say that they enjoy reading very much, with 56.8% of girls enjoying reading either very much or quite a lot compared with 43.9% of boys. Conversely, nearly twice as many boys as girls say that they don't enjoy reading at all.

The gap between boys and girls in terms of their reading enjoyment has narrowed again very slightly since 2011, with a 12.9 percentage point difference between boys and girls in 2012 compared with a 13.0 percentage point difference in 2011 and a 13.1 percentage point difference in 2010. Although the gender gap in reading enjoyment is slowly decreasing, it continues to remain wider in 2012 than in 2005, where the percentage point gap between boys and girls who enjoy reading either very much or quite a lot was 10.7.

Whether the narrowing of the enjoyment gap is linked to a narrowing in the attainment gap between boys and girls (eg at KS2 the gender gap in reading decreased from an eight percentage point difference in 2011 to a six percentage point difference in 2012) remains to be seen.

Girls not only enjoy reading more than boys but they also do it more often, with 32.55% of girls saying that they read outside of class everyday compared with 24.3% of boys. Indeed, twice as many boys as girls say that they never read outside of class.

Overall, there has been a slight decrease in the proportion of boys and girls who read daily in 2012 compared with 2011. The gender gap in daily reading has continued to narrow between 2011 and 2012 (from a 9.0 percentage point difference in 2010 to a 8.3 percentage point difference in 2012), a decrease that seems largely due to a greater drop in girls reading daily compared with boys (2.8 percentage point difference between girls reading daily in 2011 and 2012 versus a 2 percentage point difference for boys). However, comparisons with data from 2005 show that the gap between daily reading amongst boys and girls still remains wider than that evidenced in 2005.

More girls than boys also read for longer periods of time. Nearly 30% of girls compared with over two-fifths of boys (22.1%) read for one hour or longer. More girls than boys also say that they read for up to 30 minutes at a time. Conversely, more boys than girls say that they read for ten minutes when they read.

Girls and boys read different materials outside of class. More girls than boys say that they not only read technology-based formats, such as text messages, messages on social networking sites, emails and instant messages, but they also read more 'traditional' texts, such as fiction and poems as well as magazines and lyrics. By contrast, more boys than girls say that they read newspapers, comics and manuals. Girls' penchant for technology-based materials is not simply explained by girls having greater access to computers or the internet than boys; our survey showed that roughly the same proportion of boys and girls say they either own a computer (boys 77.0%; girls 77.1%), have access to one (boys 96.7%; girls 97.1%) or have the internet at home (boys 96.7%; girls 97.2%).

Boys and girls also enjoy reading different genres of fiction when they read fiction. Boys are more likely than girls to read crime, war/spy stories, science fiction and sports stories, while girls are more likely than boys to read romance and animal stories.

Finally, girls also think more positively about reading than boys. More girls than boys agreed with the statement that 'reading is cool', while more boys than girls agreed with the statements 'I prefer watching TV to reading', 'I only read when I have to' and 'I cannot find things to read that interest me'. More boys than girls also subscribed to a gendered view of reading, with 17.9% of boys agreeing that 'reading is more for girls than boys' compared with only 11.7% of girls.

Adapted from *Children and Young People's Reading in 2012: Findings from the 2012 National Literacy Trust's Annual Survey* (pages 10–14, without bar charts) by Christina Clarke, 2013, available online at www.literacytrust.org.uk.

**A.** Select the best heading for the report.

1. The gender gap in reading enjoyment
2. The difference in reading attainment between girls and boys
3. The reading habits of girls and boys
4. The gender gap in extent and regularity of daily reading

**B.** Select the best subheading to cover paragraphs 7 and 8.

1. Boys' and girls' reading preferences outside class
2. The predominance of technology-based reading
3. Boys' and girls' attitudes towards reading outside class
4. The proportion of pupils who have access to computers

**C.** From the list below, select three points that accurately convey information about boys' reading.

1. Boys are more likely to have their own computer than girls.
2. Nearly three times as many boys as girls say they don't enjoy reading at all.
3. Boys are more likely than girls to believe that reading is more for girls than boys.
4. 32.55% of boys say that they never read outside of class.
5. More boys than girls report reading for ten minutes when they read.
6. The drop in boys' daily reading between 2011 and 2012 was less than the drop in girls' daily reading.
7. Boys are more likely to read newspapers, manuals and animal stories than girls.
8. 97.2% of boys say they have access to the internet at home.
9. Fewer boys than girls agreed with the statement 'I prefer watching TV to reading.'

**D.** From the list select the two options closest to the meaning of the phrase as it appears in the context of the passage.

'Girls' penchant for technology-based formats is not simply explained by girls having greater access to computers' (paragraph 7)

1. Girls' familiarity with technology-based formats is not simply explained by girls having more expertise with computers

2. Girls' preference for technology-based formats is not simply explained by girls having more opportunities to use computers

3. Girls' resistance towards technology-based formats is not simply explained by girls having more understanding of computers

4. Girls' inclination towards technology-based formats is not simply explained by girls having more experience of using computers

5. Girls' antipathy towards technology-based formats is not simply explained by girls having more indifference towards computers

**E.** From the list below select the four main points that most accurately describe young people's reading.

1. The gap between boys and girls in terms of their reading enjoyment was narrower in 2012 than in 2005.

2. In 2012 the gap between girls' and boys' reading enjoyment decreased slightly.

3. Girls do not enjoy reading more than boys but they do it more often.

4. The proportion of boys and girls who read daily in 2012 compared with 2011 decreased slightly.

5. Nearly 30% of girls compared with 10% of boys read for one hour or longer.

6. Boys and girls read more technology-based formats than 'traditional' texts.

7. Girls and boys have different preferences when choosing genres of fiction to read.

8. The narrowing of the attainment gap between boys and girls is a result of a narrowing of the enjoyment gap.

9. More boys than girls believe that reading is an activity more appropriate for girls than boys.

# Literacy Practice Paper 2

## Spelling

For questions 1–10, select the correctly spelt word from the list of alternatives.

**1.** The new floor cushions for the library _____ the quiet reading area in the corner.

    *compliment*         *complement*         *complament*         *compelement*

**2.** Can anyone explain the _____ of the kettle from the staffroom?

    *disappearance*       *dissappearance*       *disappearence*       *disappearrance*

**3.**  We are hoping that prospective intruders will be _____ by the CCTV cameras.

    dettered            detterred            detered            deterred

**4.**  Try to resolve any _____ informally with parents before they are escalated.

    grieveances         grievances         greivances         greivences

**5.**  There is a _____ selection of lost property in the school office.

    misellaneous        miscellaneous       missellanious       miscellanious

**6.**  The Chair of Governors was _____ in persuading the Mayor to come to speech day.

    instrumental        instrumentle       instroumental      instrumentale

**7.**  _____, the year meeting due to be held today has been postponed.

    Consequentley     Consequentely     Consequently     Consequenttly

**8.**  Children should wash their hands _____ before lunch.

    immediately        imediately        immediateley       imediateley

**9.**  _____ behaviour can be a form of bullying.

    Mannipulative       Manipulativ        Manipullative       Manipulative

**10.**  There may be some _____ to the proposals for the new school day.

    resistance         resistence         resisstance        ressistence

## Grammar

A  *Complete the following passage. Select the best of the given alternatives at the points at which there are blank lines.*

*You will need to check that you have made the best overall set of choices for completing the passage.*

**This is an extract from a letter to the parents and carers of children about to go on a school trip.**

Dear Parents and Carers

Thank you for allowing your child to take part in the school trip to Benton Zoo. I have now given the coach company (Myers) our final numbers.

A.  Teachers will accompany and supervise the children, who have all been to the zoo before and are familiar with the arrangements.

B. Teachers who have all been to the zoo before will accompany and supervise the children who are familiar with the arrangements.

C. All the teachers who will accompany and supervise the children have been to the zoo before and are familiar with the arrangements.

D. All the children who have been to the zoo before will be accompanied by the teachers who are familiar with the arrangements.

We believe that this trip to the zoo will offer children not only an opportunity to learn about animals but also an experience that will be

A. an affective stimulus for their writing.

B. an effective stimulus for their writing.

C. an effectual stimulus for their writing.

D. an affecting stimulus for their writing.

Please ensure that you complete the emergency contact form; provide a packed lunch and drink; ensure your child has

A. suitable footwear, arranging to meet the coach when it returns to school at 5pm.

B. suitable footwear, please arrange to meet the coach when it returns to school at 5pm.

C. suitable footwear and arranging to meet the coach when it returns to school at 5pm.

D. suitable footwear and arrange to meet the coach when it returns to school at 5pm.

I will be writing to you again a week before the trip. By then I

A. should have had all consent forms returned to me.

B. might have had all consent forms returned to me.

C. should of had all consent forms returned to me.

D. would of had all consent forms returned to me.

Yours sincerely

Ted Bower

B  *Complete the following passage. Select the best of the given alternatives at the points at which there are blank lines.*

*You will need to check that you have made the best overall set of choices for completing the passage.*

**This is an extract from a note to Year 9 parents about progress interviews.**

Year 9 Progress Interviews

You are invited to come to a progress interview with your son/daughter. We believe that involving pupils in discussion of their progress helps them to

A. became    B. becoming    C. become    D. in becoming

more involved in their own learning.

However, we also know that communication between staff and parents plays a key role and so you will have the opportunity to discuss your child's progress with his/her form teacher

A. what     B. who     C. which     D. whom

will have an overview of your child's effort and attainment across all subjects.

We hope you will take up this opportunity

A. to attend a progress interview. The date and time rearranged if necessary.
B. to attend a progress interview, the date and time can be rearranged if necessary.
C. to attend a progress interview. The date and time to be rearranged if necessary.
D. to attend a progress interview; the date and time can be rearranged if necessary.

All interviews will take place in the Year 9 block which is the building

A. to the left of the main entrance at the rear of the school.
B. at the left of the main entrance on the rear of the school.
C. by the left of the main entrance behind the rear of the school.
D. on the left of the main entrance by the rear of the school.

C   *Complete the following passage. Select the best of the given alternatives at the points at which there are blank lines.*

*You will need to check that you have made the best overall set of choices for completing the passage.*

**This is an extract from a note to Year 8 pupils.**

**FOR THE ATTENTION OF ALL YEAR 8 PUPILS**

**Refundable laptop deposit**

At the beginning of term, pupils are required to pay a refundable deposit if they wish to take a laptop home from school to complete homework tasks. This year the deposit is £50, which will be refunded at the end of term. You will be entitled to a complete refund of your deposit provided the condition of the laptop

A. will be regarded as satisfactory.
B. is regarded as satisfactory.
C. regarded as satisfactory.
D. are regarded as satisfactory

The school has the right _____ money from the deposit to meet the cost of any damage to the laptop.

A. to retain     B. of retain     C. over retaining     D. of retaining

Please note: damage does not include

A. superfluous scratches to the case.

B. superficial scratches to the case.

C. superior scratches to the case.

D. superimposed scratches to the case.

If you have any queries about this matter,

A. parents should contact the Head of Year 8.

B. children should contact the Head of Year 8.

C. you should contact the Head of Year 8.

D. they should contact the Head of Year 8.

## Comprehension

*Read the following extract and answer the questions that follow it.*

Evidence is clear that the quality of teaching matters a great deal. It is the single most important school-based factor determining pupils' educational outcomes, and has a substantial impact on future labour market outcomes. Improving the quality of teaching is therefore a key priority for the Department; one of the ways in which we can achieve this is by raising awareness of what the most effective practice looks like, and supporting teachers to share their own experiences of what works.

Our ambition is to support the development of a 'self-improving' schools system; a system in which teachers take responsibility for identifying and addressing improvement needs (for themselves, their schools, and the system as a whole), and where outstanding teaching practice, based on strong evidence, is built and shared through collaboration and partnership. In support of the self-improving system, the Department will continue to build understanding about the impact our policies are having. However, in order for the evidence base to be of real practical use to teachers, they themselves must play an increasingly important part in building a common evidence base that can be tested and challenged.

Whilst evidence about the importance of good leaders, teachers and teaching is unequivocal, there are still some important gaps in the evidence base about how to secure the best possible teacher quality.

In terms of what teachers should be doing in the classroom, there is an important and growing international evidence base about what constitutes effective teaching practice. Responding to this, resources such as the Teaching and Learning Toolkit, for example, are providing a guide to effective teaching practice. Nevertheless, evidence gaps remain, particularly in terms of a paucity of data from the UK and studies about how best to put effective techniques into practice in the classroom.

We need to know more about how to find, nurture and develop outstanding teachers. Rigorous selection and training is essential to building a strong pool of new entrants to the profession; ultimately this will improve the competitiveness, and hence the status of teaching. This puts a premium on having in place an effective system of initial teacher training (ITT) that is able to identify and develop the best. International evidence suggests that ITT programmes linked to specific school needs can be more effective especially when training is based on demonstration and peer-review. We have therefore given schools much greater responsibility for developing and delivering ITT; it is now important that we have a clear understanding of how effectively schools are responding to these reforms.

Effective teacher supply requires more than simply getting ITT right. Teachers, and would-be teachers, are participants in the wider labour market. We know from existing evidence that some schools find it much more difficult than others to recruit teachers. We also know that there are shortages in certain subjects, where classes are often taught by non-specialist teachers. And, whilst we know that pay is not the only thing that motivates teachers, it is nevertheless important to understand the impact that pay and conditions – both nationally and between schools in an increasingly autonomous system – have on teacher recruitment and turnover. As schools increasingly develop their own pay policies and systems we will need to know which approaches are proving most effective for recruiting high-quality teachers and developing them throughout their careers, including leadership positions.

Analysis of the evidence shows that, although the quality of teaching in many parts of the schools system is good, there is more that could be done to support the teaching profession to lead and sustain its own development and improvement. Large-scale policy reforms are changing expectations of teachers; different skills and capabilities will be required in future if teachers are to continue ensuring high-quality outcomes for all pupils. We need to know how well the profession is adapting to the challenges of a changing education system.

An extract from *Research Priorities and Questions* available online at www.gov.uk/government/uploads/system/uploads/attachment_data/file/206722/Research_priorities_and_questions_-_teachers_and_teaching.pdf.

**A**  Select the most appropriate alternative for the phrase as it appears in the context of the passage.

'Whilst evidence about the importance of good leaders, teachers and teaching is unequivocal' (paragraph 3)

1. Whilst evidence about the importance of good leaders, teachers and teaching is debatable

2. Whilst evidence about the importance of good leaders, teachers and teaching is unambiguous

3. Whilst evidence about the importance of good leaders, teachers and teaching is diverse

4. Whilst evidence about the importance of good leaders, teachers and teaching is unequalled

5. Whilst evidence about the importance of good leaders, teachers and teaching is invaluable

**B** Select the most appropriate alternative for the phrase as it appears in the context of the passage.

'a paucity of data from the UK' (paragraph 4)

1. an absence of data from the UK
2. a variability of data from the UK
3. a plethora of data from the UK
4. a wealth of data
5. a lack of data from the UK

**C** Select five phrases from the list below to complete the bulleted list.

The last bullet point has been completed for you.

1.  self-improving schools will help to build the evidence base for further development
2.  effective leadership, along with good teaching, is extremely important
3.  data from the UK indicates how to put effective teaching techniques into practice
4.  more could be done to support teachers in leading and sustaining their own development
5.  the profession is adapting well to the challenges of a changing education system
6.  effective supply of teachers depends on more than simply getting ITT right
7.  quality of teaching has the most impact on the educational outcomes of pupils
8.  pay and conditions have considerable impact on recruitment and turnover
9.  rigorous selection and training is essential to building a strong profession
10. it is much more difficult for some schools than others to recruit suitable teachers
11. schools are responding effectively to reforms in initial teacher training
12. initial teacher training programmes linked to specific school needs can be more effective
13. many classes in schools are taught by non-specialist subject teachers

Evidence suggests that:

- 
- 
- 
- 
- quality of teaching has a significant effect on labour market outcomes (given answer)

**D** Read the statements below (continues overleaf) and decide whether:

- the statement is supported by the text (S)
- the statement is implied to be the case or is implicitly supported by the text (I)

- the text provides no evidence or information concerning the statement (NE)
- the statement is implicitly contradicted or implicitly refuted by the text (IC)
- the statement is contradicted by the text (C)

1. There is relatively little research evidence about what effective teaching practice in the classroom looks like.

2. Making teaching a more attractive profession is important to improving recruitment and retention in the profession.

3. Expectations of teachers are undergoing considerable change at the moment and will continue to do in the future.

4. Schools are becoming increasingly autonomous in terms of teacher recruitment which is why sharing good practice is important.

# Literacy Practice Paper 3

## Spelling

For questions 1–10, select the correctly spelt word from the list of alternatives.

1.   Pupils will be _____ in four-bed rooms in the youth hostel.

   accommodated          acommodated          accomodated          acomodated

2.   Your salary will be _____ with your qualifications and experience.

   comensurate          commencurate          commensurate          comencurate

3.   The summer fair will _____ go ahead, whatever the weather.

   definately          definitely          definitly          definiteley

4.   This has been an exceptionally _____ year for the languages faculty.

   sucessful          succesful          sucesful          successful

5.   Jakub takes a very _____ approach to this subject.

   consciencious          conscientous          conscientious          consientious

6.   There are two _____ reading groups in each class.

   parallel          paralel          parallell          paralell

7.   The school play will end at _____ 9.30 p.m.

   aproximately          approximatley          approximatly          approximately

**8.** We are lucky enough to have links with several _____ universities.

    *prestigous*          *prestigious*          *prestigioues*          *prestigiouse*

**9.** The school is hoping to _____ some new recorders for the children.

    *aquwire*          *aquire*          *acquire*          *accquire*

**10.** Children who are _____ are given additional time in school exams.

    *dyslexic*          *dyslexcic*          *dyslexsic*          *dyslexick*

## Grammar

**A** *Complete the following passage. Select the best of the given alternatives at the points at which there are blank lines.*

*You will need to check that you have made the best overall set of choices for completing the passage.*

**This is an extract from guidance for newly qualified teachers on classroom management.**

Effective classroom management is critical for effective teaching and learning. Like many other aspects of teaching, it is a skill that can be learned.

Successful classroom management

A. comprises of a number of features, including planning, relationships and a confident approach.

B. comprises in a number of features, including planning, relationships and a confident approach.

C. comprises a number of features, including planning, relationships and a confident approach.

D. comprises number of features, including planning, relationships and a confident approach.

Careful planning of lessons will help to establish

A. orderly, calm atmosphere conducive to learning.

B. enough orderly, calm atmosphere conducive to learning.

C. a orderly, calm atmosphere conducive to learning.

D. an orderly, calm atmosphere conducive to learning.

A good teacher aims to build positive relationships with pupils.

A. They should regard this as a key factor in creating a climate for learning in the classroom.

B. He/she should regard this as a key factor in creating a climate for learning in the classroom.

C. You should regard this as a key factor in creating a climate for learning in the classroom.

D. One should regard this as a key factor in creating a climate for learning in the classroom.

Having provided a sequence of engaging and challenging activities,

A. teachers should feel confident that the lesson has direction and will go smoothly.

B. pupils will be confident that the lesson has direction and will go smoothly.

C. you should feel confident that the lesson has direction and will go smoothly.

D. this will lead to the lesson having direction and going smoothly.

B   *Complete the following passage. Select the best of the given alternatives at the points at which there are blank lines.*

*You will need to check that you have made the best overall set of choices for completing the passage.*

**This is an extract from a school report.**

Dan has generally worked well this year in most subjects, although

A. his mathematics has been a bit of a let down.

B. he has fallen behind in mathematics.

C. his mathematics has been rather dodgy.

D. he hasn't come up to the mark in mathematics.

He has been an excellent member of the tutor group, always behaving

A. courteously and with a pleasant manner.

B. courteous and with a pleasant manner.

C. courteously and with a pleasantly manner.

D. courteous and with a pleasantly manner.

Dan also did well in the tennis doubles with Rhys Brown when

A. he won the match.

B. we won the match.

C. you won the match.

D. they won the match.

Overall, however, Dan needs to realise that

A. his academic studies are more important to sport.

B. his academic studies are most important than sport.

C. his academic studies are more important than sport.

D. his academic studies are greater important to sport.

**C** *Complete the following passage. Select the best of the given alternatives at the points at which there are blank lines.*

*You will need to check that you have made the best overall set of choices for completing the passage.*

**This is an extract from a note for tutors from the Head of Year 10.**

**Uniform check**

We are holding a uniform check next week.

A. Please tell your tutor group about the uniform check on Tuesday.

B. On Tuesday, please tell your tutor group about the uniform check.

C. Please tell your tutor group about the uniform check which will take place on Tuesday.

D. On Tuesday, please tell your tutor group about the uniform check which will take place.

**Bags on desks**

Please remind students that they must

A. take their bags off of their desks before the start of each lesson.

B. take their bags of their desks before the start of each lesson.

C. take their bags of of their desks before the start of each lesson.

D. take their bags off their desks before the start of each lesson.

**Christmas fair – bottle stall**

A. We have had some donations already so far for the bottle stall although not enough in my opinion to be sufficient for running the stall all afternoon.

B. We have had some donations for the bottle stall although not enough to run the stall all afternoon.

C. We have had some donations already for the bottle stall although I don't think there are enough sufficient to run the stall for the whole afternoon.

D. We have had some donations for the bottle stall, not enough to run the stall for all afternoon.

**School nurse**

Please let your tutor group know that

A. Ms Lakhani, the school nurse, who is back from maternity leave, will be in the medical room on Friday.

B. Ms Lakhani, the school nurse, that is back from maternity leave, will be in the medical room on Friday.

C. Ms Lakhani, the school nurse, whom is back from maternity leave, will be in the medical room on Friday.

D. Ms Lakhani, the school nurse, what is back from maternity leave, will be in the medical room on Friday.

### Year 10 T-shirts

Unfortunately we have run out of Year 10 T-shirts.

A.  If students had of told me before, I could have ordered some more!
B.  If students had told me before, I could have ordered some more!
C.  If students had have told me before, I could of ordered some more!
D.  If students have told me before, I could of ordered some more!

## Comprehension

*Read the following extract and answer the questions that follow it.*

The School Admissions Code 2012, which is statutory guidance, states 'Admission authorities must ensure that [...] policies around school uniform do not discourage parents from applying for a place for their child.' No school uniform should be so expensive as to leave pupils or their families feeling unable to apply to, or attend, a school of their choice, due to the cost of the uniform. School governing bodies should therefore give high priority to cost considerations. The governing body should be able to demonstrate how best value has been achieved and keep the cost of supplying the uniform under review.

When considering how the school uniform should be sourced, governing bodies should give highest priority to the consideration of cost and value for money for parents. The school uniform should be easily available for parents to purchase and schools should seek to select items that can be purchased cheaply, for example in a supermarket or other good value shop. Schools should keep compulsory branded items to a minimum and avoid specifying expensive items of uniform, eg expensive outdoor coats. Governing bodies should be able to demonstrate that they have obtained the best value for money from suppliers. Any savings negotiated with suppliers should be passed on to parents wherever possible. Schools should not enter into cash back arrangements. Exclusive single supplier contracts should be avoided unless regular tendering competitions are run where more than one supplier can compete for the contract and where best value for parents is secured.

Local authorities and academies might choose to provide school clothing grants or to help with the cost of school clothing in cases of financial hardship. Individual schools may also wish to consider running their own schemes to provide assistance, particularly for supporting new intakes of children entering the school or in the event of substantial changes to the existing uniform. Schools should avoid frequent changes to uniform specifications.

Some religions and beliefs require their adherents to conform to a particular dress code, or to otherwise outwardly manifest their belief. This could include wearing or carrying specific religious artefacts, not cutting their hair, dressing modestly, or covering their head. Pupils have the right to manifest a religion or belief, but not necessarily at all times, places or in a particular manner. Where a school has good reason for restricting an individual's freedoms, for example, the promotion of cohesion and good order in the school, or genuine health and safety or security considerations, the restriction of an individual's rights to manifest their religion or belief may be justified. The school must balance the rights of individual pupils against the best interests of the school community as a whole. Nevertheless it should be possible for most religious requirements to be met within a school uniform policy and a governing body should act reasonably through consultation and dialogue in accommodating these.

In formulating its school uniform policy, a school will need to consider its obligations not to discriminate unlawfully. For example, it is not expected that the cost of girls' uniform is significantly more expensive than boys or vice-versa, as this may constitute unlawful sex discrimination. A school should also bear in mind the concept of 'indirect' discrimination. This involves the application of a requirement, which, although applied equally to everyone, puts certain people at a particular disadvantage because of their gender, race, sexual orientation, religion or belief or gender reassignment. Such a requirement will need to be justified as a proportionate way of achieving a reasonable objective if it is to be lawful, and the policy will need to be flexible enough to allow for necessary exceptions.

Adapted from www.gov.uk/government/uploads/system/uploads/attachment_data/
file/269113/school_uniform_guidance_2013.pdf.

**A**  Read the statements below and based on the evidence provided by the passage, decide which refer to:

Schools (S)

Governing bodies (G)

Parents (P)

1.  They must be able to show they have secured value for money for school uniform suppliers.

2.  They must weigh up the rights of individual pupils against the best interests of everyone in a school.

3.  They may run schemes to assist with the purchase of school uniform, particularly for a child new to the school.

4.  They should not be deterred from selecting a particular school because of the cost of the uniform.

**B**  Identify the order in which these statements appear in the text.

1.  Some faiths require pupils to follow a particular dress code, for example covering their heads.

2.  School governing bodies should prioritise cost when making decisions about school uniform.

3.  School uniform policy has to be flexible enough to accommodate exceptions.

4.  Governors should deploy a process of consultation with the aim of meeting religious requirements linked to school uniform.

5.  Savings negotiated with school uniform suppliers must be passed on to parents.

**C**   The following groups might all be potential audiences or readers of the article, although some would find it more useful than others. Which group would find it most relevant and which group the least relevant?

- Parents
- Headteachers
- Teachers
- Local authorities
- Religious leaders

**D**   Read the statements below and decide whether

- the statement is supported by the text (S)
- the statement is implied to be the case or is implicitly supported by the text (I)
- the text provides no evidence or information concerning the statement (NE)
- the statement is implicitly contradicted or implicitly refuted by the text (IC)
- the statement is contradicted by the text (C)

1. Availability and cost are key considerations for governing bodies and schools when choosing a uniform.
2. Schools should not make profits directly or indirectly from the sale of uniform.
3. The uniform for girls and boys should be the same as far as possible.
4. School uniforms should include compulsory branded items, which are distinctive.

**E**   Match each of the following summaries to the relevant paragraph of the text: paragraphs 2, 3, 4 and 5.

1. Ensuring best value for money for parents
2. Avoiding discrimination in school uniform
3. Financial assistance with uniform for parents
4. Manifesting a religious belief through appearance or dress

**F**   From the list select the option closest to the meaning of the phrase as it appears in the context of the passage.

'discriminate unlawfully' (paragraph 4)

1. make ill-judged and prejudiced distinctions between groups of pupils
2. differentiate illicitly between pupils from different backgrounds
3. make illegal and unfair distinctions between groups of pupils
4. divide pupils illegitimately according to their different backgrounds

# Literacy Practice Paper 4

## Spelling

For questions 1–10, select the correctly spelt word from the list of alternatives.

1. We do not permit any form of _____ behaviour in this school.

   *agressive*          *aggresive*          *agresive*          *aggressive*

2. Please do not cause _____ by giving members of staff inappropriately generous gifts.

   *embarrassment*     *embarassment*      *embarrasment*     *embarasment*

3. _____ is a very important quality we want to encourage in our students.

   *Perseverence*      *Perseverance*      *Perserverance*     *Perserverence*

4. The English department _____ has spare tickets for theatre trips.

   *ocasionally*       *occassionally*     *occasionally*      *occasionnally*

5. Your handwriting is _____ in places.

   *ilegable*          *illegable*         *ilegible*          *illegible*

6. Remember you are there in a _____ capacity at all times.

   *supervisory*       *supervisery*       *supervisry*        *supervisorey*

7. It is important that children are _____ against common diseases.

   *inocullated*       *inocculated*       *inoculated*        *innoculated*

8. Mrs Jones is available in the biology _____ after lunch.

   *laboratry*         *laboratory*        *laboratery*        *laboratrey*

9. We are _____ sorry for any inconvenience caused to parents and carers.

   *sincereley*        *sinserely*         *sincerly*          *sincerely*

10. The pleasure of your _____ is requested at our end of term assembly.

    *presence*          *presents*          *presense*          *prescence*

## Grammar

A  *Complete the following passage. Select the best of the given alternatives at the points at which there are blank lines.*

*You will need to check that you have made the best overall set of choices for completing the passage.*

**This is an extract from a Governors' report.**

At Hill Top Primary School, we are very lucky to have governors

A. who have a wide range of skills and experience.

B. what have a wide range of skills and experience.

C. that have a wide range of skills and experience.

D. whom have a wide range of skills and experience.

In carrying out our responsibilities,

A. the well-being of children and staff are of paramount importance to our team ethos.

B. our team ethos is of paramount importance to the well-being of children and staff.

C. we consider our team ethos to be of paramount importance to the well-being of the children and staff.

D. the paramount importance is our team ethos to the well-being of children and staff.

This year, our established leadership team

A. have been able to take the school forward in a number of ways.

B. has being able to take the school forward in a number of ways.

C. have being able to take the school forward in a number of ways.

D. has been able to take the school forward in many ways.

From next academic year, we will become part of the Valley Federation of Schools and we believe this can only help us to achieve our aims,

A. while retaining our individual character and autonomy.

B. while allowing us to retain our individual character and autonomy.

C. while retain our individual character and autonomy.

D. while we are allowed to retaining our individual character and autonomy.

Our main aims for the year are to

A. develop children's mathematics skills, promote reading for pleasure, improve children's motivation in writing and raising boys' attainment at the end of EYFS.

B. develop children's mathematics skills, promote reading for pleasure, improve children's motivation in writing and we will raise boys' attainment at the end of EYFS.

C. develop children's mathematics skills, promote reading for pleasure, improve children's motivation in writing and raise boys' attainment at the end of EYFS.

D. develop children's mathematics skills, promote reading for pleasure, improve children's motivation in writing to raise boys' attainment at the end of EYFS.

**B** *Complete the following passage. Select the best of the given alternatives at the points at which there are blank lines.*

*You will need to check that you have made the best overall set of choices for completing the passage.*

**This is an extract from a letter to parents about sports day.**

Dear Parents

Carne Road College Sports Day will take place on 16 June. The whole school _____ as it is a normal school day

A. is expected to attend          B. are expected to attend

C. is being expected to attend    D. are being expected to attend

In the event of bad weather, for example, heavy rain, sports day will be cancelled. Otherwise students should be at Carne Road Sports Centre by 9.15 a.m.

A. In the event of a student being unwell; a parent or carer must phone the absence line as normal.

B. In the event of a student being unwell. A parent or carer must phone the absence line as normal.

C. In the event of a student being unwell, a parent or carer must phone the absence line as normal.

D. In the event of a student being unwell, a parent or carer must phone, the absence line as normal.

All students should wear

A. PE kit, tracksuit bottoms and trainers and bring a drink.

B. PE kit, tracksuit bottoms and trainers and they should bring a drink with them.

C. PE kit, tracksuit bottoms and trainers and a drink.

D. PE kit, tracksuit bottoms and trainers and a drink must be brought too.

Parents are welcome to attend sports day but unfortunately,

A. we will be unable to associate visitors in the under cover area.

B. we will be unable to accredit visitors in the under cover area.

C. we will be unable to assimilate visitors in the under cover area.

D. we will be unable to accommodate visitors in the under cover area.

**C** *Complete the following passage (see overleaf). Select the best of the given alternatives at the points at which there are blank lines.*

*You will need to check that you have made the best overall set of choices for completing the passage.*

*This is an extract from an information leaflet about fire drills.*

Schools conduct fire drills several times a year

A. to sure everyone in the building knows how to get outside quickly and quietly.

B. to be sure everyone in the building knows how to get outside quickly and quietly.

C. to assure everyone in the building knows how to get outside quickly and quietly.

D. to been sure everyone in the building knows how to get outside quickly and quietly.

A school fire drill may be scheduled and announced in advance

A. so that children can dress appropriately.

B. because children can dress appropriately.

C. in order children can dress appropriately.

D. as though children can dress appropriately.

School fire drills

A. must be take seriously – everyone in the building must participate.

B. must be taking seriously – everyone in the building must participate.

C. must be taken seriously – everyone in the building must participate.

D. must be took seriously – everyone in the building must participate.

It is important to have

A. two ways out of the school, involve your local fire station in fire drill planning for your school.

B. two ways out of the school; involve your local fire station in fire drill planning for your school.

C. two ways out of the school involve your local fire station in fire drill planning for your school.

D. two ways out of the school. Involve your local fire station in fire drill planning for your school.

## Comprehension

*Read the following extract and answer the questions that follow it.*

Safeguarding and promoting the welfare of children is defined for the purposes of this guidance as: protecting children from maltreatment; preventing impairment of children's health or development; ensuring that children grow up in circumstances consistent with the provision of safe and effective care; and taking action to enable all children to have the best outcomes. Children include everyone under the age of 18.

Where a child is suffering significant harm, or is likely to do so, action should be taken to protect that child. Action should also be taken to promote the welfare of a child in need of additional support, even if they are not suffering harm or are at immediate risk.

Everyone who comes into contact with children and their families has a role to play in safeguarding children. School and college staff are particularly important as they are in a position to identify concerns early and provide help for children, to prevent concerns from escalating. Schools and colleges and their staff form part of the wider safeguarding system for children. This system is described in statutory guidance Working Together to Safeguard Children 2013. Schools and colleges should work with social workers, the police, health services and other services to promote the welfare of children and protect them from harm.

Each school and college should have a designated safeguarding lead who will provide support to staff members to carry out their safeguarding duties and who will liaise closely with other services such as children's social care.

The Teacher Standards 2012 state that teachers, including headteachers, should safeguard children's well-being and maintain public trust in the teaching profession as part of their professional duties. All school and college staff have a responsibility to provide a safe environment in which children can learn.

All school and college staff have a responsibility to identify children who may be in need of extra help or who are suffering, or are likely to suffer, significant harm. All staff then have a responsibility to take appropriate action, working with other services as needed.

In addition to working with the designated safeguarding lead staff members should be aware that they may be asked to support social workers to take decisions about individual children.

All staff members should be aware of systems within their school or college which support safeguarding and these should be explained to them as part of staff induction. This includes the school's or college's child protection policy; the school's or college's staff behaviour policy (sometimes called a code of conduct); and the designated safeguarding lead. All staff members should also receive appropriate child protection training, which is regularly updated.

All school and college staff members should be aware of the signs of abuse and neglect so that they are able to identify cases of children who may be in need of help or protection. Staff members working with children are advised to maintain an attitude of 'it could happen here' where safeguarding is concerned. When concerned about the welfare of a child, staff members should always act in the interest of the child.

There are various expert sources of advice on the signs of abuse and neglect. Each area's Local Safeguarding Children Board (LSCB) should be able to advise on useful material, including training options. One good source of advice is provided on the NSPCC website. Types of abuse and neglect, and examples of specific safeguarding issues are described in paragraphs 20–25.

Knowing what to look for is vital to the early identification of abuse and neglect. If staff members are unsure they should always speak to children's social care.

Taken from www.gov.uk/government/uploads/system/uploads/attachment_data/
file/372753/Keeping_children_safe_in_education.pdf.

**A** The following groups might all be potential audiences or readers of the article, although some would find it more useful than others. Which group would find it the most relevant and which group the least relevant?

- Social workers
- NSPCC
- Local Safeguarding Children Board
- School and college staff
- Designated safeguarding lead

**B** Match each of the following summaries to the relevant paragraph of the text: 1, 3, 8 and 10.

1. Agencies and other authorities responsible for safeguarding
2. Definition and explanation of safeguarding
3. Sources of advice and guidance on safeguarding
4. Systems and policies which support safeguarding

**C** Read the statements below and decide which refer to

- School and college staff (SCS)
- Local Safeguarding Children Board (LSCB)
- Social workers (SW)

1. They should identify children who may be in need of additional help or who are suffering significant harm.
2. They work with schools and colleges, the police and health services to protect children.
3. They provide advice on safeguarding children, including information about the options for further training.
4. They should be made aware as part of their induction process of the systems and policies which support safeguarding.

**D** Select three phrases from the list below to complete the bulleted list.

The last bullet point has been completed for you.

1. regular training from safeguarding experts at the NSPCC
2. advising families on child protection and signs of abuse or neglect
3. reporting instances of abuse or neglect to the LSCB
4. regular training in child protection for staff
5. systems and policies which support safeguarding
6. the safeguarding lead taking sole responsibility for child protection
7. promoting the welfare of children even if they are not suffering harm
8. adopting a positive attitude, 'It couldn't happen here.'

Safeguarding in schools involves

- 
- 
- 
- safeguarding all young people under the age of 18.

**E**  Identify the order in which these statements appear in the text.

1. Teachers should maintain public trust in the teaching profession as part of their professional duties.
2. Action should be taken to protect a child who is suffering significant harm or is likely to do so.
3. Members of staff from schools and colleges form part of the wider safeguarding system for young people.
4. Recognising signs of abuse and neglect are vital to early identification of safeguarding issues.
5. The safeguarding lead in schools should liaise closely with other services such as social care.

# 4   Numeracy skills

This section introduces all the terminology, and explains all the techniques and methods, needed to pass the numeracy test.

The topics are introduced through the general areas of number, measure, statistics, presentation of data and algebra, with examples and practice questions for each topic, and then four practice papers covering all topics.

# 4.1   Number

This section introduces fractions, decimals and percentages, and how to convert between them. Fractions, decimals and percentages may also be tested within other more complex topics. The LOOK IT UP feature points ahead to the more challenging practice questions.

## FRACTIONS

**Fractions** like ½ and ⅕ are equal parts of a whole. Halve a pint of milk and you get ½ a pint of milk.

Divide a bar of chocolate between five people, and each person gets ⅕ of the bar.

The number of the top (**numerator**) is what you started with (1 whole). The number on the bottom (**denominator**) is how many equal parts resulted from the sharing.

As with whole numbers, you can count with fractions.

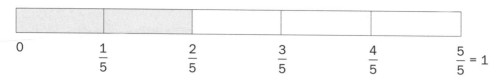

$$0 \qquad \frac{1}{5} \qquad \frac{2}{5} \qquad \frac{3}{5} \qquad \frac{4}{5} \qquad \frac{5}{5} = 1$$

$\dfrac{2}{5}$ can be thought of as $\dfrac{1}{5} + \dfrac{1}{5} = 2 \times \dfrac{1}{5}$.

It's also the same as $2 \div 5$.

| | | | | |
|---|---|---|---|---|
| | | | | |

## Simplest form/lowest terms

Multiplying (or dividing) both the top and bottom of a fraction by the same number does not change the fraction. It creates families of equivalent fractions.

$$\frac{1}{2} = \frac{2}{4} \qquad\qquad \frac{1}{5} = \frac{2}{10} = \frac{3}{15} \qquad\qquad \frac{2}{3} = \frac{4}{6} = \frac{6}{9}$$

A fraction that cannot be divided – when there is no common **factor** in the numerator and denominator – is called the **lowest term** – or simplest term.

To simplify a fraction, think of a number which divides exactly into both top and bottom. Do the division and repeat until there is no number which divides exactly into top and bottom numbers.

## Example

*In a class of twenty-four, six children go home for lunch. What fraction goes home for lunch?*

$$6 \text{ out of } 24 = \frac{6}{24}$$

Always give the answer in the lowest terms.

   6 and 24 are both even numbers, divisible by 2.

   Dividing top and bottom by 2:

$$\frac{6}{24} = \frac{3}{12}$$

   12 and 3 are both divisible by 3:

$$\frac{3}{12} = \frac{1}{3}$$

Answer: One-third of the children go home for lunch.

## Practice questions

1   A student scores fourteen out of thirty in a test. What fraction is this in its lowest form?

2   The Year 6 teacher examined the performance of her pupils at the end of Year 5.

| Level | 1 | 2 | 3 | 4 | 5 |
|-------|---|---|---|---|---|
| Boys | 2 | 3 | 4 | 5 | 1 |
| Girls | 0 | 2 | 5 | 6 | 0 |

What fraction of the boys is above level 2 and below level 5? Give your answer in its lowest terms.

**3**  In a Year 11 group, $\frac{5}{8}$ are taking part in either a sponsored walk or a sponsored swim. Of those taking part, $\frac{1}{4}$ have chosen to do the sponsored swim. What fraction of the whole year group is taking part in a sponsored swim? Give your answer as a fraction in its lowest terms.

## Fractions of amounts

To calculate a fraction of an amount, multiply the amount by the fraction.

$$\frac{1}{2} \text{ of } £56 = \frac{1}{2} \times £56$$

'Of' means multiply in fractions and percentages.

To calculate <u>mentally</u> the fraction of an amount, first share by the denominator, and then multiply by the numerator.

## Example

*Two-thirds of the pupils in class 6B bring sandwiches for lunch. There are 33 in the class. How many bring a packed lunch?*

To find $\frac{2}{3}$ of a number, first find $\frac{1}{3}$ and then double your answer.

$$\frac{1}{3} \text{ of } 33 = 33 \div 3 = 11$$

$$\frac{2}{3} \text{ of } 33 = 2 \times 11 = 22$$

Answer: 22 pupils bring a packed lunch.

<u>Using a calculator</u>, since the order of operations is immaterial for multiplication and division, multiply by the numerator and then divide by the denominator.

## Example

*Three-fifths of the pupils in class 6C have school dinners. There are thirty-five in the class. How many have school dinners?*

$$\frac{3}{5} \text{ of } 35 = \frac{3}{5} \times 35$$

Calculate: $35 \times 3 \div 5 = 21$

Answer: 21 have school dinners.

Another way of dividing by 5 is to divide by 10 and then double the answer.

## Practice questions

**4**  Two-thirds of three hundred and forty-two pupils have a hot school meal. How many pupils in total have a hot school meal?

**5**  A school has two hundred and eighty-eight pupils. Three-eighths of the pupils are eligible for free school meals. How many pupils are eligible for free school meals?

**6**  In a class of twenty-seven pupils, four out of nine are girls. How many are boys?

**7**  There are one hundred and eighty pupils in a primary school. Forty-five of these are in the Reception class. What fraction is this of the whole?

**8**  After heavy snowfall, one-third of the pupils are not able to attend their primary school on that day. The total number of pupils on the school roll is three hundred and fifty-four. How many pupils did attend that day?

**9**  Year 3 pupils carried out a survey into the pets they each had at home. A quarter of the pupils in Year 3 had a cat and one-third of those with a cat also had a dog. There are 48 pupils in Year 3. What fraction of the Year 3 pupils had a cat and a dog? Give your answer as a fraction in its lowest terms.

For more practice questions testing your knowledge of fractions, see practice questions 14–17, 19–20, 22–23, 38–39, 46–47, 62, 69, 123, 125, 128, 147, 149, 155, 178, 189.

## DECIMALS

**Decimals** are numbers with a decimal point, which indicates where the whole number part ends and the fractional part starts.

In the decimal system, the value of a digit depends on where it is placed in a number.

In 176.95, the **place value** of the 9 is nine-tenths ($\frac{9}{10}$) and the place value of the 5 is five-hundredths ($\frac{5}{100}$).

| H | T | U | . | t | h |
|---|---|---|---|---|---|
| 1 | 7 | 6 | . | 9 | 5 |

Arithmetic can be performed on decimal numbers in the same way as for whole numbers.

## Example

*A teacher organises a fun day for two classes of twenty-seven pupils and three classes of twenty-six pupils. How many pupils is that altogether?*

When multiplying 2 by 27 mentally, think of 27 as 20 plus 7. Then multiply 2 by 20 (40) and 2 by 7 (14) and add: 40 + 14 = 54.

$$2 \times 27 + 3 \times 26 = 54 + 78 = 132$$

Answer: Total number of pupils is 132.

## Practice questions

**10**   What is nought point six of four hundred and twenty?

**11**   Nought point three of the pupils in one class of thirty pupils have extra music lessons. How many pupils in the class have extra music lessons?

**12**   Nought point seven of a year group of two hundred and ten pupils took part in a sponsored walk. How many did not take part?

**13**   In a schools' athletics competition, the 4-person relay team ran their legs with these times:

87.45 secs        78.92 secs        94.38 secs        72.1 secs

What was their combined time, in seconds?

For more practice questions testing your knowledge of decimals, see practice questions 14–16, 34–37, 45, 50–53, 65–70, 77, 84, 90–91, 96–97, 109, 114, 116, 118, 121–125, 132, 141–143, 145, 148, 164, 166, 168, 182, 195, 204–206, 208.

## Conversions from fractions to decimals and vice versa, and rounding

To convert a decimal to a fraction, apply the place value for the digits after the decimal point.

$$0.1 = \frac{1}{10} \qquad 0.3 = \frac{3}{10} \qquad 0.7 = \frac{7}{10} \qquad 0.9 = \frac{9}{10} \qquad 0.01 = \frac{1}{100}$$

For factors of 10 (2 and 5) and 100 (25, 75), the fraction can be written in its lowest terms:

$$0.2 = \frac{2}{10} = \frac{1}{5} \qquad 0.25 = \frac{25}{100} = \frac{1}{4}$$

Commit to memory the most common equivalents:

$$0.5 = \frac{1}{2} \qquad 0.25 = \frac{1}{4} \qquad 0.75 = \frac{3}{4}.$$

## Example

*Of the total number of pupils in a school 0.85 have school dinners. Of those, 0.2 have special dietary requirements. What fraction of the total number of pupils in the school has school dinners and also has a special dietary requirement? Give your answer as a fraction in its lowest terms.*

$$0.2 \times 0.85 = 0.17 = \frac{17}{100} \quad \text{OR} \quad 0.85 = \frac{85}{100} = \frac{17}{20}$$

$$0.2 = \frac{2}{10} = \frac{1}{5}$$

$$\frac{17}{20} \times \frac{1}{5} = \frac{17}{100}$$

Because a fraction represents a division – the numerator divided by the denominator – converting a fraction to its decimal equivalent is achieved by division.

## Example

*What is thirty-two out of forty as a decimal?*

$$32 \text{ out of } 40 = \frac{32}{40} = \frac{16}{20} = \frac{8}{10} = 0.8$$

Answer: 32 out of 40 as a decimal is 0.8.

## Practice questions

**14**   What is nought point six five as a fraction in its lowest terms?

**15**   Nought point four pupils in a school have free school meals. What is this as a fraction? Give your answer in its lowest terms.

**16**   At the end of Key Stage two, nought point eight five pupils gained level four and above. What is this as a fraction? Give your answer in its lowest terms.

**17**   In Year 7 PE lessons, the teachers give the pupils a choice of sport. 0.4 selected football; 0.35 selected hockey and the rest selected netball or were excused PE that day. What fraction chose hockey? Give your answer in its lowest terms.

For more examples of practice questions testing your knowledge of converting from fractions to decimals and vice versa, see practice questions 34–37, 69, 97, 122, 125, 166, 168, 182.

A question may require an answer to be given to a certain number of decimal places, or the nearest whole number. With currency questions, this will usually be to the nearest penny – two decimal places for sterling amounts – or to the nearest pound.

Do not round your answer until the very end of a calculation.

Giving an answer 'to one decimal place' requires examination of the second decimal place and rounding up or down accordingly.

- 4.72 rounds to 4.7 – because $\frac{2}{100} < \frac{5}{100}$

○  4.75 rounds to 4.8 – because convention rules that $\frac{5}{100}$ is to be rounded up

○  4.78 rounds to 4.8 – because $\frac{8}{100} > \frac{5}{100}$

The same strategy applies, whatever the level of accuracy required: look at the next digit and round up/down according to that digit.

Depending on the context, it may be appropriate to round up/down, regardless of the place value of the digit to be rounded.

○  Sharing money or other items, rounding down is necessary. There will be a remainder that cannot be shared equally.

○  Sharing the cost, rounding up is necessary; otherwise there will be insufficient to pay the bill.

○  Deciding how many will fit within a space, rounding down is needed.

○  Determining, for example, how many coaches to hire for a school trip, rounding up will be necessary. This will mean spare seats but all children will be accommodated.

For questions that might involve rounding see practice questions 24–28, 33, 35, 47, 49, 56, 58, 65–69, 84, 90–91, 94, 96–97, 118, 124, 126, 130–132, 134–135, 137–138, 140–141, 148, 150–151, 154, 162, 166, 168, 172, 177, 202–203, 206, 208.

## PERCENTAGES

A percentage is an amount measured out of 100. The % symbol represents $\diagup_{100}$.

$$80\% = \frac{80}{100} = \frac{4}{5}$$

Commit to memory the most common percentages:

$10\% = \frac{1}{10}$     $12.5\% = \frac{1}{8}$     $20\% = \frac{1}{5}$

$25\% = \frac{1}{4}$     $50\% = \frac{1}{2}$     $75\% = \frac{3}{4}$

Notice that $100\% = \frac{100}{100} = 1$.

## Example

*Seven out of twenty-five pupils scored full marks in a test. What percentage of pupils scored full marks?*

Replace 'out of' with a fraction line.

7 out of 25 means $\frac{7}{25}$.

There are four 25s in 100. Multiply top and bottom by 4 to get an equivalent fraction with 100 in the denominator.

$$\frac{7}{25} = \frac{28}{100} = 28\%$$

Answer: 28% of pupils scored full marks.

## Practice questions

**18**   In a class of thirty pupils, forty per cent are boys. How many are girls?

**19**   Thirty per cent of a class of pupils have chosen history as an option in Year ten. What fraction is this?

**20**   The local museum offers a discount of seventeen and a half per cent on admission prices for school groups. What fraction of the total admission price is this discounted rate? Give your answer as a fraction in its lowest form.

**21**   A test has forty-five questions, each worth one mark. The pass mark is seventy per cent. How many questions have to be answered correctly in order to gain a pass?

**22**   The pass mark for a test is set at sixty-five per cent. What fraction of the marks must a pupil obtain to pass? Give your answer as a fraction in its lowest form.

**23**   Fifty-five per cent of a class of twenty pupils are boys. What fraction are girls?

**24**   On one day in a high school, 2.5% of 960 pupils were absent, 15.2% were not in lessons because    they were sitting exams and 5.3% were on a school trip. How many pupils were in lessons?

## Converting decimals and fractions to percentages

○   To convert a decimal to a percentage, take the number of one-hundredths:

$$0.45 = \frac{45}{100} = 45\%$$

○   To convert a fraction into a percentage, multiply it by 100%. This does not change the size of the fraction, but gives it as a percentage.

$$\frac{3}{4} = \frac{3}{4} \times 100\% = 75\%$$

Don't 'multiply a fraction by 100' unless you want to make it 100 times bigger! Instead, multiply it by 100%.  ✖

## Example

*A student scores fifty-two out of a possible eighty in a test. What is this as a percentage?*

$$52 \text{ out of } 80 = \frac{52}{80} = \frac{13}{20} = \frac{65}{100} = 65\%$$

Answer: 52 out of 80 as a percentage is 65%.

## Practice questions

**25**    A pupil scores fourteen out of a possible forty-two marks. What is this as a percentage? Give your answer to the nearest whole number.

**26**    Twenty-seven hours a week are spent in lessons. The pupils in Year 10 have four and a half hours of mathematics per week. What percentage of the total is this? Give your answer to the nearest whole number.

**27**    Sixteen out of thirty pupils chose to take extra music lessons. What is this as a percentage? Give your answer to the nearest whole number.

**28**    Students have thirty hours of lessons per week, of which six hours are devoted to English. What percentage of the total weekly lesson time is devoted to English?

**29**    A pupil scores thirty-three out of sixty in a test. What is this as a percentage?

## Percentages of amounts

'Of' means multiply in fractions and percentages.

A percentage is a fraction. To calculate the percentage of an amount, you have options:

○    Recognise the simple fractional equivalent of the percentage, and then calculate mentally as you would for a 'fraction of an amount' (page 112).

○    Revert to the $/100$ form of the percentage, and then calculate using a calculator as you would for a 'fraction of an amount' (page 112).

## Examples

*In class 6D, forty per cent of the pupils wear glasses. There are thirty-five pupils in the class. How many pupils in class 6D wear glasses?*

$$40\% = \frac{40}{100} = \frac{2}{5}$$

$\frac{1}{5}$ of 35 pupils = 7 pupils

$\frac{2}{5}$ of 35 pupils = 14 pupils

Answer: 14 pupils in class 6D wear glasses.

*A supplier offers a 12.5% discount on orders over £100. The school orders £127 worth of books. What discount is given? Round down to the nearest 1p.*

12.5% of £127 = 12.5/100 × £127

= £127 × 12.5 ÷ 100 = £15.875 = £15.87 to the nearest 1p.

Answer: £15.87 discount is given.

Using a calculator, the £ sign is not entered, so it's important to be aware of the units of your answer.

*A spring is 30 centimetres long. When stretched its length is increased by 25%. How long is the stretched spring?*

25% of 30 = $\frac{1}{4}$ of 30 = 7.5

30cm + 7.5cm = 37.5cm

Answer: The stretched spring is 37.5cm long.

Don't just calculate the extension. Remember to add it to the original length to find the stretched length.

## Practice questions

**30** In a school of four hundred and twenty pupils, fifteen per cent receive free school meals. How many pupils do not receive free schools meals?

**31** A sponsored spelling test raised sixty-five pounds, with forty-five per cent given to school funds and the remainder to charity. How much does the charity receive?

**32** Seventy per cent of the cost of a school outing is subsidised. Pupils are asked to make a contribution of fifteen pounds each. What is the total cost per pupil?

**33** The reading ages of a group of Year 6 pupils receiving additional help was assessed.

| Pupil | Actual age | | Reading age | |
|---|---|---|---|---|
| | Years | Months | Years | Months |
| 1 | 11 | 0 | 10 | 9 |
| 2 | 10 | 6 | 10 | 8 |
| 3 | 10 | 8 | 8 | 3 |
| 4 | 10 | 4 | 9 | 1 |
| 5 | 10 | 11 | 9 | 11 |
| 6 | 10 | 7 | 10 | 10 |

Look at the table and indicate all the true statements:

A: Less than 80% of the pupils had a reading age below that of their actual age.

B: Pupil 3 had 40% lower reading age compared to his actual age (to the nearest whole month).

C: 50% of the pupils had a reading age of at least 1 year 6 months below the actual age.

## Percentage points

Comparing amounts given as raw data can be difficult. Are things getting better, or worse? Converting the raw data to percentages allows a direct comparison; an improvement can be measured in **percentage points**.

If a pupil scores 40% in one test and improves by 10% in the next test, because 10% of 40% is 4%, the score in the second test is 44%. If the improvement is 10 percentage points, the score in the second test is 50%.

## Example

*Twelve out of twenty Year six pupils are predicted level four in their mathematics Key Stage two test. Fifteen actually gained a level four. What is this, as a percentage points increase?*

12 out of 20 = 60%

15 out of 20 = 75%

75% − 60% = 15%

Answer: This is 15% as a percentage points increase.

For examples of questions that refer to percentage or percentage points, see practice questions 49, 63, 94, 98, 100, 109, 114, 119, 124, 127, 129, 131–132, 134–138, 141–143, 145, 149–156, 160–162, 169–172, 174–180, 182–184, 191–196, 198, 205–208.

## PROPORTION INVOLVING FRACTIONS, PERCENTAGES AND DECIMALS

**Proportion** describes the relationship between some part of a whole, with the whole. It is usually expressed as a fraction, but can also be given as a percentage or as a decimal.

## Example

*In class 6D, there are thirty-five pupils and fourteen of them wear glasses. What proportion of class 6D wear glasses?*

$$14 \text{ out of } 35 = \frac{14}{35} = \frac{2}{5} = 40\%$$

Answer: 40% of class 6D wear glasses.

## Practice questions

**34**  Twenty-eight out of forty pupils in Year six achieved a level four or above in Key Stage two English. What proportion is this? Give your answer as a decimal.

**35**  In a survey of forty-eight pupils in Year six, sixteen pupils stated that mathematics was their favourite subject. What proportion did not state that mathematics was their favourite subject? Give your answer as a decimal to two decimal places.

**36** In a year group of one hundred and twenty-five pupils, seventy-five are boys. What proportion are boys? Give your answer as a decimal.

**37** Seven out of twenty pupils in one class are absent with flu. What proportion is this as a decimal?

**38** Pupils are studying weather patterns and record the midday temperature in °C over a period of five weeks in the winter.

| °C | Mon | Tue | Wed | Thu | Fri |
|---|---|---|---|---|---|
| Week 1 | −1 | 0 | 1 | 2 | 4 |
| Week 2 | 3 | 2 | −4 | −3 | −2 |
| Week 3 | 2 | 2 | 1 | 0 | 0 |
| Week 4 | −3 | −1 | 1 | 2 | 3 |
| Week 5 | 4 | 0 | 0 | −1 | −4 |

What proportion of the total recordings was 0°C? Give your answer as a fraction in its lowest terms.

**39** The Year 6 teacher examined the performance of her pupils at the end of Year 5.

| Level | 1 | 2 | 3 | 4 | 5 |
|---|---|---|---|---|---|
| Boys | 2 | 3 | 4 | 5 | 1 |
| Girls | 0 | 2 | 5 | 6 | 0 |

What proportion of pupils gained less than a level 4? Give your answer as a fraction in its lowest terms.

For more practice questions testing your knowledge of proportion, see practice questions 121–123, 125, 128, 132–133, 148, 155, 157–159, 168, 171, 182.

# RATIOS

Ratio describes the relationship between two parts of a whole. It is expressed using the : sign.

## Example

*In class 6E, there are 32 pupils. There are 18 girls. What is the ratio of boys to girls?*

There are 18 girls.

32 − 18 = 14

There are 14 boys.

boys:girls = 14:18 = 7:9

Answer: The ratio is 7:9.

The ordering of a ratio matters. 2:5 is not the same as 5:2.

## Practice question

**40**    The table shows the gender breakdown in each year group of a junior school.

| Year group | Boys | Girls |
|------------|------|-------|
| 3          | 28   | 32    |
| 4          | 25   | 29    |
| 5          | 31   | 26    |
| 6          | 28   | 29    |

What is the ratio of boys to girls? Give your answer in its lowest terms.

 Ratios are also used in currency conversions and in map scales; see, for example, practice questions 40, 50–58, 70, 81, 87–88, 140.

# 4.2   Measure

Measure applies to money, time, length (or distance), area and volume. Calculation can be performed using measures just as they can with whole numbers and fractional quantities.

## MONEY

The UK 'went decimal' in 1971 with 100p in £1. Prior to that, money was in pounds, shillings and pence.

Money is expressed using decimals. £1.50 means one pound and 0.5 of a pound.

### Amounts of money

**Cost** is calculated using the formula: cost = quantity × price.

### Examples

*The school magazine sells for twenty pence per copy. At the school fete, one hundred and thirty-five copies were sold. How much money was collected?*

$$135 \times 20p = 2700p = £27 \quad \text{OR} \quad 135 \times £\tfrac{1}{5} = £27$$

Another way to multiply by 20p is to remember that 20p is $\tfrac{1}{5}$ of a pound.

$\tfrac{1}{5}$ of 100 = 20. $\tfrac{1}{5}$ of 35 = 7. $\tfrac{1}{5}$ of 135 = 27.

Answer: £27 was collected.

*An educational visit will incur the following costs:*

o   *£4.50 per pupil entry fee.*

o   *14 miles each way in three school minibuses, each costing 56p per mile.*

o   *Worksheets, costing £2.40 for a set of 30. Not available in smaller amounts.*

*To go on the trip, 36 pupils have paid £6.50 each. What is the difference between the amount paid by the pupils and the total cost of the visit?*

Work out the cost of each aspect of the visit: Entry:    £4.50 × 36 = £162

Travel:    2 × 14 miles = 28 miles

28 × £0.56 × 3 = £47.04

Worksheets: 36 requires 2 sets

2 × £2.40 = £4.80

Calculate the total cost:                    £162 + £47.04 + £4.80 = £213.84

Calculate the contributions from pupils:             36 × £6.50 = £234

Calculate the difference:                    £234 − £213.84 = £20.16

Answer: The difference between the amount paid by the pupils and the total cost of the visit is £20.16.

 Avoid making mistakes; read the question carefully. The entry fee is 'per person', so multiply by the number of people. The journey is two way, so double the mileage. The worksheets are only available in sets of 30, so round up.

## Practice questions

**41**   Twenty-eight pupils each make a contribution of six pounds fifty pence towards the cost of a school trip. How much is this in total?

**42**   One hundred and fifty pupils in a school are supplied with a free hot meal every day. The cook works on a budget of three pounds fifty per meal. What is the cost in total per day?

**43**   A class did a six-mile sponsored walk for charity. In total, they raised twelve pounds forty pence per mile. How much did they raise in total?

**44**   The school newsletter costs three pence per page to produce. The Autumn edition consists of six pages. How much will it cost to produce two hundred copies? Give your answer in pounds.

**45**   A minibus travels fifty miles in one day and uses nought point three litres per mile. Fuel costs one pound thirty per litre. What is the cost of the fuel for the day?

**46**   The cost of a school trip is two hundred and forty pounds per pupil. Five-eighths of this is for accommodation. What is the cost of accommodation per pupil?

**47**   £456.42 profit has been raised from the school fete. Of this profit, $\frac{1}{3}$ was taken in the tea tent, with $\frac{5}{8}$ of this being made from the sale of cakes. How much of the total raised was made from the sale of cakes? Give your answer to the nearest penny.

**48**   A teacher submits a travel claim for attending external training sessions. Here is a summary of her claim.

| Date | Details of claim |
|------|------------------|
| 5 March | 45 miles: school to training venue and 45 miles return |
| 19 March | 36 miles school to teachers' centre and 36 miles return |
| 26 March | Return train fare: £45.50 |
| | 6 miles home to station and 6 miles return |
| | Taxi: £9.50 |

Car travel is paid at 45p per mile. What is the total cost of her claim?

**49**   A group of 30 sixth-form English students and three adults are attending a play in London. The train tickets cost £412.50 in total and the theatre tickets cost £20 for the adults. The students receive a 15% reduction on this ticket price. The total cost of the trip is to be divided evenly between everyone. How much will each person have to pay? Give your answer to the nearest whole pound.

For more examples of questions involving money calculations, see practice questions 90, 93, 99, 140, 185–187.

## Conversions from one currency to another

Different countries use different currencies. In the United Kingdom, the currency is sterling (£). In France, the currency is euros (€). To convert an amount from one currency to another, you need to know the **exchange rate**.

## Examples

*The exchange rate is €1.6 = £1. Convert £15.50 into euros.*

Answer: £15.50 = €24.80.

| | |
|---|---|
| Write the conversion rate formula starting '£1 =' | £1 = €1.6 |
| Write the sterling amount as a multiple of £1 | £15.50 = 15.50 × £1 |
| Substitute £1 for its equivalent | = 15.50 × €1.6 |
| Do the calculation | = €24.80 |
| Write the conversion rate formula starting '€1 =' | €1 = £1 ÷ 1.6 |
| Write the euro amount as a multiple of €1 | €48 = 48 × €1 |
| Substitute €1 for its equivalent | = 48 × £1 ÷ 1.6 |
| Do the calculation | = £48 ÷ 1.6 = £30 |

*The exchange rate is €1.6 = £1. Convert €48 into sterling.*

Answer: €48 = £30.

## Practice questions

**50**    There are one point four euros to a pound. How many euros in spending money will a pupil get for twenty-five pounds?

**51**    Some sixth-form students are planning on doing voluntary work in Ghana. Each pupil requires fifteen hundred cedi, the Ghanaian currency. The exchange rate is nought point two pounds to one Ghanaian cedi. How much sponsorship money is this, in sterling, per pupil?

**52**    A group of art students are planning a trip to Canada to study First Nation art. They have been told they will need one hundred and fifty pounds in spending money. One point seven Canadian dollars are equivalent to one pound. How much spending money will each pupil have in Canadian dollars?

**53**    At the end of a school trip to Germany, there are three hundred and sixty euros left in the budget. Twenty pupils were on the trip. The money left over is to be divided equally between them. How much refund will each pupil receive in pounds sterling? The rate is one point two euros to the pound.

**54**    A US dollar is worth £0.63. A piece of science equipment has been ordered from the US. It costs US$567. What is the cost in pounds sterling?

**55**    A group of geography students are going to Iceland. The exchange rate is 1:0.0052 (krona to pounds sterling). One student plans to take £65 spending money. How many Icelandic krona will he get?

**56**    The exchange rate of pounds sterling to euros is 4:5. Pupils are taking £60 in spending money. One pupil spends €50 and takes the rest home again. The exchange rate on return is €15 to £13. How much money will he have when he exchanges back to pounds sterling? Give your answer to the nearest penny.

| Accommodation (total) | €1750 |
| Channel train | £69 per person |
| Entry fees to attractions | £1000 |
| Sundries | £870 |
| Spending money | €40 per person |

**57**    The cost of a school trip for 25 pupils is summarised in the table:

What is the estimated total cost per pupil in £? Use the ratio £5 to €8.

**58**    For a school trip to Belgium, each pupil is allowed to take £75 spending money. The exchange rate on the way to Belgium was £1 = €1.23. One pupil spent €76 and exchanged the rest back into pounds sterling on her return. The exchange rate on return was £1 = €1.17. How much money did she exchange on the return journey? Give your answer to the nearest whole pound.

## TIME

There are 60 seconds in every minute, 60 minutes in every hour, 24 hours in every day and 7 days in a week. In a school, though, there are only 5 days in the week, and the important measures of time are class length and teaching day length.

Notice that questions may present time using the 12-hour clock, indicating morning with a.m. and afternoon with p.m. Alternatively, the 24-hour clock may be used, where 12:00 is noon and 24:00 is midnight.

## Examples

*Pupils in Year 9 are visiting a museum. The coach journey takes thirty-five minutes each way. They are spending four hours at the museum and must be back at school by three p.m. What is the latest time they must leave in the morning? Give your answer using the 24-hour clock.*

Calculate the total time: 4 hours + 2 × 35 minutes = 5 hours 10 minutes

Remember to multiply the 35 minutes by 2 as it is a return journey, not one way.

Calculate the time to leave: 5 hours 10 minutes back from 15:00 is 09:50

Don't use 'normal' subtraction for time: $15:00 - 5:10 \neq 9:90$

Answer: The time to leave is 09:50.

*A teacher offers after-school time slots to parents for consultations on three consecutive days. She allows 15 minutes per consultation and needs to make 28 appointments. She will start the sessions at 16:00 on the Monday and finish at 19:30 at the latest, with a break of 20 minutes at 18:00. Assuming she fills every slot consecutively, at what time will she finish on the Wednesday evening?*

15 minutes per consultation: time for 4 per hour.

28 appointments: @ 4 per hour, 7 hours needed

Session starts at 16:00 and ends at 19:30. Time available = 3.5 hours

Don't forget to allow time for the break.

Allowing for break at 18:00: 8 consultations before the break and 4 after.

Time for 12 per evening, so 24 in two evenings, Monday and Tuesday.

Third evening: Wednesday: 4 consultations remaining. Finish time: 17:00.

Answer: The finish time is 17:00 on Wednesday.

## Practice questions

**59** Each school day consists of six lessons, each of fifty minutes. How many hours per day are spent in lessons?

**60** A school day consists of four hours and forty minutes lesson time per day. How much time per week is spent in lessons? Give your answer in hours and minutes.

**61** Pupils have four hours and twenty minutes of mathematics per week. Two and a half hours of this is teacher-led. How many minutes per week do the pupils spend in class working independently?

**62** One- third of the school day is spent in registration, tutor time and breaks. The school day is six hours and thirty minutes long. How many hours are allocated to lessons?

**63** The music teacher is arranging a school concert. There are 12 planned musical items, lasting an average of 8 minutes per item. The concert starts at 19:30, with a 20-minute break in the middle. This break usually goes on for 10% longer than planned and there has to be a 3-minute break between items to allow for pupils to set up their instruments. What time should the concert finish? Give your answer in the 24-hour clock.

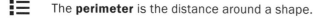

For more examples of questions involving time, see practice questions 104, 116, 118, 121–122, 151–152, 188–189, 209–212.

## DISTANCE

Distance is a measure of length, usually measured in millimetres (mm), centimetres (cm), metres (m) or kilometres (km).

10mm = 1cm    100cm = 1m    1000m = 1km

The **perimeter** is the distance around a shape.

## Examples

*An exercise book is nought point six centimetres thick. How many can be stacked on a shelf thirty-one centimetres deep?*

31cm/0.6cm = 51.66 = 51

Although 51.66 rounds to 52 when using 'to the nearest whole number', in this circumstance, it's necessary to round down. The remaining space is not big enough for an additional book.

Answer: 51 books can be stacked.

*For a charity fundraiser, pupils are asked to bring one penny coins which are laid out in a straight row. The diameter of a one penny coin is 2.1cm. Altogether 452 coins are collected. How long is the line of coins? Give your answer in metres to one decimal place.*

2.1cm × 452 = 949.2cm

100cm = 1m

949.2cm = 9.5m

Answer: The line of coins is 9.5m long.

## Practice questions

**64** A sponsored walk is taking place around the perimeter path of the school grounds, which are rectangular. The length is six hundred metres and the width is four hundred metres. What is the total distance in kilometres?

**65**   A teacher travels eight point three miles each way to a technology course, held over six sessions. How many miles does she travel to and from the course in total? Give your answer to the nearest whole mile.

**66**   A PE teacher estimates that he runs the length of the football pitch ten times in every sports lesson. The football pitch is ninety metres long and he teaches sixteen sports lessons per week. How far does he run in one week, according to his estimate? Give your answer in kilometres to one decimal place.

**67**   A box file containing exam papers measures seven centimetres in depth. How many can be stacked in one pile in a wall cupboard which is one point nought three metres deep?

**68**   A sponsored walk takes place around the school grounds, with each lap an estimated 1700m in length. The results are recorded:

| Number of laps | Number of pupils |
|:---:|:---:|
| 3 | 3 |
| 4 | 4 |
| 5 | 18 |
| 6 | 13 |

What is the total distance in kilometres walked by all the pupils? Give your answer to one decimal place.

**69**   A Duke of Edinburgh hike is divided into the following sections: $\frac{1}{3}$ flat ground; $\frac{1}{8}$ through forest; $\frac{2}{5}$ uphill; the rest is mixed terrain. The total hike is 18 miles. What is the distance over mixed terrain? Give your answer to one decimal place.

**70**   A geography class uses maps with a scale of 1:100,000. Pupils are estimating the length of a river from source to estuary by dividing it into sections on the map and measuring each section.

The distance of each section is recorded in centimetres: 1.4; 5.6; 3.9; 7.4; 2.2.

What is the estimated length of the river in kilometres based on these measurements?

For more examples of questions involving distance, see practice questions 85, 87–88, 90–92, 103, 106, 185–187, 209–212.

# AREA

Area is a two-dimensional measure and is calculated by multiplying two lengths: the length and width of an object, or its height and width. Area is usually measured in square millimetres ($mm^2$), square centimetres ($cm^2$), square metres ($m^2$) or square kilometres ($km^2$).

## Examples

*A new flowerbed is planned for the school grounds. It will measure three point two metres by one point five metres. What is its area? Give your answer in square metres.*

$3.2m \times 1.5m = 4.8m^2$

Answer: The area is $4.8m^2$.

*A sheet of A4 paper is two hundred and ten millimetres long and two hundred and ninety seven millimetres wide. What is its area? Give your answer in square centimetres.*

Area = length $\times$ width = 210mm $\times$ 297mm = 62,370mm$^2$ = 623.7cm$^2$

 1cm = 10mm but 1cm$^2 \neq$ 100mm$^2$. 1cm$^2$ = 10mm $\times$ 10mm = 100mm$^2$.

Convert the lengths to the units needed in the answer before doing the calculation.

Answer: The area is 623.7cm$^2$.

Questions on area can require other skills, like fractions.

*A small fish pond is to be made in the school grounds. Its area is planned to be one point five metres by one point two metres in an area of grass measuring nine square metres. What fraction of the area of grass is allocated to the fish pond?*

Area = 1.5m $\times$ 1.2m = 1.8m$^2$

1.8m$^2$ out of 9m$^2$ = 1.8 $\div$ 9 = $\dfrac{18}{90}$ = $\dfrac{1}{5}$

Answer: $\frac{1}{5}$ is allocated to the fish pond.

## Practice questions

**71**   The art department has a display board measuring six hundred centimetres by four hundred centimetres. What is the area in square metres?

**72**   The area of the school hockey pitch is four thousand eight hundred and sixty square metres and the length is ninety metres. What is the width?

**73**   The school football pitch is one hundred and twenty metres long and its area is six thousand square metres. What is the width of the football pitch?

**74**   Below is a cross section of the school swimming pool.

At the shallow end, the depth is 1m and at the deep end the depth is 2m. The length of the pool is 25m.

Calculate the area of the cross section. Give your answer in m$^2$.

**75**    A new classroom is to be built for the art department, 9m wide and 10m long. Windows, doors and cupboards will take up the equivalent of 9m in length. Exhibition spaces are planned for as much of the space as possible, although the maximum usable height above the floor for displays is 2m and the minimum height is 0.5m. How much area can be devoted to exhibition space?

**76**    A primary school science lesson is looking at the number of daisies per square metre on the school lawn. They divide the lawn into 15 equally sized rectangles for counting purposes. The lawn measures 6 metres by 10 metres. What is the area of one small rectangle for counting purposes?

**77**    In a mathematics lesson, Year 4 pupils are looking at the area of the school playground. They use a measuring wheel to estimate the dimensions and draw a diagram of their findings.

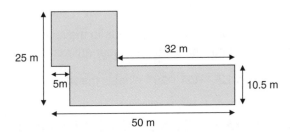

Calculate the total area of the playground.

## VOLUME AND CAPACITY

**Volume** is a three-dimensional measure and is calculated by multiplying three lengths: the height, length and width of an object. Volume is usually measured in cubic millimetres ($mm^3$), cubic centimetres ($cm^3$), cubic metres ($m^3$) or cubic kilometres ($km^3$).

**Capacity** is a measure of how much can fill a volume of space. Capacity is usually measured in millilitres (ml), centilitres (cl) or litres (l).

1 litre occupies $1000cm^3$ of space.

## Examples

*In a mathematics lesson, pupils are making cubes out of cardboard. The length of one side must be five centimetres. What is the volume of the cube?*

   $5cm \times 5cm \times 5cm = 125cm^3$

Answer: The volume is $125cm^3$.

*A packing chest is thirty centimetres by thirty centimetres by fifty centimetres. What is its volume? Give your answer in cubic metres.*

   Volume = $30cm \times 30cm \times 50cm = 4500cm^3 = 4500/1,000,000m^3 = 0.0045m^3$

Convert the lengths to the units needed in the answer before doing the calculation.

1m = 100cm but $1m^3 \neq 100cm^3$. $1m^3 = 100cm \times 100cm \times 100cm = 1,000,000cm^3$

Answer: The volume is $0.0045m^3$.

## Practice questions

**78**  What is the height of a classroom which has a volume of two hundred and twenty four cubic metres, length eight metres and width seven metres?

**79**  To prepare for some chemistry experiments, the teacher needs to divide three litres of liquid equally between seventy-five bottles. How much will be poured into each bottle? Give your answer in millilitres.

**80**  A primary school teacher planned to keep goldfish in the classroom. How many litres are needed to fill a small fish tank measuring fifty centimetres by thirty centimetres by twenty centimetres? Assume the tank will be filled to the top.

**81**  A science experiment requires dilution of acid to water in the ratio of 2:50. The teacher uses half a litre of water. How much acid should be used? Give your answer in $cm^3$.

**82**  A small storage box measures $12'' \times 12'' \times 15''$. What is the volume in $cm^3$? Use the conversion rate of 2.5cm to $1''$.

## CONVERSIONS FROM ONE MEASURE TO ANOTHER

Different countries use different units of measure. In England, distances are measured in miles. In France, kilometres (km) are used.

To convert a distance from one measure to another, you need to know the conversion formula. This is usually given as an equation.

## Examples

*Taking 5 miles to be equivalent to 8 kilometres, convert 12km into miles.*

| | |
|---|---|
| Write the conversion rate formula starting '1km =' | $1km = \dfrac{5}{8}$ miles |
| Write the kilometre distance as a multiple of 1km | $12km = 12 \times 1km$ |
| Substitute 1km for its equivalent in miles | $= 12 \times \dfrac{5}{8}$ miles |
| Do the calculation | $= 7.5$ miles |

Answer: 12km = 7.5 miles.

*Taking 5 miles to be equivalent to 8 kilometres, convert 35 miles into kilometres.*

| | |
|---|---|
| Write the conversion rate formula starting '1 mile =' | $1 \text{ mile} = \dfrac{8}{5}$ km |
| Write the distance as a multiple of 1 mile | $35 \text{ miles} = 35 \times 1 \text{ mile}$ |
| Substitute 1 mile for its equivalent in kilometres | $= 35 \times \dfrac{8}{5}$ km |
| Do the calculation | $= 56km$ |

Answer: 35 miles = 56km.

# Practice questions

**83**   Pupils travelling to France are calculating the total distance they will travel. From the French ferry port to their hotel is a distance of thirty-two kilometres. Use the approximation of five miles to eight kilometres. Calculate how many miles they will travel from the port to the hotel.

**84**   A technology teacher wants to use an old cake recipe with his class. The recipe requires eight ounces of flour. How many grams is this? Use the conversion of one ounce equals twenty-eight point four grams. Give your answer to the nearest gram.

**85**   Students are researching heights of their ancestors. One grandmother states she is five feet in height. What is this in metres? Use the conversion of thirty centimetres to one foot.

**86**   What is fifty-nine degrees Fahrenheit in degrees Centigrade? To convert from Fahrenheit to Centigrade, subtract thirty-two, then multiply by five and divide by nine.

**87**   This is a summary of the distances the school minibus will cover on a trip to France:

| | |
|---|---|
| Distance from the school to the ferry port: | 165 miles |
| Distance from ferry port in France to hotel: | 144km |
| Estimated distance covered during the stay in France | 192km |
| Odometer reading at the start (in miles) | 50,132 |

What will the odometer read at the end of the trip? Use the ratio of 5 miles to 8 kilometres.

**88**   A school trip is planned for France. From the ferry port to the hotel is a distance of 279km one way. Whilst staying in France, it is estimated that a further 186km will be travelled. From the school to the ferry is a distance of 55 miles. What is the ratio of the distance travelled in the UK to the distance travelled in France? Use the conversion rate of 5 miles to 8km.

**89**   To convert °F to °C, the pupils in a science lesson used the following method:

'Subtract 32, multiply by 5 and divide by 9'.

The pupils take two readings at set times of a liquid as it cools down. The first reading is 194°F and the second is 95°F. By how many °C has the liquid cooled?

**90**   A geography teacher is planning a short trip to the Lake District, using the school minibus.

The total distance of the trip is estimated to be 455 miles.

The fuel consumption of the minibus is estimated to be 35 miles per gallon.

Fuel costs £1.32 per litre.

Use the conversion of 1 gallon to 4.55 litres. What is the estimated cost of the fuel for the weekend? Give your answer to the nearest whole pound.

**91**    A teacher is going on a conference 45 miles away. His car does an average of 40 miles to the gallon (mpg). Use the conversion rates of 1 litre equivalent to 0.2 gallons.

How many litres of fuel will he need to travel to and from the conference? Give your answer to two decimal places.

For more examples of questions involving converting between different measures, see practice questions 211–212.

# 4.3 Statistics

When surveys are carried out and lots of data is collected, the challenge is to understand what the data can tell you. Statistics derived from the data help, allowing comparisons to be made.

## AVERAGES

An **average** is a single value chosen or calculated to represent a group of values. There are three different averages – mean, mode and median – each useful in its own way, depending on the range and spread of the data it is representing.

## Mean

The **mean** is calculated by adding up all the values and then dividing by the number of values. The mean value might not coincide with an actual data value. It represents a balance point in that there is as much above it as below. For data that is 'normal' with an even **distribution**, the mean is a useful measure but can be skewed by very low or very high results.

## Example

*A team of four children were selected for a relay race. Their best times in seconds were eighty-three point four, seventy-nine point eight, ninety-one point three and seventy-six point five. What is their mean running time in seconds? Give your answer to one decimal place.*

| | |
|---|---|
| Add up all the data items | $83.4 + 79.8 + 91.3 + 76.5 = 331$ |
| Divide by the number of data items | $331 \div 4 = 82.75$ |
| Give the answer to the required accuracy | $82.75 = 82.8$ (to 1 dp) |

Do not round the data before working out the mean.

Answer: The mean running time is 82.8 seconds (to 1 dp).

## Practice questions

**92**  A class carried out a survey to find out how far people lived from the school. In total, the twenty-five pupils lived sixty-five kilometres from the school. What is the mean distance travelled? Give your answer in metres.

**93**  A test has a maximum total of sixty marks. Pupil A scores twenty-four and pupil B scores thirty-six. What is their mean score as a percentage?

**94**  The table overleaf shows a set of test results (in %) achieved by one class.

| 34 | 46 | 67 | 76 | 23 | 98 | 67 |
| 56 | 57 | 66 | 34 | 67 | 39 | 89 |
| 45 | 67 | 99 | 67 | 43 | 56 | 77 |

What is the mean mark gained? Give your answer to the nearest whole number.

**95**  Six pupils in Year 7 are selected at random to take an additional reading test. Their actual ages to the nearest month are: 11 years 6 months; 11 years 9 months; 11 years 11 months; 11 years 2 months; 11 years 10 months; 11 years 4 months.

What is the mean age in years and months?

**96**  Pupils are studying weather patterns and record the midday temperature in °C over a period of five weeks in the winter.

|        | Mon | Tue | Wed | Thu | Fri |
|--------|-----|-----|-----|-----|-----|
| Week 1 | −1  | 0   | 1   | 2   | 4   |
| Week 2 | 3   | 2   | −4  | −3  | −2  |
| Week 3 | 2   | 2   | 1   | 0   | 0   |
| Week 4 | −3  | −1  | 1   | 2   | 3   |
| Week 5 | 4   | 0   | 0   | −1  | −4  |

What is the mean temperature in week 4? Give your answer to one decimal place.

**97**  A pupil obtained the following marks in four tests:

Test A: 13/20; Test B: 16/25; Test C: 22/40; Test D: 19/30.

What is her average mark as a decimal? Give your answer to two decimal places.

**98**  Ninety pupils take part in a sponsored walk and raise £832.50 in total. What is the mean average amount raised per pupil?

**99**  This term, 25 pupils took part in a sponsored swim. The teacher recorded the number of lengths each pupil completed.

| Number of lengths | Number of pupils |
|-------------------|------------------|
| 10                | 5                |
| 11                | 6                |
| 12                | 7                |
| 13                | 4                |
| 14                | 3                |

The mean sponsorship per length was £3.25. How much money was raised in total?

**100**   Last week, 32 pupils took a test. Their mean score was 54%. One pupil was absent and took the test on his return. He scored 21%. What is the revised mean for the group?

Age – for actual age and reading age – is measured in years and months. This may be written as year. month (where the dot is not a decimal point!) or year-month.

For more examples of questions involving calculating a mean, see practice questions 113–116, 118–119, 122, 124–125, 130, 141, 145, 162, 166, 172–173, 177, 209.

## Median

The **median** is the middlemost value when the values are arranged in order. If there is an even number of values, the mean of the middlemost two values is calculated as the median value. For large amounts of data, the data may be tallied, or grouped. The median can also be read from a **cumulative frequency** graph (see page 187 for an example of this type of graph) and may also be displayed on a **box and whisker** plot (page 178).

## Example

*A Year 7 science group is studying plant growth under different conditions. The table below records 50 plants grown in a heated environment.*

| Height | Frequency |
|--------|-----------|
| $0 < h \le 6$ | 10 |
| $6 < h \le 8$ | 16 |
| $8 < h \le 10$ | 11 |
| $10 < h \le 12$ | 7 |
| $12 < h \le 14$ | 4 |
| $14 < h \le 16$ | 1 |
| $16 < h \le 20$ | 1 |

Don't look at the middle category. Imagine all the samples lined up in a row in order of size.

*What is the median height category?*

There are 50 data items (heights of plants) so the median is the average of the 25th and 26th items. To identify these data items, extend the table to include the cumulative frequency and look where the 25th and 26th items lie.

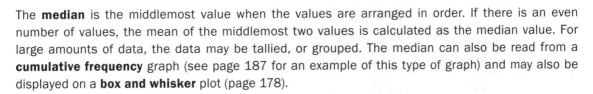

| Height | Frequency | Cumulative frequency | Height | Frequency | Cumulative frequency |
|--------|-----------|----------------------|--------|-----------|----------------------|
| $0 < h \le 6$ | 10 | 10 | $12 < h \le 14$ | 4 | 48 |
| **$6 < h \le 8$** | **16** | **26** | $14 < h \le 16$ | 1 | 49 |
| $8 < h \le 10$ | 11 | 37 | $16 < h \le 20$ | 1 | 50 |
| $10 < h \le 12$ | 7 | 44 | | | |

Check that the top value in the cumulative frequency column agrees with the total number of plants as given in the stem of the question.

Answer: The median height category is $6 < h \leq 8$.

The median is the middlemost value, not the middle of the range.

## Practice questions

**101** 25 pupils take part in a sponsored swim. The teacher records the number of lengths each pupil completes. What is the median number of lengths?

| Number of lengths | Number of pupils |
|---|---|
| 10 | \|\|\| |
| 11 | ⊞⊞ |
| 12 | \|\|\|\| |
| 13 | ⊞⊞\|\|\|\| |
| 14 | ⊞⊞\| |

If the frequency reaches 5, the four tally marks are 'crossed' with the fifth to make a 'gate' ⊞⊞.

**102** A survey of 100 pupils was carried out to determine how many siblings each had. The results were summarised:

| Number of siblings | 0 | 1 | 2 | 3 | 4 | 5 |
|---|---|---|---|---|---|---|
| Number of children | 24 | 42 | 17 | 9 | 6 | 2 |

What is the median number of siblings per child?

**103** A sponsored walk takes place around the school grounds, with each lap an estimated 1700m in length. The results are recorded:

| Number of laps | Number of pupils |
|---|---|
| 2 | 3 |
| 3 | 3 |
| 4 | 4 |
| 5 | 11 |
| 6 | 20 |

What is the median distance in kilometres walked by the pupils?

For more examples of questions involving identifying a median, see practice questions 105, 111, 114–116, 118, 140, 145, 160, 162, 164, 167, 175, 190, 197–198, 200.

## Mode

The mode is the value that occurs most frequently. It is the data value with the highest frequency. If you are presented with a lot of data, you might first need to tally the data and produce a summary of it. Because the mode provides the 'most popular' data value, it is useful to know if trying to meet the needs of as many as possible, eg in supplying uniforms to fit the majority.

## Example

*A survey is carried out on pupils' shoe sizes. What is the modal shoe size?*

| 5 | 6 | 3 | 8 | 4 |
|---|---|---|---|---|
| 7 | 6 | 10 | 7 | 8 |
| 9 | 5 | 9 | 9 | 4 |

To identify the mode, identify the smallest and largest shoe sizes (3 and 10) and create a tally chart, making one mark for every time that shoe size appears in the data.

| Size | 3 | 4 | 5 | 6 | 7 | 8 | 9 | 10 |
|------|---|---|---|---|---|---|---|----|
| Frequency | | | | | | | | | | | | | | | | | |

Answer: Size 9 is the modal show size.

## Practice questions

**104** A group of 14 pupils are timed completing a problem-solving task. The results, to the nearest whole second, are as follows:

12   15   27   14   19   22   27   13   27   22   18   22   16   22

What is the modal number of seconds taken to complete the test?

**105** This term, 25 pupils took part in a sponsored swim. The teacher recorded the number of lengths each pupil completed.

| Number of lengths | Number of pupils |
|---|---|
| 10 |卌 |
| 11 | 卌I |
| 12 | 卌II |
| 13 | IIII |
| 14 | III |

What was the median number of lengths?

**106** A sponsored walk takes place around the school grounds, with each lap an estimated 1700m in length. The results are recorded:

| Number of laps | Number of pupils |
|---|---|
| 2 | 3 |
| 3 | 3 |
| 4 | 4 |
| 5 | 11 |
| 6 | 20 |

What is the modal distance in kilometres walked by the pupils?

For more examples of questions involving identifying a mode, see practice questions 104, 106, 115, 118–119, 164, 173.

## RANGE

The range is the difference between the highest and lowest values and gives a measure of the **spread** of the data.

## Example

*A survey is carried out on pupils' shoe sizes. What is the range of shoe sizes?*

| | | | | |
|---|---|---|---|---|
| 5 | 6 | 3 | 8 | 4 |
| 7 | 6 | 10 | 7 | 8 |
| 9 | 5 | 9 | 9 | 4 |

To identify the range, identify the smallest and largest shoe sizes (3 and 10) and calculate the difference:

$10 - 3 = 7$

Answer: The range of shoe sizes is 7.

## Practice questions

**107** These are the test results achieved by one class.

| 34 | 46 | 67 | 76 | 23 | 98 | 67 |
|----|----|----|----|----|----|----|
| 56 | 57 | 66 | 34 | 67 | 39 | 89 |
| 45 | 67 | 99 | 67 | 43 | 56 | 77 |

What is the range of the marks gained?

A comparison was made between five schools' GCSE results. The tables show the percentage of pupils out of the total number gaining A*/A–C grades, rounded to one decimal place.

| School | 2012 | 2013 | 2014 |
|--------|------|------|------|
| A*/A | 62.5 | 61.9 | 59.6 |
| B | 72.8 | 75.4 | 76.9 |
| C | 45.6 | 48.9 | 50.2 |
| D | 59.6 | 58.4 | 57.9 |
| E | 86.3 | 85.4 | 79.1 |

**108** What is the range of marks in 2012?

**109** What is the difference between the range of marks in year 2013 and in year 2014?

**110** The reading ages of a group of Year 6 pupils receiving additional help was assessed.

| Pupil | Actual age | | Reading age | |
|-------|-------|--------|-------|--------|
| | Years | Months | Years | Months |
| 1 | 11 | 0 | 10 | 9 |
| 2 | 10 | 6 | 10 | 5 |
| 3 | 10 | 8 | 8 | 3 |
| 4 | 10 | 4 | 9 | 1 |
| 5 | 10 | 11 | 9 | 11 |
| 6 | 10 | 7 | 10 | 7 |

What is the difference between the ranges of actual age and reading age? Give your answer in months.

 For more examples of questions involving calculating a range, see practice questions 112, 115, 117, 119, 164, 173, 192–196, 199–200.

## Interquartile range

While the range is an indication of the spread of all the data, the interquartile range is an indication of where the middle half of the data lies.

 In the same way that the median identifies the middlemost value, when the data is arranged in order, the **lower quartile** is the middle most value of the bottom half, and the **upper quartile** is the middlemost value of the upper half.

The quartiles cut the data into quarters, and the middle two quartiles show the interquartile range.

Practice questions involving quartiles and interquartile ranges appear later as they usually relate to a box and whisker plot (page 178) or a cumulative frequency curve (page 176).

## COMBINATIONS OF MEASURES OF AVERAGE

In the test, you are not required to decide on which average to use. You will however be required to interpret the data through different averages.

 Refer to the 'Areas of numeracy' support materials available on the DfE website, for more detailed descriptions of mean, mode and median to help you to understand under what conditions each might be used.

Several questions may be set for a single set of data.

## Practice questions

Pupils are studying weather patterns and record the midday temperature in °C over a period of five weeks in the winter.

|  | Mon | Tue | Wed | Thu | Fri |
|---|---|---|---|---|---|
| **Week 1** | −1 | 0 | 1 | 2 | 4 |
| **Week 2** | 3 | 2 | −4 | −3 | −2 |
| **Week 3** | 2 | 2 | 1 | 0 | 0 |
| **Week 4** | −3 | −1 | 1 | 2 | 3 |
| **Week 5** | 4 | 0 | 0 | −1 | −4 |

**111**  What is the median temperature in week 2?

**112**  What is the range of the temperatures recorded?

**113** Point and click on the week that has the highest mean temperature.

Make sure you know which average you need to give: the mean, the median or the mode.

A single question may require you to calculate more than one type of average, or the range.

## Practice questions

**114** A comparison was made between five schools' GCSE results. The table shows the percentage of pupils out of the total number gaining five A*/A–C grades, rounded to one decimal place.

| School | 2012 | 2013 | 2014 |
|--------|------|------|------|
| A | 62.5 | 61.9 | 59.6 |
| B | 72.8 | 75.4 | 76.9 |
| C | 45.6 | 48.9 | 50.2 |
| D | 59.6 | 58.4 | 57.9 |
| E | 86.3 | 85.4 | 79.1 |

What is the difference between the mean percentage and the median percentage in 2013.

**115** Pupils are studying weather patterns and record the midday temperature in °C over a period of three weeks in the winter.

|  | Mon | Tue | Wed | Thu | Fri |
|--------|-----|-----|-----|-----|-----|
| **Week 1** | −4 | −3 | −1 | 0 | 0 |
| **Week 2** | 4 | 2 | −1 | −3 | −2 |
| **Week 3** | 0 | 2 | 2 | 4 | 5 |

Select all the true statements:

A. The median temperature is higher than the mean temperature in week 1.

B. The range of temperatures is 5°C.

C. The data is bimodal.

D. The mean temperature in week 2 is 0°C.

**116** The running times for six pupils were recorded during athletics practice.

| Pupil | Time in secs |
|-------|-------------|
| A | 94.2 |
| B | 86.1 |
| C | 92.5 |
| D | 110.4 |
| E | 108.3 |
| F | 97.1 |

What is the difference between the mean and the median running times?

**117** Test results for two groups have been summarised in the table. The maximum possible mark for the test was 100.

| Class | Lowest test score | Median | Highest test score |
|-------|------------------|--------|-------------------|
| Set 2 | 11 | 42 | 93 |
| Set 4 | 15 | 51 | 85 |

Select the true statement(s):

A.  Set 2 did better at the test than Set 4.

B.  The range of marks was greater for Set 2 than for Set 4.

C.  At least half of all the pupils taking the test scored 43 or more.

**118** The following table shows the time taken by eight Year 6 pupils to complete an obstacle course.

| Pupil | Time taken (secs) |
|-------|-------------------|
| 1 | 85.0 |
| 2 | 78.7 |
| 3 | 75.1 |
| 4 | 66.3 |
| 5 | 87.5 |
| 6 | 92.2 |
| 7 | 102.0 |
| 8 | 101.2 |

Select all the true statements:

A. There is no mode.

B. The mean time taken is 1 minute 43 secs.

C. The median time is 85.0 secs.

D. Pupil 4's was the fastest time by 9 seconds to the nearest second.

**119** A class teacher is looking at the attendance of his class over a six-week period. There are 28 children in the class.

|        | Mon | Tue | Wed | Thu | Fri |
|--------|-----|-----|-----|-----|-----|
| **Week 1** | 28  | 26  | 27  | 27  | 25  |
| **Week 2** | 25  | 26  | 23  | 22  | 24  |
| **Week 3** | 28  | 28  | 27  | 26  | 21  |
| **Week 4** | 22  | 24  | 25  | 25  | 26  |
| **Week 5** | 28  | 23  | 22  | 24  | 20  |

Select all the true statements:

A. The mean attendance on Mondays is 3 higher than the mean attendance on Fridays.

B. The range of attendance is 7.

C. The modal attendance in week 1 is 27.

# 4.4    Presentation of data

**Raw data** presented simply as a list of numbers in the order in which it is collected can be difficult to interpret. When converted to a tabulated format, or presented in diagrammatic form, this shows 'at a glance' various aspects of the data:

- ○ Most/least popular is given by

    the largest/smallest share of a pie chart

    the longest/shortest bars in a bar chart

    the highest/lowest points on a line graph.

- ○ The range or spread of the data is given by

    the axis labelling on a bar chart or graph

    the whiskers on a boxplot.

- ○ Totals can be calculated

    by adding all the number is one row, or in one column

    by reading values from a cumulative frequency curve.

## TABLES

Presenting data in tables not only requires an understanding of how to extract relevant data from the table but also allows other aspects of numeracy to be tested. You may also be asked to complete a table by filling in the missing entries.

At the simplest level, a question may require the summing of the values in a given row or column. If the data is presented such that a cross-casting sum can be used to check the total, use this as a method of ensuring accuracy. Otherwise, double-check every stage of the working.

## Simple tables

A table sets out data in a columnar format. The column headings indicate what data has been collected and collated. The row headings show what grouping, if any, has been done.

Much information is provided within the table format. It's easy to misread this information, focusing on the wrong column(s) or the wrong row(s).

# Example

*During a flu epidemic, the following table was compiled for a high school.*

| Year group | Number on roll | Proportion of pupils absent |
|---|---|---|
| 7 | 205 | 0.2 |
| 8 | 210 | 0.1 |
| 9 | 188 | 0.25 |
| 10 | 185 | 0.2 |
| 11 | 180 | 0.3 |
| 6th form | 140 | 0.15 |

*How many pupils were absent?*

Total absent: $(205 \times 0.2) + (210 \times 0.1) + (188 \times 0.25) + (185 \times 0.2) + (180 \times 0.3) + (140 \times 0.15)$

$= 41 + 21 + 47 + 37 + 54 + 21$

$= 221$

When there are so many calculations and it's essential that you arrive at the correct answer, double-check each step of your working.

Answer: 221 pupils were absent.

# Practice questions

**120** Pupils are studying weather patterns and record the midday temperature in °C over a period of five weeks in the winter.

|  | Mon | Tue | Wed | Thu | Fri |
|---|---|---|---|---|---|
| **Week 1** | 3 | 2 | −4 | −3 | −2 |
| **Week 2** | 2 | 2 | 1 | 0 | 0 |
| **Week 3** | −1 | 0 | 1 | 2 | 4 |
| **Week 4** | −3 | −1 | 1 | 1 | 3 |
| **Week 5** | 4 | 0 | 0 | −1 | −4 |

Point and click on the week in which the temperatures steadily rose.

**121** A primary school timetable is broken down into the following proportions on a Monday (see overleaf):

| Subject | Proportion of the school day |
|---|---|
| English | 0.25 |
| Mathematics | 0.25 |
| Science | 0.10 |
| PE | 0.15 |
| Other | 0.25 |

Lessons last for 5 hours per day. How much time is spent per day doing PE on Mondays? Give your answer in minutes.

**122** The running times for five pupils were recorded during athletics practice.

| Pupil | Time in secs |
|---|---|
| A | 94.2 |
| B | 86.1 |
| C | 92.5 |
| D | 110.4 |
| E | 108.3 |

What proportion of children was below the mean running time for this group? Give your answer as a decimal.

**123** The following table gives the predicted and actual proportions of pupils gaining each level in Key Stage 2.

| Level | 2 | 3 | 4 | 5 |
|---|---|---|---|---|
| Predicted | 0.10 | 0.20 | 0.44 | 0.25 |
| Actual | 0.07 | 0.10 | 0.62 | 0.21 |

What was the proportional increase from the predicted to actual grades in level 4? Give your answer as a fraction in its lowest terms.

**124** A comparison was made between five schools' GCSE results. The table shows the percentage of pupils out of the total number gaining A*/A–C grades, rounded to one decimal place.

| School | 2012 | 2013 | 2014 |
|---|---|---|---|
| A | 62.5 | 61.9 | 59.6 |
| B | 72.8 | 75.4 | 76.9 |
| C | 45.6 | 48.9 | 50.2 |
| D | 59.6 | 58.4 | 57.9 |
| E | 86.3 | 85.4 | 79.1 |

What is the difference between the mean in 2012 and the mean in 2014? Give your answer to one decimal place.

**125**  A food technology group is comparing different pastry recipes.

| Proportion | Recipe 1 | Recipe 2 | Recipe 3 | Recipe 4 |
|---|---|---|---|---|
| Flour | 0.5 | 0.7 | 0.35 | 0.75 |
| Fat | 0.5 | 0.3 | 0.65 | 0.25 |

What is the mean amount of fat needed for the four recipes? Give your answer as a fraction in its lowest terms.

**126**  In a portfolio-based qualification, there are three grades: distinction, merit and pass. This table shows the results for classes 1, 2 and 3.

| Class | Number of portfolios | | |
|---|---|---|---|
| | Pass | Merit | Distinction |
| 1 | 15 | 9 | 4 |
| 2 | 12 | 16 | 8 |
| 3 | 11 | 6 | 9 |

For the purposes of internal moderation, the school has a policy of selecting $\frac{1}{6}$ of each category to the nearest next whole number above. For example, if there are 9 in a category, the moderator will select 2.

How many portfolios will be selected in total?

## Completion of missing entries

The next set of questions requires the completion of missing entries in tables.

## Practice questions

**127**  A learning support assistant used some new resources with a small group of pupils in a mathematics class. She tested the pupils before and after they used the new resources and analysed the results.

| Pupil | Test results (%) | | % difference |
|---|---|---|---|
| | Before | After | |
| A | 55 | 74 | +19 |
| B | 42 | 48 | +6 |
| C | 39 | 35 | |
| D | 22 | 23 | |
| E | 44 | 56 | |

Select and place the % differences into the correct cells.

| -12 | -4 | -1 | 0 | +1 | +4 | +8 | +10 | +12 |

**128** A school's prediction for Key Stage 2 results is shown in the table.

| Level | Number of pupils predicted for each grade | | |
| | English | Mathematics | Science |
|---|---|---|---|
| 2 | 2 | 4 | 6 |
| 3 | 9 | 11 | |
| 4 | 28 | 25 | 20 |
| 5 | 7 | 6 | 8 |

Complete the table and then calculate the proportion of the year group that is predicted to gain below a level 5 in science. Give your answer as a fraction in its lowest terms.

**129** The table shows the achievement of pupils at Key Stage 2 over a three-year period.

| Year | Level 3 | Level 4 | Level 5 |
|---|---|---|---|
| 2012 | 6 | 8 | 4 |
| % of total | 33 | 44 | |
| 2013 | 6 | 12 | |
| % of total | | 50 | 25 |
| 2014 | 7 | | 9 |
| % of total | 22 | 50 | 28 |

Select from the numbers below to insert in the correct boxes.

| 6 | 12 | 16 | 22 | 23 | 25 | 50 | 75 |

**130** Reading ages were compared between boys and girls in Years 4, 5 and 6.

| | Mean reading age (years-months) | | |
| | Year 4 | Year 5 | Year 6 |
|---|---|---|---|
| **Boys** | 8-1 | 9-0 | 10-2 |
| **Girls** | 8-7 | 9-5 | 10-5 |

What is the mean difference in reading ages (to the nearest whole number) between boys and girls for years 4, 5 and 6?

Drag and drop the correct values to complete the table:

| 2 | 3 | 4 | 5 | 6 |

| Difference between boys' and girls' mean reading ages (months) | | | Mean difference for years 4, 5 and 6 |
|---|---|---|---|
| Year 4 | Year 5 | Year 6 | |
|  | 5 |  |  |

## Multiple questions set against one table

More than one question could be set from a single table of data.

Read the question carefully to establish which row/column of which table holds the data to be used to work out the answer.

## Practice questions

A table has been produced to show which pupils in a primary school live in the village in which the school is situated.

| Class | Number of pupils | Number of pupils living in the village |
|---|---|---|
| R | 16 | 7 |
| 1 | 18 | 10 |
| 2 | 22 | 12 |
| 3 | 17 | 13 |
| 4 | 19 | 11 |
| 5 | 25 | 18 |
| 6 | 19 | 14 |

**131** What percentage of pupils in the school live in the village in which the school is situated? Give your answer to the nearest whole number.

**132** Taking each individual year group, calculate the largest proportion of pupils living in the village in which the school is situated. Give your answer as a percentage to one decimal place.

The table shows the achievement of pupils at Key Stage 2 over a three-year period.

| Year | Level 3 | Level 4 | Level 5 |
|---|---|---|---|
| 2012 | 6 | 8 | 4 |
| 2013 | 6 | 12 | 6 |
| 2014 | 3 | 15 | 6 |

**133**  In which year did the smallest proportion of pupils gain level 5?

**134**  What percentage of pupils gained level 4 in year 2012? Answer to the nearest whole number.

| 8 | 23 | 42 | 44 | 47 | 50 | 63 |
|---|----|----|----|----|----|----|

The Key Stage 2 levels of Year 6 pupils in a large primary school were analysed by the class.

| Level | Class 6 (1) | Class 6 (2) | Class 6 (3) |
|-------|-------------|-------------|-------------|
| 2 | 2 | 4 | 0 |
| 3 | 7 | 7 | 6 |
| 4 | 12 | 13 | 16 |
| 5 | 8 | 2 | 4 |
| 6 | 0 | 0 | 1 |

**135**  What percentage of the total year group achieved level 4 and above, to the nearest whole number?

| 56 | 68 | 69 | 76 | 82 | 86 | 93 |
|----|----|----|----|----|----|----|

**136**  Point and click on the class which achieved the highest percentage of level 3 grades at Key Stage 2.

A school analyses its GCSE results in the core subjects of English, mathematics, science and a humanities subject. The results are summarised in the table below. All percentages are rounded to the nearest whole number.

| Grade | Number of pupils | | | |
|-------|---------|-------------|---------|------------|
| | **English** | **Mathematics** | **Science** | **Humanities** |
| A*–A | 45 | 42 | 52 | 57 |
| B–C | 88 | 79 | 67 | |
| D–E | 56 | | 52 | 46 |
| F–G | 22 | 41 | 40 | 34 |
| | 211 | 211 | 211 | 211 |
| | **English** | **Mathematics** | **Science** | **Humanities** |
| % A*–C | 63 | | 56 | 27 |
| % A*–E | | 81 | | 84 |
| % A*–G | 100 | 100 | 100 | 100 |

**137**  Drag and drop the correct values to complete the table.

| 37 | 43 | 44 | 49 | 5 | 59 | 64 | 74 | 81 | 90 |
|----|----|----|----|---|----|----|----|----|----|

**138** The English department has set a target of increasing the number of A*–C grades by 6 percentage points for the following academic year. Assuming there will be the same number of pupils taking GCSEs, how many more pupils will need to achieve grades A*–C?

## Multiple tables

More than one table may be provided!

## Practice questions

**139** A group of pupils was tested for their reading age on two different occasions.

| Autumn term | | | | Summer term | | |
|---|---|---|---|---|---|---|
| Pupil | Actual age years-months | Reading age years-months | | Pupil | Actual age years-months | Reading age years-months |
| A | 8-11 | 7-5 | | A | 9-5 | 7-9 |
| B | 8-4 | 8-4 | | B | 8-10 | 9-0 |
| C | 8-6 | 8-8 | | C | 9-0 | 9-2 |
| D | 8-7 | 8-9 | | D | 9-1 | 9-9 |
| E | 9-1 | 9-3 | | E | 9-7 | 10-3 |
| F | 8-3 | 8-11 | | F | 8-9 | 9-7 |
| G | 8-1 | 8-0 | | G | 8-7 | 8-7 |
| H | 8-4 | 9-3 | | H | 8-10 | 9-9 |

Click on the letters for pupils who showed an improvement of more than 4 months in the difference between the actual age and the reading age between the autumn and the summer terms.

**140** At the end of the summer term, a school has a fund-raising week. Pupils select to do different activities for charity. The tables summarise three of the fund-raising events. The money raised is to be divided between charity A and charity B in the ratio of 3:2.

| Sponsored activities | | School fete | | Sales in school | |
|---|---|---|---|---|---|
| Activity | Amount raised | Item | Amount raised | Type | Amount raised |
| Swimming | £89.45 | Refreshments | £167.22 | Magazine | £67.50 |
| Walking | £93.87 | Tombola | £75.50 | Cakes | £35.20 |
| Running | £145.35 | Stalls | £105.43 | Craft | £68.30 |

Select all the true statements:

A. Of the activities listed, the highest total amount of money raised was at the school fete.

B. Charity A will receive £509 to the nearest whole £.

C. The median amount raised of all the items listed is £89.45.

More than one question could be set from such tables of data. Note that question 143 also requires completion of entries.

## Practice questions

From 2011 to 2014, a primary school's pupils' performance in reading in Key Stage 1 was tested and compared with the national averages.

| Year | Percentage of boys at level 2 and above (school) | Percentage of boys at level 2 and above (national average) | Percentage of girls at level 2 and above (school) | Percentage of girls at level 2 and above (national average) |
|------|------|------|------|------|
| 2011 | 76.4 | 75.3 | 86.3 | 85.9 |
| 2012 | 79.6 | 78.7 | 87.4 | 86.2 |
| 2013 | 75.8 | 78.3 | 88.1 | 87.5 |
| 2014 | 78.5 | 78.7 | 89.2 | 87.4 |
| 2015 |      |      |      |      |

*Source*: www.gov.uk/government/collections/statistics-key-stage-2

**141**  What is the difference between the mean average over the four-year period 2011–2014, between the boys' performance in the school and the national average for the boys? Give your answer to one decimal place.

**142**  Select the correct statements:

A. The performance of the boys in the school is consistently below the national average.

B. The percentage of girls in the school achieving level 2 and above has increased every year.

C. The girls in the school consistently outperform the boys.

D. In 2013, the boys in the school were performing at 2.5% below the national average for that year.

**143**  The school predicts that the percentage of pupils in the school achieving level 2 and above will increase in 2015 by 0.6% for both boys and girls. The national averages are expected to rise by 0.2%.

Drag and drop the correct amounts into the table:

| 75.5 | 77.0 | 78.7 | 78.9 | 79.1 | 79.3 | 86.1 | 86.9 | 87.6 | 88.0 | 89.4 | 89.8 | 91.5 |

Ten pupils in a Year 5 group were given additional mathematics support in an attempt to raise their achievement. They were given a task before and after the additional support. The task was marked out of 40 and the results analysed according to gender.

| Pupil | Girls' task score before additional support | Girls' task score after additional support |
|---|---|---|
| A | 15 | 22 |
| B | 20 | 25 |
| C | 32 | 34 |
| D | 16 | 19 |
| E | 25 | 21 |

| Pupil | Boys' task score before additional support | Boys' task score after additional support |
|---|---|---|
| F | 20 | 32 |
| G | 16 | 19 |
| H | 17 | 28 |
| I | 29 | 33 |
| J | 31 | 38 |

**144**  Point and click on the pupil who made the most improvement after the additional support.

**145**  Indicate the true statement(s):

    A. All the boys achieved improved scores after the additional support.

    B. 20% of the girls achieved a lower score after the additional support.

    C. The mean difference in the boys' scores before and after the additional support was 7.4.

    D. The median girls' score after the additional support was 25 marks.

    E. Pupil G scored 47.5% in the task after additional support.

## Two-way tables

**Two-way tables** allow comparison of different sets of tables.

Totals are usually shown on the opposite side of the table from the category heading.

Be sure to read the correct row and column from the correct table!

## Practice questions

**146** A student teacher is researching into a possible link between ability in mathematics and in music. She presents the GCSE results of a group of pupils in a two-way table.

| GCSE mathematics | | GCSE music | | | |
|---|---|---|---|---|---|
| | GCSE grade | A*–A | B–C | D–E | F–G |
| | A*–A | 5 | 6 | 2 | 0 |
| | B–C | 4 | 7 | 3 | 1 |
| | D–E | 3 | 4 | 5 | 2 |
| | F–G | 0 | 1 | 1 | 7 |

Indicate all the true statements:

A. Approximately $\frac{1}{10}$ of the pupils who took GCSE mathematics and GCSE music gained grades A* or A in both subjects.

B. More than $\frac{1}{6}$ of the pupils taking both GCSE mathematics and GCSE music gained grades F or G in mathematics.

C. $\frac{3}{4}$ of the pupils who gained C and above in mathematics, gained A or A* in music.

More than one two-way table might be given and more than one question may be set for them.

## Practice questions

A comparison is made between pupils' GCSE results in mathematics and their results in French and in music. This comparison is summarised in the two-way tables below and at the top of page 157.

| | | GCSE French | | | | |
|---|---|---|---|---|---|---|
| | GCSE grade | A*–A | B–C | D–E | F–G | Total |
| GCSE mathematics | A*–A | 5 | 8 | 1 | – | 14 |
| | B–C | 2 | 11 | 5 | – | 18 |
| | D–E | 3 | 9 | 11 | 12 | 35 |
| | F–G | 1 | 1 | 2 | 14 | 18 |
| | Total | 11 | 29 | 19 | 26 | |

| | GCSE music | | | | |
|---|---|---|---|---|---|
| GCSE grade | A*–A | B–C | D–E | F–G | Total |
| A*–A | 3 | 2 | 2 | – | 7 |
| B–C | 1 | 9 | 5 | – | 15 |
| D–E | – | 3 | 2 | 2 | 7 |
| F–G | – | 1 | 1 | – | 2 |
| Total | 4 | 15 | 10 | 2 | |

(GCSE mathematics labels the rows)

**147** What fraction of pupils taking both mathematics and French GCSEs gained E and above in both subjects? Give your answer as a fraction in its lowest terms.

**148** The proportion of pupils achieving C and above in both GCSE music and in GCSE mathematics as a decimal to one decimal place is:

| 0.3 | | 0.31 | | 0.4 | | 0.48 | | 0.5 |
|---|---|---|---|---|---|---|---|---|

# CHARTS

Data can be presented in chart form for a quick appreciation of proportion, as in shares of a pie chart, or for comparison, one against another, as in a bar chart.

## Pie charts

In a pie chart, each sector of the circle represents a share of the total **population**.

The shares of the 'pie' can show actual values (as in practice questions 149, 150) or the percentages (as in practice questions 151, 152).

Multiple pie charts provide an easy way to compare two sets of data, eg from two different classes, different schools, different years: see for example practice questions 153–157.

## Practice questions

The pastoral team at one high school is concerned about the eating habits of Years 7 and 8. A pie chart is created to look at lunchtime arrangements made by Year 7 and 8 pupils.

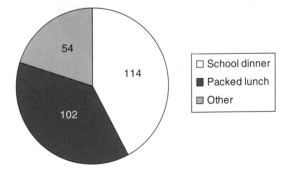

**149** Select all the true statements:

A. More than 40% of pupils in Years 7 and 8 have school dinners.

B. One-fifth of the pupils make other arrangements.

C. Less than 1 in 3 pupils has a packed lunch.

**150** The school puts in place a strategy to encourage more pupils to have school dinners. The following term, 24 more pupils had school dinners. What percentage of pupils now has school dinners (to the nearest whole number)?

| 24 | 29 | 47 | 51 | 54 | 126 | 138 |
|----|----|----|----|----|-----|-----|

The ICT teacher investigated how long the 74 pupils in the computer club spent playing computer games at home. She produced the pie chart below.

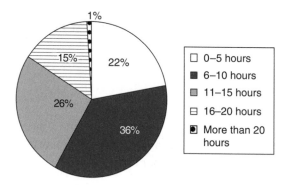

**151** How many pupils spent more than 20 hours playing computer games?

**152** Three more pupils join the computer club. They each played computer games for between 11 and 15 hours per week.

Point and click on the pie chart below which represents the new data.

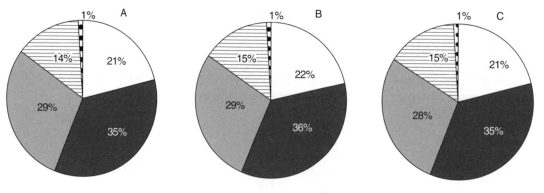

 When a question asks 'how many pupils', consider whether you should round up to the nearest whole number.

**153** A group of pupils was surveyed in Year 7 and again in Year 10 to see which school clubs they attended. The results are shown in the pie charts below.

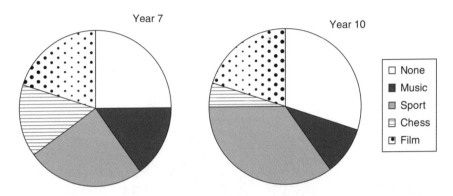

Year 7        Year 10

☐ None
■ Music
☐ Sport
☐ Chess
☐ Film

The number going to film club remains the same. Drag and drop the correct percentage values into the table below:

| 10 | 15 | 20 | 20 | 25 | 25 | 30 | 90 |

|  | **None** | **Music** | **Sport** | **Chess** | **Film** |
|---|---|---|---|---|---|
| **% Year 7** |  | 15 | 25 |  |  |
| **% Year 10** | 30 | 10 | 35 | 5 |  |

The same pair of pie charts could be used for more than one question:

## Practice questions

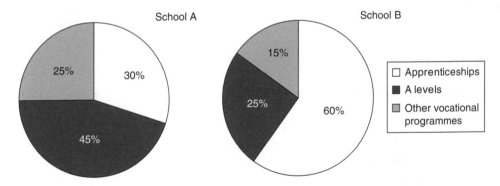

School A        School B

25%    30%

45%

15%

25%    60%

☐ Apprenticeships
■ A levels
☐ Other vocational programmes

Two local high schools compare the chosen study programmes of pupils at the end of Year 11. The pie charts show the percentage of pupils taking each option.

**154** School A has 103 pupils in Year 11. School B has 95 pupils in Year 11. How many pupils in total from the two schools are intending to do A levels?

**155**  Select all the true statement(s):

A.  A greater proportion of pupils are taking A levels at school B than at school A.

B.  One-quarter of the pupils at school A are planning on taking other vocational programmes.

C.  More than half the pupils at school B are planning on doing an apprenticeship.

The head of the mathematics department compares GCSE results for Year 11 over a two-year period and produces pie charts:

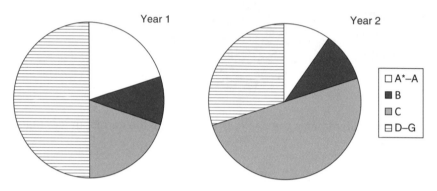

**156**  Select all the true statements:

A.  The proportion of pupils achieving A*–A improved in year two.

B.  The proportion of D–G grades remained the same.

C.  The proportion of pupils achieving A*–C grades improved in year two.

D.  We are not able to tell whether more pupils achieved a C and above in year two.

**157**  In year one, there were 130 pupils in Year 11. In year two, 30% of Year 11 achieved grades D–G from a total year group of 120. How many more pupils achieved grades D–G in year one than in year two?

As many as four pie charts might be given.

## Practice questions

The pie charts show the proportions of levels achieved by pupils in one school at Key Stage 2.

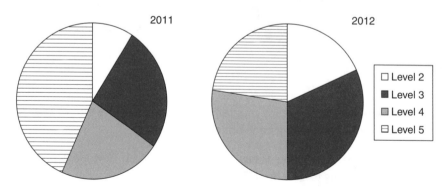

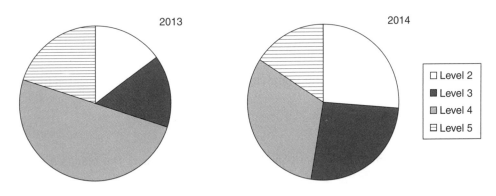

2013

2014

- □ Level 2
- ■ Level 3
- ▣ Level 4
- ⊟ Level 5

**158** Point and click on the pie for the year which shows the best results for pupils achieving level 5.

**159** Point and click on the pie for the year in which exactly half of the pupils achieve level 4 or 5.

**160** A headteacher is reviewing the Key Stage 2 results of the Year 6 classes in four local schools. She produces the pie charts below.

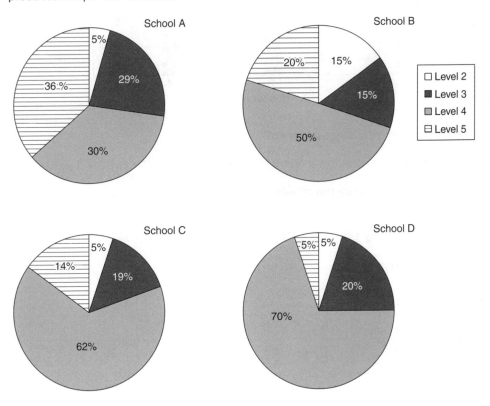

School A

5%
29%
36.%
30%

School B

20%  15%
15%
50%

- □ Level 2
- ■ Level 3
- ▣ Level 4
- ⊟ Level 5

School C

5%
14%
19%
62%

School D

5% 5%
20%
70%

What is the median percentage of pupils achieving level 4 and above in the four schools?

| 18.75 | 53 | 56 | 51.6 | 70 | 71.5 | 72.5 |

## Bar charts

 Read carefully all titles: of the diagram and the axes. What does the data represent?

 A **bar chart** presents data as vertical or horizontal bars. The length of the bar indicates frequency of a data value.

## Example

*A survey was carried out to find the number of siblings per pupil in Year 6. The results are displayed in a bar chart:*

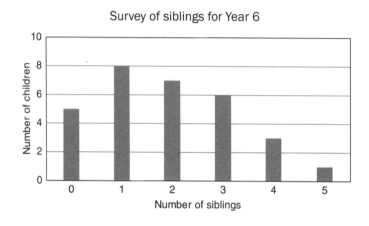

*What is the median number of siblings per child?*

   Reading from the vertical axis, total number of pupils = 5 + 8 + 7 + 6 + 3 + 1 = 30

 Read the vertical axis carefully. Here the 'number of children' are marked in 2s – so half-way between is worth 1 child.

   The 'middle' pupils are the 15th and 16th.

   Considering the cumulative data:

| Number of siblings | 0 | 1 | 2 | 3 | 4 | 5 | Total |
|---|---|---|---|---|---|---|---|
| Number of children | 5 | 8 | 7 | 6 | 3 | 1 | 30 |
| Cumulative frequency | 5 | 13 | 20 | 26 | 29 | 30 | |

   The 15th and 16th pupils appear in the third group, those with 2 siblings.

Answer: the median number of siblings is 2.

A simple bar chart can be used to illustrate categorical data or grouped data – see practice questions 161–169. More complex bar charts present two (or more) sets of bars against one axis as in practice question 170 and/or present stacked bars with each column showing the amounts (or share) of various subcategories within that data – see practice questions 171–180.

# Practice questions

**161** The French department wishes to compare their GCSE results with those from other departments.  75 pupils took French GCSE and 40 achieved grades A*–C.

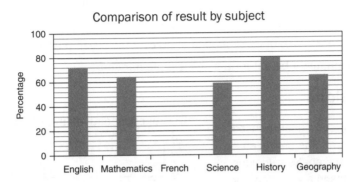

Comparison of result by subject

Select and place the correct bar on to the chart above.

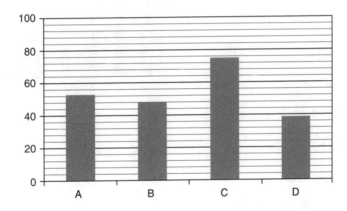

**162** The Art department has analysed the percentage of GCSE grades A*–C over seven years.

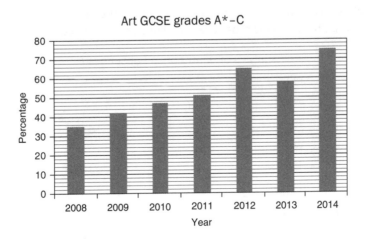

Art GCSE grades A*–C

Indicate all the true statement(s):

A. The mean percentage of GCSE grades A*–C for the first four years of the chart was 44% (to the nearest whole number).

B. The percentage of GCSE grades A*–C in 2008 was less than half of that in 2014.

C. The percentage of grades A*–C increased each year.

D. The median percentage of GCSE grades A*–C over the seven-year period was 51%.

More than one question might be set for a single simple bar chart.

## Practice questions

A headteacher analysed unauthorised absence over half a term. She produced a bar chart to help with the analysis, looking at where pupils have taken a single day, or more than one consecutive day.

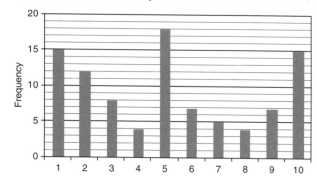

Analysis of consecutive days of unauthorised absences

**163** The total number of days' unauthorised absence is:

| 5 | 10 | 20 | 49 | 90 | 150 | 491 | 501 |

**164** Select all the true statements:

A. The range of days of unauthorised absence is 10.

B. The modal number of consecutive days of unauthorised days of absence is 5.

C. The median number of consecutive days of unauthorised absence is 5.5.

The headteacher of a small primary school is concerned about the increase in unauthorised absences over a number of years. She compiles a bar chart to illustrate her concerns.

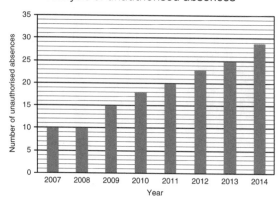

Analysis of unauthorised absences

**165** Point and click on the year that shows the greatest increase in unauthorised absences.

**166** What is the mean number of unauthorised absences over the 8-year period? Give your answer to two decimal places.

**167** What is the median number of unauthorised absences over the 8-year period?

| 10 | 17 | 18 | 19 | 20 |
|----|----|----|----|----|

A school offers three modern foreign languages for GCSE study. Pupils in Year 9 can choose to study one or two modern foreign languages. There are 104 pupils in Year 9. The diagram shows the choices made by those who chose to study two foreign languages:

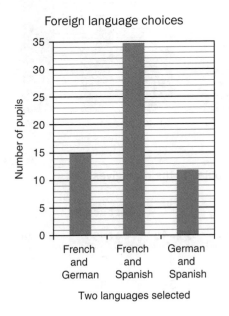

**168** What proportion of the pupils in Year 9 has chosen to study two foreign languages? Give your answer as a decimal to one decimal place.

**169** In addition, a further 25 pupils have chosen to study German at GCSE level as their only modern foreign language. What percentage of pupils will be studying German at GCSE?

| 24% | 30% | 45% | 50% | 60% | 84% |
|-----|-----|-----|-----|-----|-----|

To compare two (or more) sets of data, the bars can be set side by side for each data value on the x-axis. Read the legend to establish which bars relate to which data category.

## Example

*A geography class has 30 pupils. The teacher gives them a test at the beginning (test 1) and at the end (test 2) of the autumn term and compares the results.*

*Point and click on the test score where the greatest difference occurs between test 1 and test 2.*

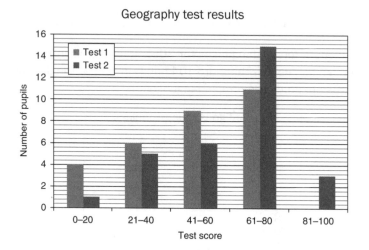

Geography test results

Reading the graph and tabulating the data gives:

| | Test score | | | | |
|---|---|---|---|---|---|
| | **0–20** | **21–40** | **41–60** | **61–80** | **81–100** |
| **Test 1** | 4 | 6 | 9 | 11 | 0 |
| **Test 2** | 1 | 5 | 6 | 15 | 3 |
| **Difference** | 3 | 1 | 3 | **4** | 3 |

 The difference is found by subtraction: the smaller from the larger.

Visually, without having to do any calculation, the largest difference is seen by comparing heights of pairs of bar.

Answer: The greatest difference is in test score 61–80.

## Practice question

**170** Answer this question using the bar chart above. Indicate the true statement(s):

A. The overall results in test 2 were higher than in test 1.

B. The scores between 41 and 60 decreased in test 2 by one-third.

C. 85% of pupils scored more than 40% in test 2.

Single bars may be subdivided to show additional information about the data. The bars can be coded for different categories to show actual data values, one on top of another, or the share of the data.

For the upper part of a bar, calculate the length of that part of the bar by reading the upper and lower  values and finding the difference.

## Example

*A headteacher is concerned about punctuality in the mornings and analyses methods of transport of a random sample of pupils across four different year groups.*

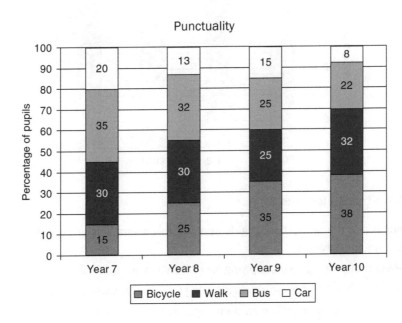

The ratio of pupils travelling to school by car to the number travelling to school by bus in its lowest terms is:

*56:114   28:57   57:28   114:56*

      Number travelling by car: 20 + 13 + 15 + 8 = 56

      Number by bus: 35 + 32 + 25 + 22 = 114

Answer: ratio is 56:114 = 28:57.

56:114 is not correct because the simplified version is required.

Order matters with ratios. 28:57 is not the same as 57:28.

## Practice questions

**171** A comparison was made in the sixth form of one high school to determine the proportion of students who apply to university. The data was further broken down into gender, and bar charts produced.

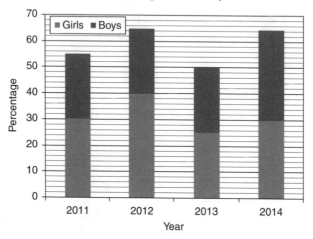

Proportion of girls and boys applying to university in a school's sixth form

Identify all the true statements:

A. In all four years, the proportion of girls applying to university is greater than the proportion of boys applying for university.

B. The highest proportion of boys applying for university was in 2012.

C. The highest proportion of all students applying for university was in 2012.

D. In each year, 50% or more of the students applied for university.

Five pupils took three advanced algebra tests after receiving extra mathematical support. Each test was marked out of 40. The bar chart shows a summary of their results:

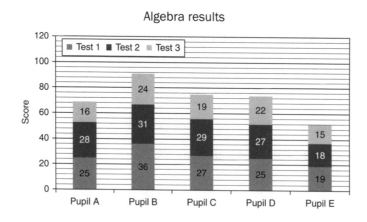

Algebra results

**172** What is pupil C's mean mark as a percentage to the nearest whole number?

**173**  Select all the true statements:

A. The mean mark for test 1 is 25.

B. The range of marks in tests 3 is 9.

C. The lowest marks were achieved in test 1.

D. The modal mark over all three tests was 25.

Over a period of five years, Year 9 pupils in one high school had to select one technology subject to study to GCSE. Their selections are analysed to produce these composite bar charts:

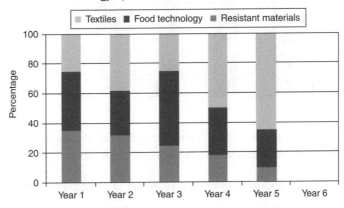

Technology option selections of Year 9 pupils

**174**  The popularity of *resistant materials* has decreased from year one to year five by:

| 10% | 20% | 25% | 35% | 40% |

**175**  What is the median percentage of pupils choosing textiles as their technology option in years one to five?

**176**  In the sixth year, Year 9 pupils have just made their selections for the new academic year.

| Subject | Resistant materials | Food technology | Textiles |
|---|---|---|---|
| % of pupils choosing that subject | 35 | 25 | 40 |

Which of these bars shows the data for the sixth year?

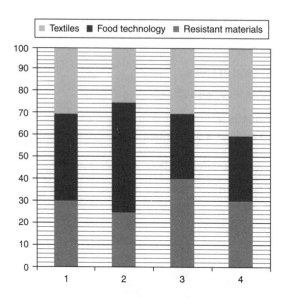

As part of a quality improvement initiative, three schools' senior management teams carried out classroom observations and made comparisons between the schools.

Quality improvement initiative: result of classroom observation

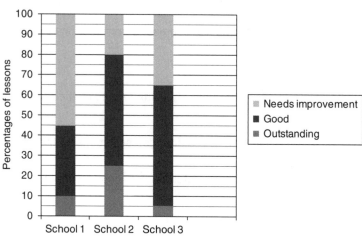

**177** What is the mean percentage of lessons graded 'needs improvement' across the three schools? Give your answer to the nearest whole percentage.

**178** Select the true statement(s):

A. In school 3, 65% were graded as 'Needs improvement'.

B. More than half the lessons in school 1 were graded 'Needs improvement'.

C. In school 2, ⅘ of the lessons were graded 'good' or 'outstanding'.

**179** In school 2, five lessons were graded as 'outstanding'. How many lessons observations were carried out in school 2?

| 6 | 10 | 20 | 25 | 50 | 100 | Not possible to tell |
|---|----|----|----|----|-----|----------------------|

**180** A fourth school joins the comparison exercise. Their classroom observation grades are as follows:

| Outstanding | Good | Needs improvement |
|:-----------:|:----:|:-----------------:|
| 15 | 75 | 10 |

Select the bar which represents this data.

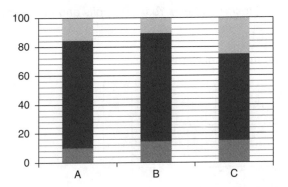

Read the axes carefully and be aware of the starting and ending values, the scale of the axes and the units for the data.

# GRAPHS

Four types of graph appear in the numeracy skills test: scatter graphs, line graphs and cumulative frequency curves, and box and whisker diagrams.

All of these graphs present data pictorially, with points plotted against two axes: the vertical axis and the horizontal axis.

## Scatter graphs

A scatter graph compares two paired sets of data by recording, as a single point, each pair. Each point represents, for example, one person.

Scatter graphs can be used to identify, for example, pupils whose performance is unusual or requires attention.

If the points on a scatter graph are clustered along a line, this indicates a relationship – correlation – between the two variables.

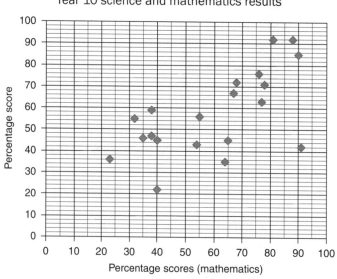

To compare one data set with the other, a line drawn joining points where the data is equal will separate the data into two subsets: one where one data reading is higher than the other and one where it is lower.

## Example

*Science and mathematics teachers are comparing test results for Year 10 pupils and plot a scatter graph to show the results.*

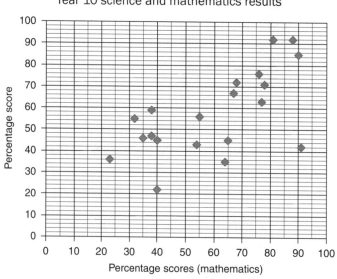

*Which points represent these pupils?*

(a) *The pupil who scored the highest in mathematics*
Mathematics scores are on the horizontal axis. Look for the point furthest to the right.
Answer: (91, 42).

(b) *The pupil who came bottom in science*
Science scores are on the vertical axis. Look for the lowest point.
Answer: (40, 22).

(c) *The pupil who got between 50% and 60% in both tests*
Look between pairs of parallel lines at 50 and 60 from both axes.
Answer: (55, 56).

## Practice questions

*Using the scatter diagram above, now answer these practice questions.*

**181** Point and click on the pupil who has the greatest difference between their mathematics and their science scores.

**182** The proportion of pupils who scored 50% or more in both subjects is:

| 50% | 0.45 | $\frac{8}{20}$ | Not able to tell |

## Line graphs

**Line graphs** offer a visual representation of the relationship between two sets of related data. The axes are labelled with the data being measured (eg scores against years). Points are plotted and a line drawn to join these points, thus showing a **trend**.

## Example

*In a small primary school, Ofsted has praised the music teacher because the number of pupils in Year 6 learning a musical instrument has consistently risen over a four-year period.*

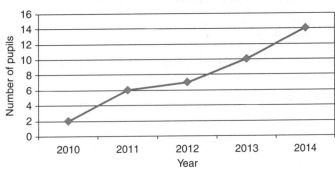

Number of pupils learning a musical instrument

*There were 25 pupils in Year 6 in 2010 and 28 pupils in Year 6 in 2014. What is the percentage increase in pupils learning a musical instrument between 2010 and 2014?*

Make sure the data for the correct years is used in the calculation.

2010: 2 pupils                    2014: 14 pupils

$\frac{2}{25} \times 100\% = 8\%$            $\frac{14}{28} \times 100\% = 50\%$

$50\% - 8\% = 42\%$

Answer: the percentage increase is 42%.

On one set of axes, more than one graph may be shown, so that a comparison between the two sets of data can be made.

## Example

*Two pupils' marks are compared in a series of mathematics tests.*

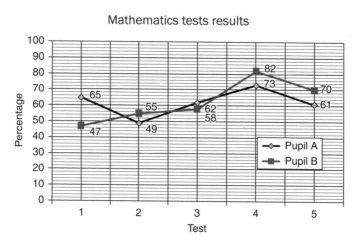

*The mean difference between the pupils' marks is:*

| 0.4 | 4 | 23 | 62 | 62.4 |
|-----|---|----|----|------|

✖ Read the axes carefully and be aware of the starting and ending values, the scale of the axes and the units for the data.

For Pupil A:

Marks = 65 + 49 + 62 + 73 + 61 = 310

Average = 310/5 = 62

For Pupil B:

Marks = 47 + 55 + 58 + 82 + 70 = 312

Average = 312/5 = 62.4

Difference in averages = 62.4 − 62 = 0.4

Answer: The mean difference is 0.4.

OR

Difference between marks = 18 + −6 + 4 + −9 + −9 = −2

Mean difference = 2/5 = 0.4

More than one question might be set for a single graph.

## Practice questions

The senior management team is making a comparison with the percentage of pupils achieving five A*–C grades at the end of Year 11 with the national averages over a six-year period.

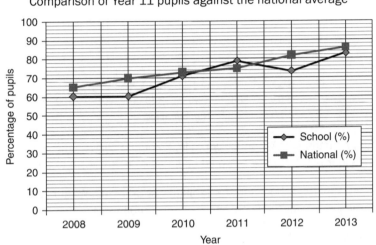

Comparison of Year 11 pupils against the national average

**183**  Point and click on the year when the school did better than the national average.

**184**  Select all the true statements:

   A. The school's highest percentage score was in 2011.

   B. 2010 was the year when the school made the greatest amount of improvement in percentage points.

   C. The percentage of pupils gaining 5 A*–C grades in the school fell in 2012.

   D. The school is performing consistently below the national average.

An art teacher is planning a school trip to an exhibition. She is making comparisons between two coach companies to obtain the best price.

○   The Dotty Coach Company charges a flat rate per trip of £4 and an additional cost per mile.

○   The Dashed Company charges £5 per mile.

She produces a graph (see overleaf) to show the difference between the prices of the two companies.

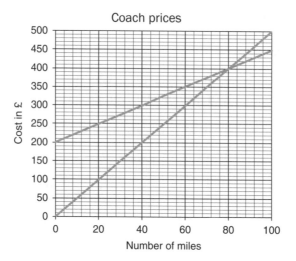

Coach prices

**185** A third company charges £300 then £1 per mile. Point and click on the correct place on the graph to show where a journey of 100 miles would be if this company were to be used.

**186** The distance between the school and the exhibition is 30 miles. What is the difference in the cost of this part of the journey for the Dotty and Dashed companies?

**187** Select the true statement(s):

A. For a distance of 20 miles, the Dotty Company charges £125 more than the Dashed Company.

B. Both companies charge the same amount for a distance of 80 miles.

C. The cost of hiring the Dashed Company for a journey of 120 miles is £600.

D. The Dotty Company is cheaper for all journeys up to 60 miles.

# Cumulative frequency curves

The cumulative frequency is the total number of data items up to a given data value. It can be plotted on a cumulative frequency graph, and this allows other information to be read from the graph, such as the median, and the upper and lower quartiles and hence the interquartile range. Having plotted a cumulative frequency curve, the data could be represented using a box and whisker diagram (page 178).

The cumulative frequency is always plotted on the vertical axis, with the graph curving from the bottom left to the upper right.

# Example

*A survey was carried out in one high school to determine how much time 150 pupils had spent watching television during the school week. How many watched more than 10 hours?*

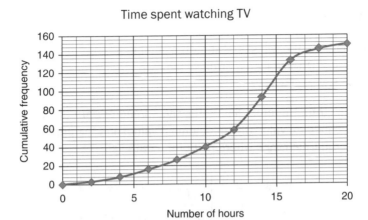

Time spent watching TV

Reading the graph up from 10 hours, the number of pupils is 40, but this shows the number who watched less than 10 hours.

Read the question carefully to determine whether you need to find 'more than' or 'less than' a particular value.

150 − 40 = 110

Answer: 110 pupils watched more than 10 hours television during the school week.

## Practice questions

A survey was carried out to determine how much time pupils in Year 7 spent doing homework per week. The results were plotted on a cumulative frequency graph.

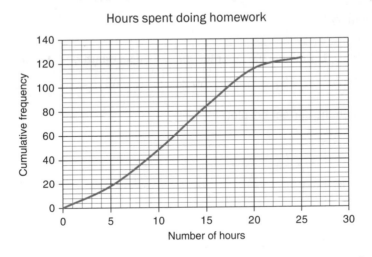

Hours spent doing homework

**188** How many pupils spent more than ten hours per week doing homework?

**189** Select the true statements:

   A. Altogether, 126 pupils took part in the survey.

   B. Half the pupils did less than 15 hours per week.

   C. Approximately 48 pupils did less than 10 hours per week.

   D. Exactly 12 pupils did more than 20 hours per week.

## Box and whisker diagrams

In a box and whisker diagram, the 'whiskers' show the complete range of the data, and the 'box' shows where half of the data lies. Often called a boxplot, the extent of the box is achieved by identifying the upper quartile and the lower quartile.

The box and whisker diagram therefore illustrates the spread of data (distance between the lowest and highest values), the median value (the middlemost value) and the upper and lower quartiles, and within the box, the interquartile range where half of the data lies.

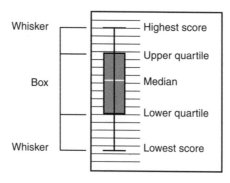

 Read the axes carefully and be aware of the starting and ending values, the scale of the axes and the units for the data.

## Practice question

190   The results of one class test are analysed and a boxplot produced.

The data summary is:

| Lowest value | Lower quartile | Median | Upper quartile | Highest value |
|---|---|---|---|---|
| 20 | 35 | 50 | 65 | 80 |

Point and click on the correct boxplot.

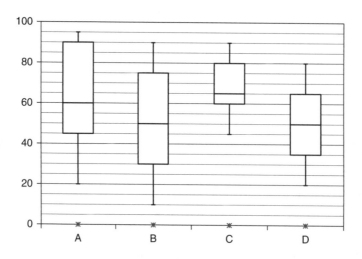

Several questions can be asked of the data presented in a single box and whisker diagram.

## Practice questions

The history department set two tests for Year 10 pupils. The results are shown in the boxplots.

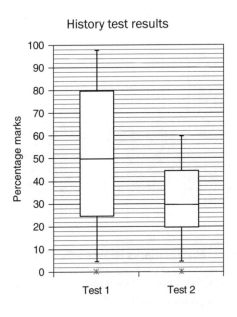

History test results

**191** Forty-eight pupils took test 1. How many pupils scored between 50% and 80%?

**192** Select all the true statements:

A. Many pupils found test 2 easier than test 1.

B. The interquartile range of test 1 is more than twice that of the interquartile range of test 2.

C. The range of marks for test 2 is 60.

D. 25% of the pupils gained 80% or more in test 1.

**193** The marks for test 2 are standardised and all pupils' marks are increased by 13 percentage points.

The new interquartile range for test 2 is:

| 5 | 13 | 20 | 25 | 30 | 51 | 60 | 68 | 80 |

The diagram below shows the percentage test marks in English for two class groups.

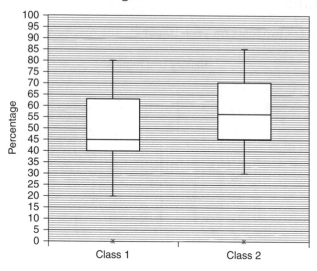

194   What is the difference in the range of marks between the two classes?

195   The marks are standardised and all pupils' percentage marks in class 2 were reduced by 5%. What is the revised interquartile range for class 2?

| 20 | 22.5 | 23.75 | 25 | 40 | 42.75 | 52.25 | 55 | 51 | 66.5 |

Boxplots have been created to display the examination results for two Year 10 classes, each containing 28 pupils.

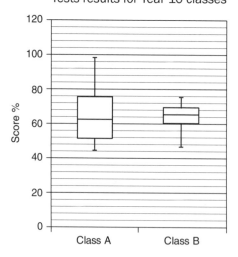

196   Indicate all the true statement(s):

A. The range of marks for class B is lower than for class A.

B. Fewer people in class A gained over 76% than in class B.

C.  21 pupils in class B scored 60 or more in the test.

D.  Seven pupils in class A gained more than 80%.

**197**  The results for Class C in Year 10 are summarised in the table below:

| Lowest mark | Lower quartile | Median | Upper quartile | Highest mark |
|:-----------:|:--------------:|:------:|:--------------:|:------------:|
| 30 | 50 | 70 | 80 | 85 |

Select and place the correct boxplot into the chart above.

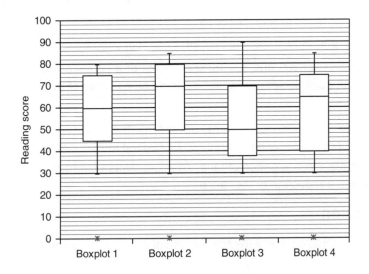

The reading ages of a group of pupils have been analysed over a three-year period. Boxplots have been created to show the results.

### Analysis of reading age

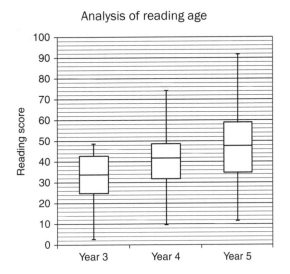

**198** The maximum reading score is 100. The increase in the median score between year four and year five is:

| 3% | 6% | 14% | Not able to tell |

**199** What is the difference in the interquartile range between Year 4 and Year 5?

**200** Select all the true statements:

A. The median has increased by 16 points over the three-year period.

B. There is a greater range of scores in year five than in either of the other two years.

C. The interquartile range in year four is 18.

D. All pupils have improved in reading over the three-year period.

Comparing box and whisker diagrams, say for the results of a series of tests, can lead to teachers asking questions about pupil performance and deciding on a course of action to address any issues identified.

○   If the tests were taken at approximately the same time, but on different topics, and the results vary widely, then perhaps some topics need to be revised more thoroughly.

○   If the tests were taken over a period of time, an improvement might be expected in the median score together with a reduction in the range.

## Practice question

**201** Boxplots were used to compare the test results of a year group over a period of time.

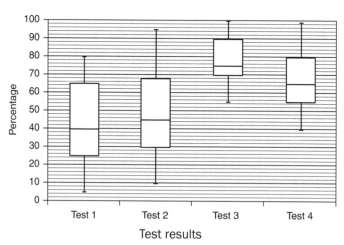

Click on the boxplot for the test which appeared to be the easiest.

# 4.5   Algebra

Algebra is the part of mathematics where letters are used instead of numbers.

## USING SIMPLE FORMULAE

A formula is a statement in words, or an equation using letters, to describe the relationship between two or more variables.

## Example

*One method of predicting A level results is to use a formula based on GCSE points.*

> *(21.71 × GCSE points score) − 44.69*

*What is a pupil's predicted A level points score for a pupil with a mean GCSE points score of 6.9? Give your answer to one decimal place.*

Substitute the value 6.9 into the formula:

$21.71 \times 6.9 - 44.69$

$= 149.799 - 44.69$

$= 105.109$

$= 105.1$ (to 1 dp)

Answer: The predicted A level points score for a pupil with a mean GCSE points score of 6.9 is 105.1 (1 dp).

## Practice question

**202** An internal test taken by 104 Year 8 pupils is marked by the relevant class teacher. The head of faculty then samples the marking to ensure consistency, according to a formula where n is the number of pupils taking the test.

(n/10) + 7

How many scripts must the head of faculty check?

When measuring temperature, there are two scales: Celsius or Fahrenheit. Using C as the temperature in degrees Celsius and F as the temperature in degrees Fahrenheit:

○   the formula to convert from Fahrenheit to Celsius is $C = (F - 32) \times 5/9$
○   the formula to convert from Celsius to Fahrenheit is $F = C \times 9/5 + 32$

## Practice question

**203**   The formula for changing °C to °F is

$$C = \frac{5(F-32)}{9}.$$

What is 75°F in °C? Give your answer to the nearest whole number.

## WEIGHTING

Pupils sit two papers in an examination, Paper 1 and Paper 2, but their total mark is a combined weighted score. Paper 2 carries double the weight of Paper 1. Using S1 as the score on Paper 1 and S2 as the score on Paper 2, the total score S, is given by

S = S1 + 2 × S2.

## Example

*For an end of year test, 25% of the marks were allocated to the practical work and the rest to the written paper. The practical was marked out of 30 and the written paper out of 120.*

*A pupil scored 15 for the practical and 95 for the written paper.*

*What was the pupil's final percentage mark? Give your answer to the nearest whole number.*

Obey the 'order of operations' when evaluating a formula. BIDMAS: Brackets first, then Indices, then Division/Multiplication working left to right, then Addition/Subtraction working left to right.

Practical:      15/30 × 25% = 12.5%

Written:      95/120 × 75% = 59.4%

Total mark:   12.5% + 59.4% = 71.9% = 72% to the nearest whole number

Retain the decimal places through the calculation. Round only at the very end.

Answer: The pupil's final mark is 72.

## Practice questions

**204**   A pupil's final mark for a test is calculated as follows:

Part one × 0.6 + Part two × 0.4

To gain a grade A, a pupil needs a total score of 70 or more.

One pupil gains 65 marks in Part one. What is the lowest mark he must gain to be awarded an A?

**205** A test is divided into two parts. 0.4 of the score of test one and 0.6 of the second test make up the final overall mark. A pupil scores 18 out of a possible 45 for the first test and 28 out of a possible 60 for the second. What is her overall mark as a percentage?

**206** A test paper is made up of two papers. Paper 1 is worth 30% of the total and paper 2 is worth 70% of the total amount.

Here are the results for two pupils.

| Pupil | Paper 1 marked out of 80 | Weighted score (%) | Paper 2 marked out of 65 | Weighted score (%) |
|---|---|---|---|---|
| A | 45 | 16.9 | 38 | 40.9 |
| B | 63 | | 49 | |

Weighted scores are rounded to one decimal place. Drag and drop the correct amounts to complete the table.

22.6   23.6   23.7   52.7   52.8   55.1   75.3   78.8

**207** Two exams are taken at the end of Year 10 in geography. The final score consists of 20% of the marks gained from the first paper and 80% of the marks gained for the second paper. A pupil scored 16 out of 40 for the first paper and 45 out of 80 for the second paper. What is the pupil's final score as a percentage?

**208** An internal school examination is made up of three parts (tests a, b and c). A formula is then used to calculate each pupil's overall result:

$$\text{Final mark}(\%) = \frac{0.3a + 0.5b + 0.2c}{2.5}.$$

One pupil achieves the following results:

| Test a | Test b | Test c |
|---|---|---|
| 105 | 96 | 125 |

What is his overall percentage score? Give your answer to the nearest whole number.

# SPEED/TIME/DISTANCE

Some questions on the topic of time require you to use a formula to work out the time it will take to travel a given distance. The formula is:

distance = speed × time.

## Example

*A bus travels at 40mph. How far does it travel in 1.5 hours?*

1.5 hours means 1½ hours, ie 1 hour 30 minutes, not 1 hour 50 minutes.

Distance = 40 miles/hour × 1.5 hours = 60 miles

Answer: It travels 60 miles in 1.5 hours.

## Practice questions

**209**  The venue for a school outing is 125 miles from the school. The students need to arrive at the venue at 11:00. The estimated mean speed of the coach is 50mph. What is the latest time the coaches must leave school?

**210**  A school sponsored walk is to cover 12km. Two breaks of 15 minutes each are planned and it is expected that the pupils will walk at an average of 5km per hour. They will start out at 09:00. At what time will they be expected to complete the walk?

**211**  A school trip to France is planned. The ferry is due to arrive in Calais at 11:15 and it normally takes a further 30 minutes to disembark. It is 48km from the ferry port to the hotel where the pupils will be staying. The average speed of the coach is estimated to be 45 miles per hour. At what time is the coach expected to arrive at the hotel? Use the conversion of 5 miles to 8km.

**212**  A party of school pupils is returning to the UK after staying in France. They need to be at the ferry port no later than 16:30. It is estimated that the coach will travel the 120km distance at an average speed of 50mph. What is the latest time they need to leave their accommodation? Use the conversion of 5 miles to 8km.

# 4.6   Numeracy practice papers

The answers to these questions appear on page 223.

Aim to complete each of these four papers under examination conditions.

## Numeracy Practice Paper 1

### Mental questions

1   At a parents' evening, each interview is timed to last ten minutes. How long must the teacher allow in order to see twenty sets of parents? She is to have one break of fifteen minutes. Give your answer in hours and minutes.

2   A group of students decided to split the proceeds from a sponsored swim equally between three charities. The class raised two hundred and fifty-three pounds and five pence. How much will each charity receive?

3   Twenty-four pupils each pay two pounds fifty towards a school trip. How much money did the pupils pay in total?

4   The perimeter of the local park is one point two kilometres. A sponsored walk is planned for four circuits of the park. What is the total distance of the walk in kilometres?

5   A test is marked out of eighty. Pupils need sixty-five per cent for a grade A. How many marks is this?

6   As part of a school visit to Germany, pupils visited an exhibition. The total entrance fee was three hundred and sixty euros. What was the total entrance fee in pounds? Use the conversion of one euro equivalent to nought point eight pounds.

7   There are one thousand and seventy-four pupils in a high school. Two-thirds of the pupils have school meals at lunchtime. Each table in the dining room seats ten pupils. How many tables are needed?

8   A cross-country run covers three laps, each of two kilometres. The estimated speed of running is eight kilometres per hour. How long should the run take? Give your answer in minutes.

9   A high school's target for English GCSE results is that at least eighty per cent achieve grade C and above. How many pupils will need to achieve grade C and above from a cohort of two hundred and forty pupils in order to meet the target?

10   What is nought point four multiplied by seven point three?

11   A pupil achieves fifty-one out of sixty in a test. What is this as a percentage?

12   A primary school teacher estimates that his pupils will use six exercise books each during the school year. There are twenty-five pupils in his class. There are forty exercise books in a pack. How many packs must he order for the year?

# Onscreen questions

**1**  A survey was carried out to find the number of siblings per pupil in Year 6. The results are displayed in a bar chart:

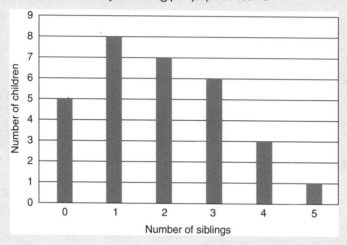

Survey of sibling per pupil in Year 6

What is the mean number of siblings per child? Give your answer to one decimal place.

**2**  A survey of the methods of transport used by a sample of staff at a high school is carried out. The results are:

|          | Bus | Car | Bicycle |
|----------|-----|-----|---------|
| **Male**   | 6   | 9   | 5       |
| **Female** | 8   | 7   | 1       |

What percentage of the staff cycle to the school? Give your answer to two decimal places.

**3**  A teacher analyses the results of the end of year tests for her German class. There were two tests – one oral and one written. The results are shown in the scatter graph.

Written versus oral results

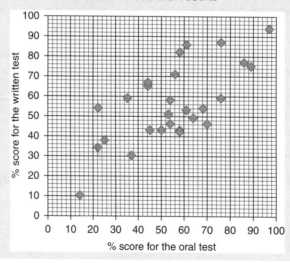

There were 28 in the German class. What proportion of pupils did better in the written test than in the oral test? Give your answer as a decimal to one decimal place.

**4** A class teacher is looking at the attendance of his class over a five-week period. There are 28 children in the class.

|  | Mon | Tue | Wed | Thu | Fri | Total |
|---|---|---|---|---|---|---|
| **Week 1** |  | 26 | 27 | 27 | 25 | 133 |
| **Week 2** | 25 | 26 |  | 22 |  | 123 |
| **Week 3** | 24 | 27 | 27 | 26 | 21 | 125 |
| **Week 4** | 22 | 24 | 28 | 25 | 26 | 125 |
| **Week 5** | 28 |  | 22 | 24 | 25 | 122 |
| **Total** | 127 | 126 | 130 | 124 | 121 | 628 |

Select and place the correct values in the table.

| 23 | 24 | 25 | 26 | 27 | 28 | 29 | 30 |
|---|---|---|---|---|---|---|---|

**5** A pupil who plays in the school netball team will be selected to play for the county if her mean number of goals in seven matches exceeds 5. After six games, her mean score is 4.8 (to 1dp). What is the least number of goals she must score in the next game in order to be selected?

**6** Boxplots were used to compare the test results of a year group over a period of time

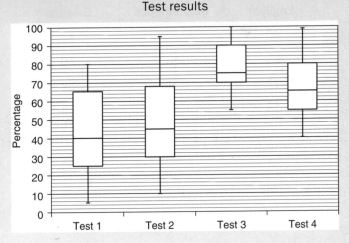

Test results

Indicate all the true statements:

A. Test 3 has the smallest range of marks

B. Test 2 was found to be the most difficult

C. The interquartile range for test 1 was 40

D. Over half the pupils achieved over 65% in test 4

**7**   42 pupils from Year 9 English groups and 6 teachers are going on an outing to see a play at the theatre. The group rate for theatre tickets is £15.55, with one free place for every 15 paid tickets. The train fare costs £18 per person. How much will each person have to pay for the outing? Give your answer to the nearest penny.

**8**   A school analyses its GCSE results in the core subjects of English, mathematics, science and a humanities subject. The results are summarised in the table below.

| Grade | Number of pupils | | | |
|---|---|---|---|---|
| | English | Mathematics | Science | Humanities |
| A*–A | 46 | 37 | 42 | 51 |
| B–C | 89 | 81 | 79 | 79 |
| D–E | 27 | 30 | 34 | 35 |
| F–G | 18 | 32 | 25 | 15 |

The English department has set a target of increasing the number of A*–C grades by 6% for the following academic year. Assuming there will be the same number of pupils taking GCSEs, how many more pupils will need to achieve grades A*–C?

**9**   A school analyses its GCSE results in the core subjects of English, mathematics, science and a humanities subject. The results are summarised in the tables below.

| Grade | Number of pupils | | | |
|---|---|---|---|---|
| | English | Mathematics | Science | Humanities |
| A*–A | 46 | 37 | 42 | 51 |
| B–C | 89 | 81 | 79 | 79 |
| D–E | 27 | 30 | 34 | 35 |
| F–G | 18 | 32 | 25 | 15 |

What is the mean percentage of A*–A grades across the four core subjects to the nearest whole number?

| 21 | 23 | 24 | 25 | 26 | 29 |
|---|---|---|---|---|---|

**10** A school governing body is looking at the age profile of the teachers in the school over a five-year period. The data is shown in the pie charts below:

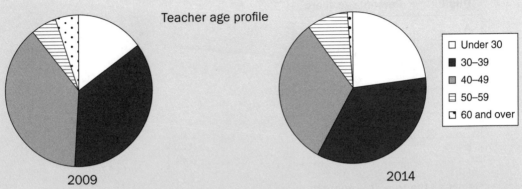

Teacher age profile

☐ Under 30
■ 30–39
▨ 40–49
▤ 50–59
▱ 60 and over

2009                    2014

Select all the true statements:

A. There are more teachers under the age of 30 in the school in 2014 than in 2009.

B. The age profile of the teachers in 2009 was generally younger than in 2014.

C. Approximately 75% of teachers in the school in 2009 were aged between 30 and 49 years.

**11** Four pupils were given additional support in a mathematics class and their test results analysed over a period of time. The results were plotted on a line graph.

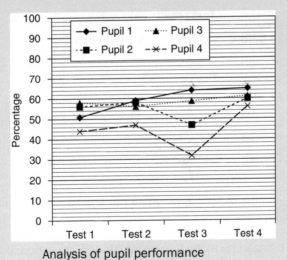

Analysis of pupil performance

Which pupil had the greatest range of marks?

**12** This table shows the percentage score achieved by six pupils in an additional mathematics test.

| Pupil | Percentage score |
|-------|------------------|
| A | 74 |
| B | 65 |
| C | 87 |
| D | 39 |
| E | 65 |
| F | 62 |

Select all the true statements:

A. The mode and the median are the same.

B. The mean is lower than the median.

C. The range is 48.

**13** A learning support assistant used some new resources with a small group of pupils in a mathematics class. She tested the pupils before and after they used the new resources and analysed the results.

| Pupil | Test results (%) | | |
|-------|------|-------|--------------|
| | Before | After | % difference |
| A | 55 | 69 | |
| B | 42 | 48 | |
| C | 69 | 55 | |
| D | 22 | 23 | |
| E | 44 | 56 | |

Point and click on the letter representing the pupil who made the most progress in terms of their % difference.

**14** Pupils are attending a play at the theatre, which is 35 miles from the school. The play starts at 19:30. The teacher wishes to arrive at least 15 minutes before the start. It is estimated that the coach will be travelling at an average speed of 30 miles per hour. What is the latest time they must leave the school? Give your answer according to the 24-hour clock.

**15** A survey of the methods of transport used by a sample of staff at a high school is carried out. The results are:

|  | Bus | Car | Bicycle |
|---|---|---|---|
| **Male** | 6 | 8 | 6 |
| **Female** | 8 | 6 | 3 |

There are plans to build a car park for the school's 250 staff. Assuming that the above survey is representative of all staff, how many car-parking spaces are required to meet the current demand?

**16** Year 11 form teachers are interested to determine how much additional study time their pupils undertook in the three-week period leading up to the GCSE examinations. The results are plotted on a cumulative frequency chart.

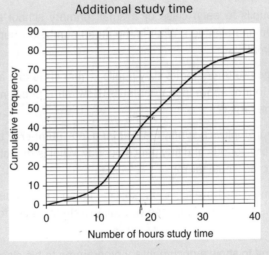

Additional study time

What is the median amount of additional study time undertaken by the Year 11 pupils?

| 15 | 18 | 20 | 22 | 40 | 80 |
|---|---|---|---|---|---|

# Numeracy Practice Paper 2

## Mental questions

**1** In a school of two hundred pupils, there are eighty pupils with English as an additional language. What proportion is this? Give your answer as a decimal.

**2** A pupil scores eighteen out of twenty-five in one test and sixteen out of twenty in a second test. What is her average score across the two tests? Give your answer as a percentage.

**3** In a sample of two hundred and twenty schools' Ofsted grades, thirty-three were graded as unsatisfactory. What fraction of the schools in the sample were graded unsatisfactory? Give your answer as a fraction in its lowest form.

**4** A school purchases a new television set. The cost is two hundred and sixty pounds plus VAT at twenty per cent. What is the full cost of the television when VAT is included?

**5** What is nought point three multiplied by five point seven?

**6** A science experiment requires pupils to cut thin wire into lengths of nought point four five metres. The wire comes in five-metre rolls. How many pieces can be cut from one roll?

**7** The national statistics for Key Stage two in mathematics showed that forty-four point three one per cent of pupils achieved level four and forty point six nine per cent achieved level five. What proportion of pupils achieved either level four or level five? Give your answer as a fraction.

**8** The numbers of pupils in each class of a small primary school are: twenty, twenty-two, seventeen, nineteen and eighteen. What is the mean number of pupils per class? Give your answer to one decimal place.

**9** A school's Key Stage two target for its sixty pupils in Year six is that at least seventy per cent will achieve a level four or above in mathematics. How many pupils must achieve a level four or above to meet the target?

**10** In one term, a school employs a supply teacher for a total number of thirty-three days, costing one hundred and sixty pounds and fifty pence per day. What is the total cost of employing the supply teacher over the whole term?

**11** A group of sixth formers are travelling to Japan. One Japanese yen equals nought point nought nought five pounds. How many Japanese yen will the students get for one hundred and fifty pounds?

**12** A teacher is planning to show a documentary programme to his class. The programme lasts forty-seven minutes and he wants to allow at least fifteen minutes afterwards for discussion. The lesson finishes at eleven o'clock. What is the latest time he must start the documentary?

## Onscreen questions

**1** A junior school's daily lesson times are as follows:

09:15–10:45   11:05–12:30   13:20–14:20   14:30–15:30

How many hours and minutes per week are spent in lessons?

**2**   The test results for a group of pupils was recorded in the following table:

|  | Test 1 | Test 2 | Test 3 | Test 4 | Test 5 |
|---|---|---|---|---|---|
| **Pupil A** | 43 | 34 | 52 | 49 | 63 |
| **Pupil B** | 84 | 89 | 78 | 87 | 75 |
| **Pupil C** | 94 | 89 | 78 | 80 | 71 |
| **Pupil D** | 38 | 45 | 52 | 61 | 67 |

Indicate all the true statements:

A. The average mark for test 5 was higher than any other test.

B. The greatest range of marks was achieved in test 2.

C. The median mark for test 1 was 63.5.

D. Pupil A achieved the lowest mean score.

**3**   The test results for a group of pupils were recorded in the following table:

|  | Test 1 | Test 2 | Test 3 | Test 4 | Test 5 |
|---|---|---|---|---|---|
| **Pupil A** | 43 | 34 | 52 | 49 | 63 |
| **Pupil B** | 84 | 89 | 78 | 87 | 75 |
| **Pupil C** | 94 | 89 | 78 | 80 | 71 |
| **Pupil D** | 38 | 45 | 52 | 61 | 67 |

Pupil E's marks for the same test are as follows:

| Test 1 | Test 2 | Test 3 | Test 4 | Test 5 |
|---|---|---|---|---|
| 86 | 92 | 76 | 58 | 72 |

What is the difference between the mean and median scores for all the pupils for test 4?

**4**   An end of year test in science uses the following formula to calculate the pupils' overall tests scores:

$$\frac{M + 2P + 3W}{6}$$

M is the score for a multi-choice paper, P is the score for the practical and W is the score for the written test.

Three pupils results were as follows:

| Pupil | Test type | | |
|---|---|---|---|
| | M | P | W |
| A | 45 | 52 | 75 |
| B | 63 | 61 | 62 |
| C | 82 | 65 | 61 |

Point and click on the pupil who gained the highest score, using the formula.

5   The marks obtained by 60 pupils over two tests have been displayed in the following cumulative frequency charts:

Test results

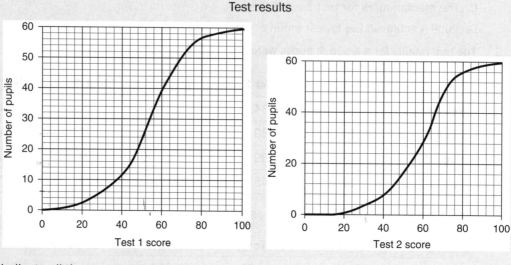

Indicate all the true statements:

A. The median mark for test 2 is higher than the median mark for test 1.

B. The interquartile range is higher in test 2 than in test 1.

C. 25% of pupils in test 1 obtained less than 40 marks.

D. The overall marks for test 2 are higher than for test 1.

**6**   As part of road safety week, pupils' bicycles were checked for faults. A table of results was compiled.

| Number of faults | Number of bicycles |
|:---:|:---:|
| 0 | 12 |
| 1 | 15 |
| 2 | 22 |
| 3 | 14 |
| 4 | 9 |
| 5 | 2 |
| 6 | 1 |

What is the mean number of faults per bicycle? Give your answer to the nearest whole number.

**7**   National statistics for attainment in the Key Stage 2 reading test in England are displayed in the line graph below (*Source*: www.gov.uk/government/collections/statistics-key-stage-2).

Attainment in Key Stage 2 reading test

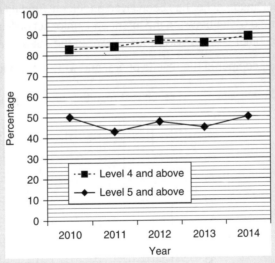

Select the true statements:

A. The percentage of pupils achieving level 4 and above has steadily increased over the last five years.

B. The best results of the last five years were achieved in 2014.

C. In 2011, 57% of pupils at Key Stage 2 achieved scores below level 4.

D. In 2010 and in 2014, half of all pupils achieved level 5 and above.

**8**    A Year 2 group is doing a project about looking after pets. The bar chart shows the number of pets each child has at home.

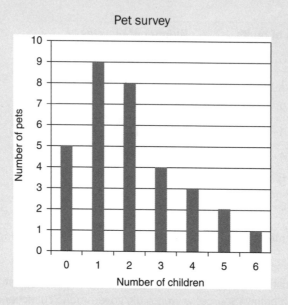

Pet survey

What is the mean number of pets? Give your answer to two decimal places.

**9**    A primary school headteacher has been given additional funding of £7054. She allocates the funding in the ratio of 3:4 between the infant and junior school classes. How much funding is allocated to the junior classes? Give your answer to the nearest whole £.

**10**    A French teacher compared the results of oral and written tests for a class of pupils.

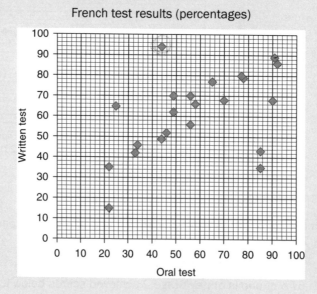

French test results (percentages)

Point and click on the pupil who scored 50 points more on the oral test than on the written test.

**11** A teacher is calculating the cost of a school trip to Sweden, based on 30 pupils. So far, she has estimated the following costs:

| Transport (total) | £2352 |
|---|---|
| Accommodation (total) | 54,360 SEK |
| Food, sundries (per pupil) | 1184 SEK |

The currency conversion rate is £1 = 12.08 Swedish kroner (SEK).

Calculate the cost per pupil based on the teacher's estimates.

**12** In mock GCSE examinations in a high school, 84 out of a possible 115 pupils achieved five A* to C grades. In the real GCSE examinations, 101 actually achieved five A* to C grades. What is this as a percentage increase? Give your answer to one decimal place.

**13** The following table shows the pupil numbers by gender in three local primary schools.

| | Number of boys | Percentage of boys | Number of girls | Percentage of girls | Total |
|---|---|---|---|---|---|
| **School A** | 97 | 46 | 113 | 54 | 210 |
| **School B** | 56 | 52 | 52 | 48 | 108 |
| **School C** | 73 | 48 | 79 | 52 | 152 |

What is the average percentage of girls in the three schools? Give your answer to one decimal place.

**14** A primary school with a total of 207 pupils has adopted a healthy-living initiative and has monitored how the children travel to school over a three-year period. The pie charts (two below and a third overleaf) show the results.

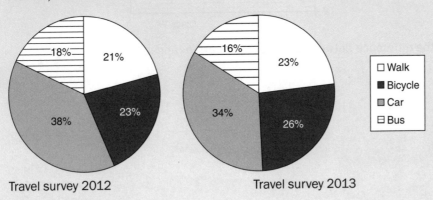

Travel survey 2012    Travel survey 2013

□ Walk
■ Bicycle
▨ Car
▤ Bus

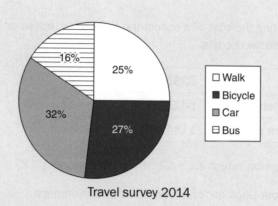

Travel survey 2014

How many more children either walk or go by bicycle to school in 2014 than in 2012?

**15** The reading scores of two Year 6 classes are shown on the boxplots.

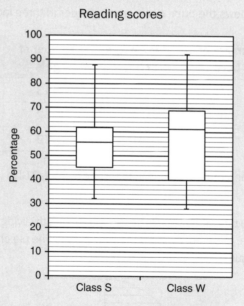

What is the difference between the two interquartile ranges?

**16** Year 6 teachers at a primary school compared the results of the mathematics Key Stage 2 results.

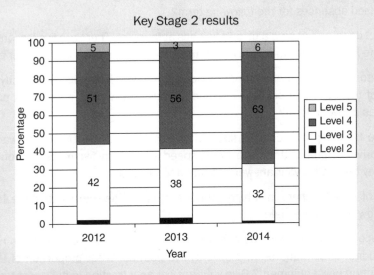

| Year | 2012 | 2013 | 2014 |
|---|---|---|---|
| **Number of pupils** | 32 | 35 | 28 |

How many more pupils achieved level 4 and above in 2014 compared to 2012?

# Numeracy Practice Paper 3

## Mental questions

1   In a school, there are three hundred and fifteen pupils and fifteen teachers. What is the ratio of teachers to pupils? Give your answer as a fraction in its lowest form.

2   In one GCSE examination, nought point nought nought five pupils were ungraded. How many times more candidates did achieve a grade?

3   How much would it cost in pounds for thirty pupils to visit a museum in Germany at a cost of twenty euros per person? Use the exchange rate of one euro equals nought point eight pounds.

4   A new textbook costs eight pounds fifty pence. A teacher wants to buy forty and will receive a ten percent discount. What is the total cost of forty textbooks after the discount has been applied?

5   A primary school fete raises one thousand seven hundred and sixty-four pounds. The headteacher decides to allocate the money between the infant and junior schools in the ratio three to four. How much will be allocated to the junior school?

**6**   A high school records eighty-four unauthorised absences in one term. The headteacher wishes to reduce this by twelve per cent for the following term. What is the target number of unauthorised absences for the following term?

**7**   The school day starts at nine a.m. and finishes at four p.m. There are five lessons per day, each lasting one hour and five minutes. How much time is spent each day in other activities?

**8**   In a sponsored run, the mean number of laps completed by pupils was exactly six. The mean amount of money raised per lap was nine pounds. Thirty-eight pupils took part. How much money was raised in total?

**9**   Pupils are travelling to a concert sixty miles from the school. On the outward journey, the minibus driver estimates that the average speed will be forty-five miles per hour. How long will the journey take? Give your answer in hours and minutes.

**10**   Four out of nine teachers in a high school are male. There are sixty-three teachers in the school. How many are female?

**11**   The science department has spent four hundred and twenty-five pounds on new equipment from a budget of six hundred and seventy-five pounds. What proportion of the budget has been spent on new equipment? Give your answer as a fraction in its lowest terms.

**12**   Find the cost of fifty-two calculators each costing five pounds fifty pence.

## Onscreen questions

**1**   A school's governing body is considering changes to the times of the school day. At present, school starts at 9:00 and finishes at 15:45, with total breaks of 1½ hours. The proposal is to start the school day at 08:45, finishing at 15:50, with the total break time being reduced to 1¼ hours. By how many minutes will the school day, excluding breaks, be increased?

**2**   The cumulative frequency chart shows the test results for Year 8 mathematics. How many pupils achieved 40 or more marks?

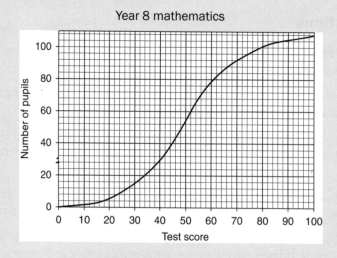

Year 8 mathematics

**3** The art department of a high school buys card in sheets of A1, each of which has an area of 0.5m². The teacher needs to cut the card into size A4, with an area of 625cm². The teacher needs 30 pieces of A4 card. How many sheets of A1 will he need?

**4** The cost of a school trip is summarised in the table below:

| Coach hire | £250 |
|---|---|
| Additional miles | 45 @ 65p per mile |
| Entrance to museum | £4.50 per pupil, with one free place per 20 pupils |

35 pupils are going on the trip. What is the cost per pupil?

**5** The English and mathematics test scores of one year group are plotted on a scatter graph.

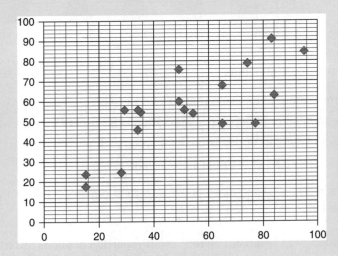

Point and click on the pupil who achieved the highest mean score over the two tests.

**6** A pupil obtained the following marks in five tests:

Test A: 28/35   Test B: 14/20   Test C: 13/30   Test D: 23/30   Test E: 11/15

What is her average mark as a decimal? Give your answer to two decimal places.

**7** A technology department uses an estimate that $\frac{4}{11}$ of the allocated budget is spent on textbooks. Its departmental allocation for one year is £5654. How much does the department allocate to textbooks? Give your answer to the nearest pound sterling.

**8** It is planned to create a new five-a-side football pitch in the school grounds. The pitch will measure 2500cm by 1650cm, with a border of 6m all the way round. What area of land is required in total to create the new pitch? Give your answer in m².

**9**    The bar chart shows the number of pupils on roll in Years 7 to 11.

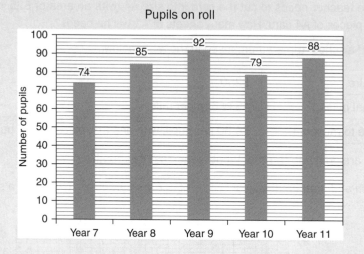

Select all the true statements:

A. The total number of pupils in years 7 to 11 is 418.

B. The mean number of pupils per year group is 83 (to the nearest whole number).

C. The median number of pupils per year group is 85.

D. Approximately 21% of the pupils are in year 11.

**10**    Following a heavy snowfall, many pupils in a rural primary school were unable to travel to school. The following table was compiled.

| Year group | Number on roll | Proportion of pupils absent |
|---|---|---|
| R | 24 | 0.3 |
| 1 | 22 | 0.4 |
| 2 | 16 | 0.5 |
| 3 | 21 | 0.7 |
| 4 | 28 | 0.4 |
| 5 | 24 | 0.75 |
| 6 | 17 | 0.6 |

How many pupils did attend school that day?

**11**  The following table shows the time taken by a small group of pupils to solve a mathematical problem. .

| Pupil | Time taken (mins:secs) |
|-------|------------------------|
| A     | 4:26 |
| B     | 3:52 |
| C     | 5:25 |
| D     | 2:55 |
| E     | 9:29 |
| F     | 4:17 |

What is the mean time taken? Give your answer in minutes and seconds.

**12**  The results of an initial numeracy test given to all Year 7 pupils at one high school are recorded over a three-year period.

Results of initial numeracy test

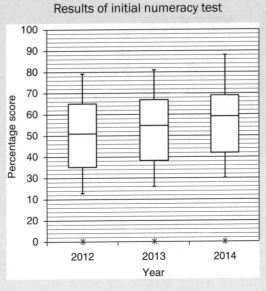

What is the difference in the interquartile ranges for 2012 and 2014?

**13** A sponsored run took place on the school's 400m running track. The results were tabulated as follows:

| Number of laps | Number of pupils |
|---|---|
| 1 | 3 |
| 2 | 26 |
| 3 | 48 |
| 4 | 36 |
| 5 | 28 |
| 6 | 10 |
| 7 | 1 |

What is the total distance covered by all the pupils who took part? Give your answer in kilometres.

**14** A sponsored run took place on the school's 400m running track. The results were tabulated as follows:

| Number of laps | Number of pupils |
|---|---|
| 1 | 3 |
| 2 | 26 |
| 3 | 48 |
| 4 | 36 |
| 5 | 28 |
| 6 | 10 |
| 7 | 1 |

What is the median number of laps completed?

**15** One year, an awarding body had 2643 requests for a review of the grade awarded at GCSE in one subject. Of these, 59.4% resulted in a change of grade. How many reviews resulted in a change of grade?

**16** A survey was made of 28 Year 7 and 35 Year 8 pupils into how much time they were spending playing computer games per day. The findings are shown in the pie charts below.

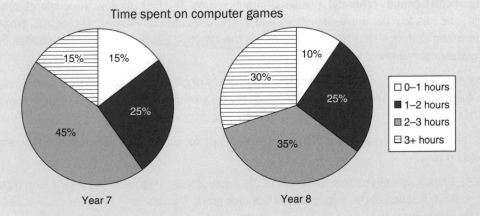

Time spent on computer games

Year 7

Year 8

Legend:
☐ 0–1 hours
■ 1–2 hours
▨ 2–3 hours
⊟ 3+ hours

Select all the true statements:

A. Fewer Year 8 children spend more than three hours playing computer games per day than Year 7 children.

B. More than 50% of the Year 8 pupils surveyed play computer games for more than two hours per day.

C. Of the Year 7 children surveyed, only 4 play computer games for less than one hour per day.

# Numeracy Practice Paper 4

## Mental questions

**1** A new playing field has been created in the school grounds. It will be fifty-eight point five metres wide and seventy-five metres long. What is the area of the playing field? Give your answer in square metres.

**2** A primary school with sixty pupils spends six thousand five hundred and twenty-five pounds on new resources. What is the mean amount spent per pupil?

**3** In a charity events week, fourteen out of a total of three hundred and twenty-two pupils each raised more than one hundred pounds. What fraction of pupils raised more than one hundred pounds?

**4** A class of pupils use different methods to estimate the height of a room. The highest estimate is six point nine metres and the lowest estimate is three point four two metres. What is the range of the estimates?

5    The ratio of male to female teachers in one primary school is seven to thirteen. What proportion of teachers is male? Give your answer as a decimal.

6    A school cross-country team did a series of practice runs. The first run was three kilometres, the second was four point five kilometres and the third was five point seven kilometres. What is the mean distance that the team ran over the practice sessions? Give your answer in kilometres and metres.

7    Pupils are supporting a charity by donating small boxes of gifts. They make up their own boxes from card. The boxes measure, in centimetres, thirty by twenty by fifteen. What is the volume of a box? Give your answer in cubic centimetres.

8    On a very foggy day, eighteen out of thirty pupils are late for school. What percentage of pupils arrived on time?

9    In GCSE English, nought point seven eight of the pupils achieved grade C or above in one high school. What fraction of the pupils did not achieve grade C or above? Give your answer as a fraction in its lowest form.

10   A group of technology students are researching obesity. One student states that his weight is twelve stones. What is this in kilograms? Use the conversion of one stone equals six point three five kilograms.

11   A high school's target for GCSE science is that at least seventy-six per cent of its pupils will achieve a grade C or above. One hundred and twenty pupils are taking GCSE science. How many must achieve a grade C or above for the school to meet its target?

12   A pupil took two tests. He achieved sixteen out of twenty in the first test and eighteen out of thirty in the second. What is his average score? Give your answer as a percentage.

## Onscreen questions

1    A science group is following the instructions for a basic experiment where the expected temperatures have been given in degrees Fahrenheit.

The pupils have been given the formula to convert the temperatures to centigrade:

$$C = \frac{5(F - 32)}{9}$$

Using this formula, convert 79°F to °C, giving your answer to the nearest whole number.

2    The Year 6 teachers examined the performance of their pupils midway through the year.

| Level | 1 | 2 | 3 | 4 | 5 |
|-------|---|---|---|---|---|
| Boys  | 2 | 4 | 9 | 6 | 1 |
| Girls | 1 | 3 | 5 | 8 | 3 |

What proportion of pupils gained level 4 and above? Give your answer as a fraction in its lowest terms.

**3** A teacher offers after-school time slots to parents for consultations on two consecutive days. She allows 20 minutes per consultation and needs to make 16 appointments. She will start the sessions at 15:30 on the Monday and finish at 19:00 at the latest, with a break of 15 minutes at 17:30. Assuming she fills every slot consecutively, what time will she finish on the Tuesday evening?

**4** The boxplots show the results of five tests taken by a class of geography students.

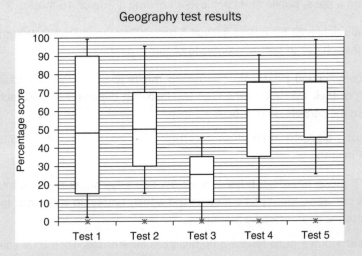

Geography test results

Point and click on the boxplot which best represents the following statement:

The test appeared to be too difficult for most of the students.

**5** As part of a quality-improvement initiative, a school's senior management team carried out classroom observations in four different departments.

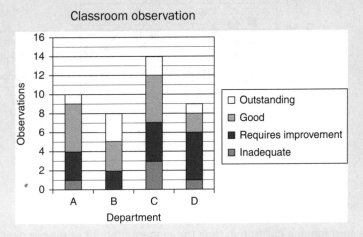

Classroom observation

What percentage of lessons was graded as 'good' across all four departments?

| 0.36% | 15% | 17% | 36.6% | 41% |

**6**    A new textbook is to be ordered. Each book costs £9.50. For orders over 50 in quantity, a discount of 15% can be applied. The teacher needs 45 books, but realises that it will be cheaper to order 50. What is the difference between the cost of 45 books and the cost of 50 books?

**7**    The final grade for a qualification, consisting of three parts, is calculated as follows:

Part A: 0.2; Part B: 0.3; Part C: 0.5

To obtain a pass, pupils must achieve an overall grade of 45 marks.

One pupil achieves 52 marks in Part A and 49 marks in Part B. What is the lowest mark she must achieve in part C in order to obtain a pass?

**8**    The recommended classroom size for 25 pupils is 51m². Pupils measure the length and breadth of their classroom and note the following dimensions: 300 inches by 290 inches. They use the conversion of 2.5cm = 1 inch.

How much bigger is their classroom than the recommended minimum size? Give your answer in cm².

**9**    A Year 6 group has English lessons for 4¾ hours per week out of a total of 21¾ hours of lessons per week. What percentage of the weekly timetable is devoted to English? Give your answer to the nearest whole number.

**10**   Three sixth-form groups have set up business enterprises. Their total sales over a four-week period are displayed below.

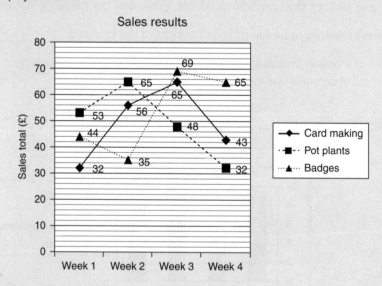

Sales results

Select all the true statements:

A.  The card-making enterprise took the highest amount of money over the four weeks.

B.  The lowest sales were made by the pot-plant enterprise in week 4.

C.  The range of sales totals is £37.

D.  The mean sales total of the badge-making group is £50.58.

11  The dimensions of a piece of A4 paper are 210mm by 297mm. What is the area of a piece of A4 paper? Give your answer in cm².

12  A primary school's pupils' performance in reading in Key Stage 1 was tested and compared with the national averages.

| Year | Percentage of boys at level 2 and above (school) | Percentage of boys at level 2 and above (national average) | Difference |
|------|------|------|------|
| 2011 | 76.4 | 75.3 | + 1.1 |
| 2012 | 79.6 | 78.7 | + 0.9 |
| 2013 | 75.8 | 78.3 | −2.5 |
| 2014 | 78.5 | 78.7 | −0.2 |
|  |  |  | Mean difference: |

| Year | Percentage of girls at level 2 and above (school) | Percentage of girls at level 2 and above (national average) | Difference |
|------|------|------|------|
| 2011 | 86.3 | 85.9 | 0.4 |
| 2012 | 87.4 | 86.2 | 1.2 |
| 2013 | 88.1 | 87.5 | 0.6 |
| 2014 | 89.2 | 87.4 | 1.8 |
|  |  |  | Mean difference: |

Select and place the correct values, to one decimal place, for the mean differences.

| 0.7 | −0.2 | 0.2 | 1.0 | 1.2 | 4.0 |

13  A comparison was made between four schools' Key Stage 2 results. The tables show the percentage of pupils out of the total number achieving level 4 or above, rounded to one decimal place.

| School | 2013 | 2014 |
|--------|------|------|
| A | 77.8 | 78.7 |
| B | 76.4 | 79.9 |
| C | 81.5 | 83.4 |
| D | 75.5 | 79.2 |

What is the percentage increase in the mean between 2013 and 2014?

**14** In one high school's sixth form, there were 76 school leavers in 2013 and 85 school leavers in 2014. The pie charts show the destinations of the school leavers over the two-year period.

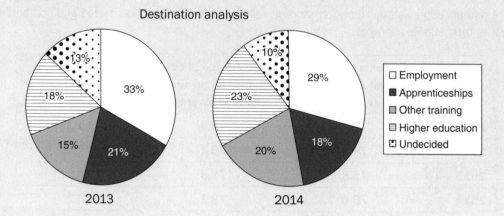

Destination analysis

2013

2014

Legend:
- □ Employment
- ■ Apprenticeships
- ▨ Other training
- ▤ Higher education
- ⊡ Undecided

How many more pupils were intending to go in to higher education in 2014 than in 2013?

**15** A primary school's average points score for science at Key Stage 2 was 26.4. The following year it was 28.5. What is the percentage increase in the average point score? Give your answer to one decimal place.

**16** The cost of a school trip for 20 pupils is summarised in the table:

| | |
|---|---|
| Accommodation and meals (total) | €4400 |
| Channel train | £75 per person |
| Entry fees to attractions (total) | £580 |
| Sundries (total) | £675 |
| Spending money | €50 per person |

What is the estimated total cost per pupil in £?

Use the ratio £5 to €8.

# Answers

## Answers to literacy practice questions

1   Please accept this as the only **acknowledgement** of your application.

2   Regular attendance at school will increase the **likelihood** of your child doing well in his or her exams.

3   The PE team has been ably **led** by Mrs Suzanne Williams for the last four years.

4   Sahira has really **benefited** from the one-to-one tuition she has had this term.

5   The proposed reorganisation of the pastoral system may be **controversial**.

6   The new assessment policy will **supersede** all previous versions.

7   In this school, we celebrate **excellence**, wherever it is demonstrated.

8   Your interpretation of the set topic was both **humorous** and moving.

9   Once they reach Year 11, students have the **privilege** of leaving the college at lunchtime.

10   This is a good subject to take at GCSE for anyone wishing to pursue **business** studies later on.

11   Aim to teach students a range of **strategies** for tackling unfamiliar spellings.

12   There are three new **syllabuses** available from different awarding organisations.

13   Some **irregularities** have been noticed in the way examination entries have been completed.

14   The relevant graphs are included in the **appendices** at the end of the report.

15   I would like us to reach a **consensus** on how to proceed in this matter.

16   Please make sure you attend every **practice** session between now and half term.

**17** Once pupils' cursive handwriting is sufficiently well formed, they will be given a pen **licence**.

**18** If you need help with your project, your class teacher can **advise** you.

**19** The threat of a detention usually has an immediate **effect** on pupil behaviour.

**20** Please complete the **relevant** paperwork and return it to me tomorrow.

**21** This schedule for completing reports should be **manageable** for everyone.

**22** The pupils **panicked** when faced with a test format that they had not encountered before.

**23** Please supply the relevant details as **concisely** as possible.

**24** Grammar is taught in three **discrete** sessions each week.

**25** The most important **principle** to bear in mind when carrying out research is 'do no harm'.

**26** Please make sure that the school hamster has **its** cage covered each evening.

**27** The trip will only go ahead if the **weather** is fine and suitable for outdoor pursuits.

**28** Jan was **apparently** unaware that he should have been in the hall with the rest of the class.

**29** Some children are becoming too **dependent** on the support of a teaching assistant.

**30** Ali Khan, the educational **psychologist**, will be in school on Friday.

**31** Students will need to demonstrate considerable **commitment** if they wish to take part in this dance project.

**32** Offering both courses will **necessitate** all members of the department teaching Year 10.

**33** Please check through the **programme** for the Christmas concert by tomorrow.

**34** The school's anti-bullying policy covers sexual and racial **harassment**.

**35** You will **automatically** receive a reminder when your library book is due back.

**36** The incident that **occurred** in the playground has been dealt with by Mr Thomas.

**37** Winning the silver cup was a huge **achievement** for the netball team.

**38** We hope that students will **seize** this opportunity to take part in an exciting local event.

**39** Your stories should be imaginative and engaging for the reader but also **believable**!

**40** Please find enclosed a **receipt** for the money you kindly donated to the school fund.

**41** D

| | | | | | |
|---|---|---|---|---|---|
| **42** | C | **73** | D | **104** | B |
| **43** | D | **74** | B | **105** | A |
| **44** | B | **75** | C | **106** | B |
| **45** | C | **76** | A | **107** | D |
| **46** | A | **77** | D | **108** | B |
| **47** | C | **78** | C | **109** | D |
| **48** | D | **79** | B | **110** | B |
| **49** | B | **80** | A | **111** | B |
| **50** | B | **81** | D | **112** | A |
| **51** | A | **82** | A | **113** | C |
| **52** | C | **83** | B | **114** | B |
| **53** | B | **84** | C | **115** | B |
| **54** | D | **85** | D | **116** | D |
| **55** | A | **86** | C | **117** | C |
| **56** | C | **87** | C | **118** | A |
| **57** | A | **88** | A | **119** | B |
| **58** | B | **89** | D | **120** | B |
| **59** | C | **90** | B | **121** | A |
| **60** | D | **91** | C | **122** | D |
| **61** | B | **92** | B | **123** | B |
| **62** | C | **93** | C | **124** | A |
| **63** | A | **94** | D | **125** | D |
| **64** | C | **95** | A | **126** | B |
| **65** | C | **96** | C | **127** | D |
| **66** | D | **97** | B | **128** | B |
| **67** | B | **98** | D | **129** | C |
| **68** | C | **99** | B | **130** | B |
| **69** | A | **100** | A | **131** | D |
| **70** | B | **101** | C | **132** | A |
| **71** | D | **102** | B | **133** | C2: 1, 3, 5 |
| **72** | B | **103** | D | **134** | C8: 1 |
| | | | | **135** | C6: 5 |

**136**  C4: 2, 6, 8

**137**  C1: 1 S; 2 P; 3 LA; 4 S; 5 LA

**138**  C3: 2, 5, 4, 6, 1, 3

**139**  C9: M = Local authorities; L = Ofsted inspectors

**140**  C1: 1 R; 2 S; 3 S; 4 HSE; 5 R

**141**  C3: 4, 2, 1, 3, 5

**142**  C6: 2 and 5

**143**  C7: 1 S; 2 C; 3 I; 4 NE

**144**  C4: 2, 4, 7, 8

**145**  C8: 4

**146**  C9: L = HM Government; M = Teachers leading school visits

**147**  C8: 2

**148**  C8: 1

**149**  C6: 3 and 5

**150**  C2: 3, 4, 6

**151**  C9: L = Headteachers of junior schools; M = School governors

**152**  C5: 1 para. 6; 2 para. 1; 3 para. 4; 4 para. 9

**153**  C7: 1 S; 2 C; 3 I; 4 NE

**154**  C3: 4, 3, 1, 6, 5, 2

**155**  C1: 1 AI; 2 SI; 3 AI; 4 SST; 5 AI

**156**  C5: 1 para. 5; 2 para. 7; 3 para. 2; 4 para. 6

**157**  C2: 1, 4, 6

**158**  C7: 1 S; 2 I; 3 NE; 4 I

**159**  C9: L = Bus drivers; M = Local authorities

**160**  C3: 5, 2, 1, 4, 6, 3

**161**  C2: 1, 4, 6

**162**  C8: 2

**163**  C9: L = The headteacher at Bold Hill Academy; M = The staff at Bold Hill Primary School

**164**  C1: 1 W; 2 G; 3 S; 4 G; 5 W

**165**  C5: 1 para. 2; 2 para. 7; 3 para. 1; 4 para. 9

**166**   C6: 3 and 6

**167**   C1: 1 S; 2 H; 3 H; 4 T

**168**   C3: 2, 4, 6, 1, 3, 5

**169**   C4: 3, 5, 9

**170**   C6: 3 and 6

**171**   C5: 1 para. 6; 2 para. 5; 3 para. 2; 4 para. 7

**172**   C2: 2, 3, 6

**173**   C7: 1 S; 2 IC; 3 S; 4 I

# Answers to literacy practice papers

## Literacy Practice Paper 1

### Spelling

**1**   Worksheets should be **accessible** to all pupils in the class.

**2**   Students who are **persistently** late should be sent to their head of year.

**3**   Children **normally** play outside during the lunch break.

**4**   The new benches for the hall are more **manoeuvrable** than the seating we had before.

**5**   The clash of dates presents the leadership team with a **dilemma**.

**6**   You can ask your form teacher to provide a **reference** for you.

**7**   The audience was visibly **affected** by the children's performance.

**8**   The **calendar** for next year is now on the notice board in the staffroom.

**9**   There has been an **extraordinary** response to my request for help at parents' evening.

**10**   Children were **irresistibly** drawn to the puppet show at the school summer fair.

### Grammar

**A**: A, D, C, B, C, A        **B**: C, B, A        **C**: C, D, A

### Comprehension

A: 3        B: 1        C: 3, 5, 6        D: 2, 4        E: 2, 4, 7, 9

# Literacy Practice Paper 2

## Spelling

1   The new floor cushions for the library **complement** the quiet reading area in the corner.

2   Can anyone explain the **disappearance** of the kettle from the staffroom?

3   We are hoping that prospective intruders will be **deterred** by the CCTV cameras.

4   Try to resolve any **grievances** informally with parents before they are escalated.

5   There is a **miscellaneous** selection of lost property in the school office.

6   The Chair of Governors was **instrumental** in persuading the Mayor to come to speech day.

7   **Consequently**, the year meeting due to be held today has been postponed.

8   Children should wash their hands **immediately** before lunch.

9   **Manipulative** behaviour can be a form of bullying.

10   There may be some **resistance** to the proposals for the new school day.

## Grammar

**A**: C, B, D, A          **B**: C, B, D, A          **C**: B, A, B, C

## Comprehension

A: 2          B: 5          C: 2, 4, 7, 10, 12          D: 1: C; 2: I; 3: S; 4: S

# Literacy Practice Paper 3

## Spelling

1   Pupils will be **accommodated** in four-bed rooms in the youth hostel.

2   Your salary will be **commensurate** with your qualifications and experience.

3   The summer fair will **definitely** go ahead, whatever the weather.

4   This has been an exceptionally **successful** year for the languages faculty.

5   Jakub takes a very **conscientious** approach to this subject.

6   There are two **parallel** reading groups in each class.

7   The school play will end at **approximately** 9.30 p.m.

8   We are lucky enough to have links with several **prestigious** universities.

9   The school is hoping to **acquire** some new recorders for the children.

10   Children who are **dyslexic** are given additional time in school exams.

## Grammar

**A**: C, D, B, A　　　　**B**: B, A, D, C　　　　**C**: C, D, B, A, B

## Comprehension

A: 1: G; 2: S; 3: S; 4: P　　　B: 2, 5, 1, 4, 3　　　C: L = Religious leaders; M = Headteachers

D: 1: S; 2: I; 3: NE; 4: C　　　E: 1: para 2; 2: para 5; 3: para 3; 4: para 4　　　F: 3

# Literacy Practice Paper 4

## Spelling

1　We do not permit any form of **aggressive** behaviour in this school.

2　Please do not cause **embarrassment** by giving members of staff inappropriately generous gifts.

3　**Perseverance** is a very important quality we want to encourage in our students.

4　The English department **occasionally** has spare tickets for theatre trips.

5　Your handwriting is **illegible** in places.

6　Remember you are there in a **supervisory** capacity at all times.

7　It is important that children are **inoculated** against common diseases.

8　Mrs Jones is available in the biology **laboratory** after lunch.

9　We are **sincerely** sorry for any inconvenience caused to parents and carers.

10　The pleasure of your **presence** is requested at our end of term assembly.

## Grammar

**A**: A, C, D, B, C　　　　**B**: A, C, B, D　　　　**C**: B, A, C, D

## Comprehension

A: L = NSPCC; M = Designated safeguarding lead

B: 1: para 3; 2: para 1; 3: para 10; 4: para 8

C: 1: SCS; 2: SW; 3: LSCB; 4: SCS　　　D: 4, 5, 7　　　E: 2, 3, 5, 1, 4

# Answers to numeracy practice questions

1   $\dfrac{7}{15}$

2   $\dfrac{3}{5}$

3   $\dfrac{5}{32}$

4   228

5   108

6   15

7   $\dfrac{1}{4}$

8   236

9   $\dfrac{1}{12}$

10   252

11   9

12   63

13   332.85

14   $\dfrac{13}{20}$

15   $\dfrac{2}{5}$

16   $\dfrac{17}{20}$

17   $\dfrac{7}{20}$

18   18

19   $\dfrac{3}{10}$

20   $\dfrac{7}{40}$

21   32

22   $\dfrac{13}{20}$

23   $\dfrac{9}{20}$

24   739

25   33%

26   17

27   53%

28   20%

29   55%

30   357

31   £35.75

32   £50

33   A

34   0.7

35   0.67

36   0.6

37   0.35

38   $\dfrac{1}{5}$

39   $\dfrac{4}{7}$

40   28:29

41   £182

42   £525

43   £74.40

44   £36

45   £19.50

46   £150

47   £95.09

48   £133.30

49   £30

50   €35

51   £300

52   255 Canadian dollars

53   £15

54   £357.21

55   12,500 krona

56   £21.67

57   £212.55

58   £14

59   5 hours

60   23 hours + 20 minutes

61   110 minutes

62   4 hours 20 minutes

63   21:58

64   2km

65   100

66   14.4km

67   14

68   328.1km

| 69 | 2.6 miles |
|----|-----------|
| 70 | 20.5km |
| 71 | 24m$^2$ |
| 72 | 54m |
| 73 | 50m |
| 74 | 37.5$^2$ |
| 75 | 43.5m$^2$ |
| 76 | 4m$^2$ |
| 77 | 733.5m$^2$ |
| 78 | 4m |
| 79 | 40ml |
| 80 | 30 litres |
| 81 | 20cm$^3$ |
| 82 | 33750cm$^3$ |
| 83 | 20 miles |
| 84 | 227g |
| 85 | 1.5m |
| 86 | 15°C |
| 87 | 50762 |
| 88 | 22:93 |
| 89 | 55°C |

| 90 | £78 |
|-----|------|
| 91 | 11.25 litres |
| 92 | 2600m |
| 93 | 50% |
| 94 | 61 |
| 95 | 11 years 7 months |
| 96 | 0.4°C |
| 97 | 0.62 |
| 98 | £9.25 |
| 99 | £955.50 |
| 100 | 53% |
| 101 | 13 |
| 102 | 1 |
| 103 | 8.5km |
| 104 | 22 |
| 105 | 12 |
| 106 | 10.2km |
| 107 | 76 |
| 108 | 40.7 |
| 109 | 7.6 |
| 110 | 22 months |

| 111 | −2°C |
|-----|------|
| 112 | 8°C |
| 113 | Week 1 |
| 114 | 4.1 |
| 115 | A, C and D |
| 116 | 2.45 seconds |
| 117 | B and C |
| 118 | A and D |
| 119 | C |
| 120 | Week 3 |
| 121 | 45 minutes |
| 122 | 0.6 |
| 123 | $\dfrac{9}{50}$ |
| 124 | 0.6 |
| 125 | $\dfrac{17}{40}$ |
| 126 | 18 |
| 127 | Pupil C: −4; Pupil D: +1; Pupil E: +12 |
| 128 | $\dfrac{19}{23}$ |

**129**

| Level 3 | Level 4 | Level 5 |
|---------|---------|---------|
| 6 | 8 | 4 |
| 33 | 44 | 22 |
| 6 | 12 | 6 |
| 25 | 50 | 25 |
| 7 | 16 | 9 |
| 22 | 50 | 28 |

**130**  6, 3, 5

**131**  63% to the nearest whole %

**132**  (Year 3) 76.4%

**133**  2012

**134**  44

**135**  68%

**136**  Class (2) 27%

**137**

| English | Mathematics | Science | Humanities |
|---------|-------------|---------|------------|
| 45 | 42 | 52 | 57 |
| 88 | 79 | 67 | **74** |
| 56 | **49** | 52 | 46 |
| 22 | 41 | 40 | 34 |
| 211 | 211 | 211 | 211 |

| English | Mathematics | Science | Humanities |
|---------|-------------|---------|------------|
| 63 | **57** | 56 | 27 |
| **90** | 81 | **81** | 84 |
| 100 | 100 | 100 | 100 |

**138**  13

**139**  Pupils D and E

**140**  All statements are true

**141**  0.2

**142**  B, C and D

**143**

Boys:

| 2015 | 79.1 | 78.9 |
|------|------|------|

Girls:

| 2015 | 89.8 | 87.6 |
|------|------|------|

**144**  Pupil F

**145**  A, B, C and E

**146**  A and B

**147**  $^{11}\!/_{17}$

**148**  0.5

**149**  A and B

**150**  51

**151**  1

**152**  A

**153**

|    | N | M | S | C | F |
|----|---|---|---|---|---|
| **7**  | 25 | 15 | 25 | 15 | 20 |
| **10** | 30 | 10 | 35 | 5  | 20 |

| | | | | | |
|---|---|---|---|---|---|
| **154** | 70 | **173** | B | **193** | 25 |
| **155** | B and C | **174** | 25% | **194** | 5 |
| **156** | C and D | **175** | 35 | **195** | 25 |
| **157** | 29 pupils | **176** | Column 4 | **196** | A and C |
| **158** | 2011 | **177** | 37% | **197** | 2 |
| **159** | 2012 | **178** | B and C | **198** | 6 |
| **160** | 72.5 | **179** | 20 | **199** | 7 |
| **161** | A | **180** | B | **200** | B and C |
| **162** | A, B and D | **181** | (91, 42) | **201** | Test 3 |
| **163** | 491 | **182** | 0.45 | **202** | 17 |
| **164** | B | **183** | 2011 | **203** | 24°C |
| **165** | 5 is the greatest increase, in 2009 | **184** | B and C | **204** | 78 |
| | | **185** | (100, 400) | **205** | 44% |
| **166** | 18.75 | **186** | £125 | **206** | 23.6% and 52.8%, respectively |
| **167** | 19 | **187** | B and C | | |
| **168** | 0.6 | **188** | 76 | **207** | 53% |
| **169** | 50% | **189** | B and C | **208** | 42 |
| **170** | A and B | **190** | D | **209** | 08:30 |
| **171** | D | **191** | 12 pupils | **210** | 11:54 |
| **172** | 63% | **192** | B and D | **211** | 11:25 |
| | | | | **212** | 15:00 |

# Answers to numeracy practice papers

# Numeracy Practice Paper 1

## Mental questions

| | | | | | |
|---|---|---|---|---|---|
| **1** | 3 hrs 35 mins | **5** | 52 | **9** | 192 |
| **2** | £84.35 | **6** | £288 | **10** | 2.92 |
| **3** | £60 | **7** | 72 | **11** | 85% |
| **4** | 4.8km | **8** | 45 mins | **12** | 4 |

## Onscreen questions

| | | | | | |
|---|---|---|---|---|---|
| 1 | 1.9 | 5 | 6 | 11 | Pupil 4 |
| 2 | 16.17% | 6 | A, C and D | 12 | A and C |
| 3 | 0.4 | 7 | £32.58 | 13 | A |
| 4 | Mon. wk 1: 28; Tue. wk 5: 23; Wed. wk 2: 26; Fri. wk 2: 24 | 8 | 11 | 14 | 18:05 |
| | | 9 | 24% | 15 | 95 |
| | | 10 | A and C | 16 | 18 hours |

# Numeracy Practice Paper 2

## Mental questions

| | | | | | |
|---|---|---|---|---|---|
| 1 | 0.4 | 5 | 1.71 | 9 | 42 |
| 2 | 76% | 6 | 11 | 10 | £5296.50 |
| 3 | $\frac{3}{20}$ | 7 | $\frac{17}{20}$ | 11 | 30,000 Yen |
| 4 | £312 | 8 | 19.2 | 12 | 9:58 |

## Onscreen questions

| | | | | | |
|---|---|---|---|---|---|
| 1 | 24 hrs 35 mins | 7 | B and D | 13 | 51.9% |
| 2 | C and D | 8 | 2.03 | 14 | 17 |
| 3 | 6 | 9 | £4031 | 15 | 12 |
| 4 | C | 10 | (85, 35) | 16 | 1 |
| 5 | A and D | 11 | £326.41 | | |
| 6 | 2 | 12 | 14.8 | | |

# Numeracy Practice Paper 3

## Mental questions

| | | | | | |
|---|---|---|---|---|---|
| 1 | 21:1 | 5 | £1008 | 9 | 1 hr 20 mins |
| 2 | 199 | 6 | 74 | 10 | 35 |
| 3 | £480 | 7 | 1 hr 35 mins | 11 | $\frac{17}{27}$ |
| 4 | £306 | 8 | £2052 | 12 | £286 |

### Onscreen questions

| | | | | | |
|---|---|---|---|---|---|
| **1** | 35 mins | **7** | £2056 | **13** | 220km |
| **2** | 78 | **8** | 1054.5m² | **14** | 3 |
| **3** | 4 | **9** | A, C and D | **15** | 1570 |
| **4** | £12.35 | **10** | 74 | **16** | B and C |
| **5** | (96, 85) | **11** | 5:04 | | |
| **6** | 0.69 | **12** | 3 | | |

## Numeracy Practice Paper 4

### Mental questions

| | | | | | |
|---|---|---|---|---|---|
| **1** | 4387.5m² | **5** | 0.35 | **9** | $^{11}/_{50}$ |
| **2** | £108.75 | **6** | 4km 400m | **10** | 76.2kg |
| **3** | $^{1}/_{23}$ | **7** | 9000cm² | **11** | 91 |
| **4** | 3.48m | **8** | 40% | **12** | 70% |

### Onscreen questions

| | | | | | |
|---|---|---|---|---|---|
| **1** | 26°C | **7** | 40 | **13** | 2.5% |
| **2** | $^{3}/_{7}$ | **8** | 33,750cm² | **14** | 6 |
| **3** | 18:05 | **9** | 22% | **15** | 8.0% |
| **4** | Test 3 | **10** | C | **16** | £306.50 |
| **5** | 36.6 | **11** | 623.7cm² | | |
| **6** | £23.75 | **12** | −0.2, 1.0 | | |

# Show me: solutions to numeracy practice questions

**1** 14 out of 30 = $\dfrac{14}{30}$ = $\dfrac{7}{15}$

**2** Number of boys: 2 + 3 + 4 + 5 + 1 = 15

Number of boys at levels 3 or 4: 4 + 5 = 9

9 out of 15 = $\dfrac{9}{15}$ = $\dfrac{3}{5}$

**3** $\dfrac{1}{4}$ of $\dfrac{5}{8}$ = $\dfrac{1}{4} \times \dfrac{5}{8}$ = $\dfrac{5}{32}$

**4** $\dfrac{1}{3}$ of 342 = 342 ÷ 3 = 114

$\dfrac{2}{3}$ of 342 = 114 × 2 = 228

**5** $\dfrac{1}{8}$ of pupils = $\dfrac{288}{8}$ = 36

$\dfrac{3}{8}$ of pupils = 36 × 3 = 108

**6** 4 out of 9 are girls

5 out of 9 are boys

$\dfrac{5}{9}$ of 27 = 5/9 × 27 = 15

**7** 45 out of 180 = 45/180 = $\dfrac{1}{4}$

**8** $\dfrac{1}{3}$ did not attend; $\dfrac{2}{3}$ did attend

$\dfrac{1}{3}$ of 354 = 118

$\dfrac{2}{3}$ of 354 = 236

Read the question carefully. Watch out for negatives such as 'are <u>not</u> able'.

**9** Cat: $\dfrac{1}{4}$ of 48 = 12

Dog: $\dfrac{1}{3}$ of 12 = 4

4 out of 48 = $\dfrac{4}{48}$ = $\dfrac{1}{12}$

To find a fraction of a fraction, multiply the fractions together: $\dfrac{1}{4}$ of $\dfrac{1}{3}$ = $\dfrac{1}{4} \times \dfrac{1}{3}$ = $\dfrac{1}{12}$.

**10** 0.6 of 420 = 0.6 × 420 = 252

**11** 0.3 of 30 = 0.3 × 30 = 9

**12** 0.7 of 210 = 147

210 − 147 = 63

Read the question carefully. Watch out for negatives such as 'did <u>not</u> take part'.

**13**   332.85

**14**   $0.65 = \dfrac{65}{100} = \dfrac{13}{20}$

**15**   $0.4 = \dfrac{4}{10} = \dfrac{2}{5}$

**16**   $0.85 = \dfrac{85}{100} = \dfrac{17}{20}$

**17**   $0.35 = \dfrac{35}{100} = \dfrac{7}{20}$

**18**   40% girls; 60% boys

$60\%$ of $30 = 0.6 \times 30 = 18$

**19**   $30\% = \dfrac{30}{100} = \dfrac{3}{10}$

**20**   $17.5\% = \dfrac{175\%}{10} = \dfrac{175}{1000} = \dfrac{7}{40}$

**21**   $70\%$ of $45 = 0.7 \times 45 = 31.5$

Round up as 31 is not enough to pass.

**22**   $65\% = \dfrac{65}{100} = \dfrac{13}{20}$

**23**   $100\% - 55\% = 45\%$

$45\% = \dfrac{45}{100} = \dfrac{9}{20}$

**24**   Absent: $2.5\%$ of $960 = 0.025 \times 960 = 24$

Exams: $15.2\%$ of $960 = 0.152 \times 960 = 146$

Trip: $5.3\%$ of $960 = 0.053 \times 960 = 51$

In lessons: $960 - (24 + 146 + 51) = 739$

**25**   14 out of $42 = \dfrac{1}{3}$

$= \dfrac{1}{3} \times 100\% = 33\dfrac{1}{3}\%$

$= 33\%$ to the nearest whole number

**26**   $4\dfrac{1}{2} = 4.5$

4.5 out of 27 as a percentage

$= 4.5 \div 27 \times 100\%$

= 9 ÷ 54 × 100%

= 17% to the nearest whole number

Double top and bottom (9/54).

**27**   16 out of 30 as a percentage = 16 ÷ 30 × 100% = 53% to the nearest whole number

**28**   6 out of 30 as a percentage = 6 ÷ 30 × 100% = 20% to the nearest whole number

**29**   33 out of 60 as a percentage = 33 ÷ 60 × 100% = 55%

**30**   15% receive school meals

15% of 420 pupils = 63

Number not receiving free school meals = 420 − 63 = 357

Read the question carefully. Watch out for negatives such as 'not'.

**31**   100% − 45% = 55%

55% of £65 = 0.55 × £65 = £35.75

**32**   100% − 70% = 30%

£15 is 30% of total cost

£15/30 is 1%

£15/30 × 70 = £35

£35 + £15 = £50

**33**   Statement A: Less than 80% of the pupils had a reading age below that of their actual age.

Number of pupils = 6

Pupils with reading age below their actual age: 1, 3, 4, and 5

Number of pupils with reading age below their actual age = 4

4 out of 6 = 4/6 × 100% = 67% < 80%

Statement A is true.

Statement B: Pupil 3 had 40% lower reading age compared to his actual age (to the nearest whole month).

Pupil 3's actual age = 10 × 12 months + 8 months = 128 months

Pupil 3's reading age = 8 × 12 months + 3 months = 99 months

Difference = 128 months − 99 months = 29 months

29 out of 128 = 29/128 × 100% = 22.6%

Statement B is not true.

Statement C: 50% of the pupils had a reading age of at least 1 year 6 months below the actual age.

Only pupil with reading age at least 1 year 6 months below the actual age is pupil 3.

1 out of 6 = 1/6 × 100% = 17% ≠ 50%

Statement C is not true.

**34**   28 out of 40 = $\dfrac{28}{40}$ = $\dfrac{7}{10}$ = 0.7

**35**   16 out of 48 = 1 out of 3 = 0.33     OR

1 − 0.33 = 0.67                          48 −16 = 32

$\dfrac{32}{48}$ = $\dfrac{2}{3}$ = 0.67

Read the question carefully. Watch out for negatives such as 'not'.

**36**   75 out of 125 = 75 ÷ 125 = 3 ÷ 5 = 0.6

**37**   7 out of 20 = 7 ÷ 20 = 0.35

**38**   5 recordings of 0°C.

5 out of 25 = $\dfrac{5}{25}$ = $\dfrac{1}{5}$

**39**   Number < level 4:

2 + 3 + 4 + 0 + 2 + 5 = 16

Total number of pupils:

16 + 5 + 1 + 6 + 0 = 28

Proportion:

16 out of 28 = $\dfrac{16}{28}$ = $\dfrac{4}{7}$

**40**   Total boys = 28 + 25 + 31 + 28 = 112

Total girls = 32 + 29 + 26 + 29 = 116

Ratio of boys to girls = 112:116

Dividing both by 4, gives, in lowest terms, the ratio as 28:29

**41**   28 × £6.50 = £182

**42**   150 meals × £3.50 per meal = £525

**43**   6 miles × £12.40 per mile = £74.40

**44**   200 copies × 6 pages per copy = 1200 pages

1200 pages × 3p per page = 3600p = £36

**45**  $50 \times 0.3 \times £1.30 = £19.50$

**46**  $\frac{5}{8}$ of £240 = £150

**47**  $\frac{1}{3}$ of £456.42 = £456.42/3 = £152.14

$\frac{5}{8}$ of £152.14 = $\frac{5}{8} \times$ £152.14 = £95.09 (nearest penny)

**48**  5 March:

$2 \times 45$ miles = 90 miles

90 miles @ 45p/mile = £40.50

19 March:

$2 \times 36$ miles = 72 miles

72 miles @ 45p/mile = £32.40

26 March:

$2 \times 6$ miles = 12 miles

12 miles @ 45p/mile = £5.40

£5.40 + £45.50 + £9.50 = £60.40

Total cost:

£40.50 + £32.40 + £60.40 = £133.30

**49**  Student ticket price: $0.85 \times £20 = £17$

Total ticket price: $(3 \times £20) + (30 \times £17) = £60 + £510 = £570$

Total cost of trip: £570 + £412.50 = £982.50

£982.50 ÷ 33 = £30 (to the nearest whole pound)

**50**  £25 = $25 \times €1.40 = €35$

€1.40 = £1

**51**  1 cedi = £0.2; 1500 cedi = $1500 \times £0.2 = £300$

**52**  £1 = 1.7CAD; £150 = $150 \times 1.7\text{CAD} = 255\text{CAD}$

**53**  €360 ÷ 20 = €18

£1 = €1.20; €1 = £1/1.2

€18 = £18 ÷ 1.20 = £180 ÷ 12 = £15

**54**  US$1 = £0.63; US$567 = $567 \times £0.63 = £357.21$

**55**  1 krona = £0.0052; £1 = 1/0.0052 krona

£65 = 65/0.0052 krona = 12,500 krona

**56**  £4 = €5

£1 = €(5 ÷ 4)

For the spending money: £60 = 60 × 5 ÷ €4 = €75

€75 − €50 = €25

For the €25 remaining: €15 = £13

€1 = £13 ÷ 15

€25 = 25 × £13 ÷ 15 = £21.67

**57**  £5 = €8

€1 = £⅝

Total accommodation: €1750 = 1750 × £⅝ = £1093.75

Accommodation per pupil = £1093.75/25 = £43.75

Train cost per pupil: £69

Entry fees per pupil = £1000/25 = £40

Sundries per pupil = £870/25 = £34.80

Spending money per pupil: €40 = 40 × £⅝ = £25

Total per pupil = £43.75 + £69 + £40 + £34.80 + £25 = £212.55

**58**  Belgium exchange £1 = €1.23

Euros taken: £75 = 75 × €1.23 = €92.25

€92.25 − €76 = €16.25

Return exchange £1 = €1.17; €1 = £1/1.17

€16.25 = 16.25 × £1/1.17 = £13.88 = £14 (to nearest pound)

**59**  6 × 50 minutes = 300 minutes

300 minutes ÷ 60 minutes/hour = 5 hours

**60**  5 days in the week

Hours: 5 × 4 hours = 20 hours

Minutes: 5 × 40 minutes = 200

200 minutes ÷ 60 minutes/hour = $3\frac{1}{3}$ hours = 3 hours 20 minutes

20 hours + 3 hours + 20 minutes = 23 hours + 20 minutes

**61**  Total mathematics time = 4 hours 20 minutes = 4 × 60 minutes + 20 minutes
= 260 minutes

Teacher-led = 2 hours 30 minutes = 2 × 60 minutes + 30 minutes = 150 minutes

260 − 150 = 110

**62**   $\frac{1}{3}$ of 6 hours 30 mins = 2 hours 10 mins

6 hours 30 mins − 2 hours 10 mins = 4 hours 20 mins

OR

$\frac{2}{3}$ of 6 hours 30 mins = 2 × 2 hours 10 mins = 4 hours 20 minutes

**63**   12 × 8 minutes = 96 minutes of musical items

10% of 20 minutes = 2 minutes

20 minutes + 2 minutes = 22 minutes break

10 × 3 minutes = 30 minutes setting up

Total time = 96 + 22 + 30 = 148 minutes

19:30 + 2 hours and 28 mins = ...

Time to finish = 21:58

**64**   Perimeter = 600m + 400m + 600m + 400m = 2000m = 2km

**65**   8.3 × 2 × 6 = 99.6 = 100 to the nearest mile

**66**   10 times per lesson: 10 × 90m = 900m in one lesson

16 lessons per week: 16 × 900m = 14,400m in one week

14,400m = 14.4km

**67**   1.03m = 1.03 × 100cm = 103cm

Change to centimetres first.

103cm ÷ 7cm = 14.7 (to 1 dp) = 14 (rounded down to the nearest whole number)

**68**   Totals number of laps: (3 × 3) + (4 × 4) + (18 × 5) + (13 × 6) = 9 + 16 + 90 + 78 = 193

193 laps of 1700m/lap = 328,100m

328,100m = 328,100/1000km = 328.1km

**69**   $\frac{1}{3} + \frac{1}{8} + \frac{2}{5} = \frac{103}{120}$   OR   $\frac{1}{3}$ of 18 = 6 (flat)

$\frac{17}{120} \times 18 = 2.6$        $\frac{1}{8}$ of 18 = 2.25 (forest)

$\frac{2}{5}$ of 18 = 7.2 (uphill)

Mixed: 18 − 6 − 2.25 − 7.2 = 2.55 = 2.6 to 1 dp

**70** Total distance on map:

1.4cm + 5.6cm + 3.9cm + 7.4cm + 2.2cm = 20.5cm

Ratio 1:100,000

20.5cm: 20.5 × 100,000cm

Length is 2,050,000cm = 20.5km

**71** 600cm × 400cm = 6m × 4m = 24m$^2$

**72** 4860m$^2$ ÷ 90m = 54m

**73** 6000m$^2$ ÷ 120m = 50m

**74** Area of trapezium = average depth × length

= (1m + 2m)/2 × 25m

= 1.5m × 25m

= 37.5m$^2$

OR

Rectangle measuring 25m × 1m = 25m$^2$

Plus triangle = $\frac{1}{2}$ × 25m × 1m = 12.5m$^2$

Area of trapezium = 25m + 12.5m = 37.5m$^2$

**75** Perimeter = 10m + 9m + 10m + 9m = 38m

Losing 9m for doors etc, leaves  38m − 9m = 29m around the walls.

Available area = 29m × available height.

Available height = 2m − 0.5m = 1.5m

Available wall space = 29m × 1.5m = 43.5m$^2$

**76** Lawn area = 6m × 10m = 60m$^2$

Area of 1 rectangle for counting purposes = 60m$^2$ ÷ 15 = 4m$^2$

**77** Method 1: Calculating the overall rectangle and subtracting the two cut-outs

Top right cut-out rectangle is 32m by (25 − 10.5)m

Bottom left cut-out rectangle is 5m by 10.5m

50m × 25m − (5m × 10.5m) − (32m × 14.5m)

1250m$^2$ − 52.5 m$^2$ − 464m$^2$ = 733.5m$^2$

Method 2: Dividing the area into two rectangles

14.5 × 18 + 45 × 10.5 = 733.5

**78**   $224m^3 \div 8m \div 7m = 4m$

**79**   3 litres = 3000ml

Change to millilitres first.

3000ml $\div$ 75 = 40ml

**80**   50cm $\times$ 30cm $\times$ 20cm = 30,000cm$^3$

1000cm$^3$ = 1 litre

30,000cm$^3$ = 30 litres

**81**   Acid : water = 2:50 = $\dfrac{2}{50}$ : 1

Water : acid = 1:$\dfrac{2}{50}$

$\dfrac{1}{2}$ litre: $\dfrac{2}{50} \times \dfrac{1}{2}$ litre

$\dfrac{2}{50} \times \dfrac{1}{2}$ litre = $\dfrac{1}{50}$ litre

1 litre = 1000cm$^3$

$\dfrac{1}{50} \times 1000cm^3 = 20cm^3$

**82**   1″ = 2.5cm

Convert first.

12″ = 12 $\times$ 2.5cm = 30cm

15″ = 15 $\times$ 2.5cm = 37.5cm

30cm $\times$ 30cm $\times$ 37.5cm = 33,750cm$^3$

OR

12″ $\times$ 12″ $\times$ 15″ = 2160 cu in

2.5cm = 1″

2.5cm $\times$ 2.5cm $\times$ 2.5cm = 1 cu in

2160 cu in = 2160 $\times$ 2.5 $\times$ 2.5 $\times$ 2.5cm$^3$ = 33,750cm$^3$

**83**   5 miles $\cong$ 8 kilometres

1 kilometre = $\dfrac{5}{8}$ miles

32 kilometres = 32 $\times$ $\dfrac{5}{8}$ miles = 20 miles

**84**   1 oz ≅ 28.4g

8oz = 8 × 28.4g = 227.2g = 227g to the nearest gram

**85**   30cm ≅ 1 foot

5 feet = 5 × 30cm = 150cm = 1.5m

**86**   59 − 32 = 27

27 × 5 = 135

$\dfrac{135}{9}$ = 15

**87**   UK travel: 2 × 165 miles = 330 miles

French travel: 2 × 144km + 192km = 288km + 192km = 480km

8km = 5 miles; 1km = $\dfrac{5}{8}$ miles

480km = 480 × $\dfrac{5}{8}$ miles = 300 miles

Total mileage: 330 miles + 300 miles = 630 miles

50,132 + 630 = 50,762

**88**   Distance travelled in the UK: 55 miles × 2 = 110 miles

Distance travelled in France: (279km × 2) + 186km = 744km

5 miles = 8km; 1km = (5 ÷ 8) miles

744km = 744 × 5 ÷ 8 miles = 465 miles

Ratio of UK travel to French travel = 110:465

Dividing both by 5, gives, in lowest terms, the ratio as 22:93

**89**   $(194°F − 32) × \dfrac{5}{9}$ = 90°C

$(95°F − 32) × \dfrac{5}{9}$ = 35°C

90°C − 35°C = 55°C

**90**   Fuel needed: 455 miles @ 35 mpg = $\dfrac{455}{35}$ gallons = 13 gallons

1 gallon = 4.55 litres

13 gallons = 13 × 4.55 litres = 59.15 litres

59.15 litres @ £1.32 per litre = 59.15 × £1.32 = £78.078 = £78 (to nearest pound)

**91**   Distance = 2 × 45 miles = 90 miles

Fuel needed: 90 miles @ 40 mpg = $\dfrac{90}{40}$ gallons = 2.25 gallons

1 litre = 0.2 gallons; 1 gallon = $\dfrac{1}{0.2}$ litres

2.25 gallons = 2.25 × $\dfrac{1}{0.2}$ litres = 11.25 litres

**92**    Mean distance $= \dfrac{65km}{25} = \dfrac{65,000m}{25} = 2600m$

**93**    Mean $= \dfrac{(24+36)}{2} = \dfrac{60}{2} = 30$      OR      $\dfrac{24}{60} \times 100\% = 40\%$

30 out of 60 $= \dfrac{30}{60} = 50\%$              $\dfrac{36}{60} \times 100\% = 60\%$

Mean: $\dfrac{40\%+60\%}{2} = 50\%$

**94**    Total marks: 34 + 46 + 67 + 76 + 23 + 98 + 67 + 56 + 57 + 66 + 34 + 67 + 39 + 89 + 45 + 67 + 99 + 67 + 43 + 56 + 77 = 1273

Number of results = 21

Mean $= \dfrac{1273}{21} = 60.619 = 61$ (to the nearest whole number)

**95**    Total years: $6 \times 11 = 66$

Total months: 6 + 9 + 11 + 2 + 10 + 4 = 42

66 ÷ 6 = 11 years

42 ÷ 6 = 7 months

11 years 7 months

**96**    Week 4 in table: $-3°C + -1°C + 1°C + 2°C + 3°C = 2°C$

$\dfrac{2°C}{5} = 0.4°C$

**97**    Test A: $\dfrac{13}{20} = 0.65$

Test B: $\dfrac{16}{25} = 0.64$

Test C: $\dfrac{22}{40} = 0.55$

Test D: $\dfrac{19}{30} = 0.63$

Average $= \dfrac{0.65+0.64+0.55+0.63}{4}$

$= \dfrac{2.47}{4} = 0.62$ (2 dp)

**98**    £832.50/90 = £9.25

**99**    Total number of lengths = (5 × 10 lengths) + (6 × 11 lengths) + (7 × 12 lengths) + (4 × 13 lengths) + (3 × 14 lengths) = 50 lengths + 66 lengths + 84 lengths + 52 lengths + 42 lengths = 294 lengths

Total money = 294 lengths × £3.25/length = £955.50

**100**   Total score = 32 × 54% = 1728%

1728% + 21% = 1749%

Number of scores = 32 + 1 = 33

1749%/33 = 53%

**101**   Interpreting the tally marks, the total number of pupils:

3 + 5 + 4 + 9 + 6 = 27

Middle pupil is number 14

3 + 5 + 4 = 12

The 14th pupil is in the next group

13 lengths

**102**   Middle pupil of 100: need to average data for pupils 50 and 51

24 + 42 = 66 > 50

Pupils 50 and 51 each have 1 sibling.

**103**   Number of pupils: 3 + 3 + 4 + 18 + 13 = 41 pupils.

Middle pupil is pupil number 21

3 + 3 + 4 = 10

3 + 3 + 4 + 18 = 28

21st pupil's distance is in the 4th group

Number of laps: 5

5 × 1700m = 8500m = 8.5km

**104**   Producing a tally chart:

| 12 | \| |
|----|----|
| 13 | \| |
| 14 | \| |
| 15 | \| |
| 16 | \| |
| 18 | \| |
| 19 | \| |
| 22 | \|\|\|\| |
| 27 | \|\|\| |

22 occurs the most number of times

**105**  Interpreting the tally marks, the highest number of pupils (7) complete 12 lengths

**106**  The highest number of children (20) complete 6 laps; 6 × 1700m = 10,200m = 10.2km

**107**  Highest mark = 99; Lowest mark = 23; Range = 99 − 23 = 76

**108**  2012: 86.3 − 45.6 = 40.7

**109**  2013: 85.4 − 48.9 = 36.5

2014: 79.1 − 50.2 = 28.9

36.5 − 28.9 = 7.6

**110**  Actual age range = 8 months

Reading age range = 30 months

30 − 8 = 22 months

**111**  Temperatures in week 2, in order:

−4°C; −3°C; −2°C; 2°C; 3°C

Median is middle value: −2°C

**112**  Lowest temperature recorded = −4°C

Highest temperature recorded = 4°C

Range is 8°C

**113**

| | Mon | Tue | Wed | Thu | Fri | Sum of temperatures |
|---|---|---|---|---|---|---|
| **Week 1** | **−1** | **0** | **1** | **2** | **4** | **−1 + 1 + 2 + 4 = 6** |
| **Week 2** | 3 | 2 | −4 | −3 | −2 | 3 + 2 + −4 + −3 + −2 = −4 |
| **Week 3** | 2 | 2 | 1 | 0 | 0 | 2 + 2 + 1 = 5 |
| **Week 4** | −3 | −1 | 1 | 2 | 3 | −3 + −1 + 1 + 2 + 3 = 2 |
| **Week 5** | 4 | 0 | 0 | −1 | −4 | 4 + −1 + −4 = −1 |

All the samples are the same size, so you only need to add. Dividing by 5 for each one is unnecessary.

**114**  Mean percentage in 2013: (61.9 + 75.4 + 48.9 + 58.4 + 85.4)/5 = 330/5 = 66

Median percentage: 61.9

Difference: 66 − 61.9 = 4.1

**115**  Statement A:

Week 1 mean in °C = (−4 + −3 + −1 + 0 + 0)/5 = −8/5 = −1.6

Week 1 median in °C = −1

Statement A is true.

Statement B:

Range: $-4\,°C$ to $+5\,°C = 9\,°C$

Statement B is not true.

Statement C:

| °C | −4 | −3 | −2 | −1 | 0 |
|---|---|---|---|---|---|
| freq | 1 | 2 | 1 | 2 | 3 |

| °C | 1 | 2 | 3 | 4 | 5 |
|---|---|---|---|---|---|
| freq | 0 | 3 | 0 | 2 | 1 |

Modes at $0\,°C$ and $2\,°C$: bimodal

Statement C is true.

Statement D:

Week 2 mean in $°C = (4 + 2 + -1 + -3 + -2)/5 = 0$

Statement D is true.

**116**   Mean: $(94.2 + 86.1 + 92.5 + 110.4 + 108.3 + 97.1)$ secs $\div 6 = 588.6$ secs $\div 6 = 98.1$ secs

Median: 6 data items; median is mean of third and fourth items when in order

$(94.2 + 97.1)$ secs $\div 2 = 95.65$ secs

Difference: 98.1 secs − 95.65 secs = 2.45 secs

**117**   Statement A: Set 2 did better at the test than Set 4.

The highest test score for Set 2 exceeds that for Set 4 (93 > 85) but the median is lower (42 < 51) and the lowest score is also lower (11 < 15).

Statement A is not true.

Statement B: The range of marks was greater for set 2 than for set 4.

Range for Set 2 = 93 − 11 = 82

Range for Set 4 = 85 − 15 = 70

82 > 70

Statement B is true.

Statement C: At least half of all the pupils taking the test scored 43 or more.

Half of Set 2 scored 43 or more. Half of Set 4 scored 52 or more.

Statement C is true.

**118**    Statement A: All values are different so there is no modal value.

Statement A is true.

Statement B: Mean = sum of values ÷ number of values

= (85.0 + 78.7 + 75.1 + 66.3 + 87.5 + 92.2 + 102.0 + 101.2) secs/8

= 688 secs/8 = 86 secs

Statement B is not true.

Statement C:

Putting the times in order, the median is the mean of the fourth and fifth data items.

= (85.0 + 87.5) seconds/2

= 86.25 seconds

Statement C is not true.

Statement D:

Pupil 4's time = 66.3 seconds

Next fastest pupil's time = 75.1 seconds

Difference = (75.1 − 66.3) seconds = 8.8 seconds = 9 seconds to the nearest second

Statement D is true.

**119**    Statement A: The mean attendance on Mondays is 3 higher than the mean attendance on Fridays.

Monday: 28 + 25 + 28 + 22 + 28 = 131

131/5 = 26.2

Friday: 25 + 24 + 21 + 26 + 20 = 116

116/5 = 23.2

Statement A is true.

Statement B: The range of attendance is 7.

Range is 28 − 20 = 8

Statement B is not true.

Statement C: The modal attendance in week 1 is 27.

Mode for week 1 is 27 (occurs twice)

Statement C is true.

**120** Looking for data which shows the temperature staying the same or dropping:

In Week 1, the temperature dropped on Tuesday

In Week 2, it stayed the same on Tuesday

In Week 4, it stayed the same on Thursday

In Week 5, it dropped on Tuesday

Only in Week 3 did the temperature rise every day.

**121** Selecting data from the PE row:

$0.15 \times 5$ hours $\times 60$ minutes/hour $= 45$ minutes

**122** Mean running time = total time $\div 5$

Total time (in secs) $= 94.2 + 86.1 + 92.5 + 110.4 + 108.3 = 491.5$

$491.5$ secs $\div 5 = 98.3$ secs

Three of the 5 children were below this time: A, B and C

3 out of $5 = \dfrac{3}{5} = 0.6$

**123** Difference $= 0.62 - 0.44 = 0.18 = \dfrac{18}{100} = \dfrac{9}{50}$

**124** 2012 mean: $(62.5 + 72.8 + 45.6 + 59.6 + 86.3)/5 = 326.8/5 = 65.36$

2014 mean: $(59.6 + 76.9 + 50.2 + 57.9 + 79.1)/5 = 323.7/5 = 64.74$

Difference in the means: $65.36 - 64.74 = 0.6$

**125** Total fat: $0.5 + 0.3 + 0.65 + 0.25 = 1.7$

Mean fat: $1.7/4 = 0.425 = \dfrac{425}{1000} = \dfrac{17}{40}$

**126**

| Portfolios | Selected |
|---|---|
| 0–6 | 1 |
| 7–12 | 2 |
| 13–18 | 3 |

| Pass | Merit | Distinction |
|---|---|---|
| 3 | 2 | 1 |
| 2 | 3 | 2 |
| 2 | 1 | 2 |

Total of entries = 18

**127**   Pupil C: 35 − 39 = −4; Pupil D: 23 − 22 = +1; Pupil E: 56 − 44 = +12

**128**   Looking at English: 2 + 9 + 28 + 7 = 46

46 in the year group

Looking at science: 46 − 6 − 20 − 8 = 12

Number of pupils predicted level 3 science = 12

Below level 5: 6 + 12 + 20 = 38

38 out of 46 = $\dfrac{38}{46} = \dfrac{19}{23}$

**129**   2012 % of total = $\dfrac{4}{18} \times 100\% = 22\%$

2013: level 5 total is 25% = 12 ÷ 2 = 6

2013 level 3% of total = 100 − (50 + 25) = 25

2014: 50% = 7 + 9 = 16

**130**   Year 4: 8–7 − 8–1 = 0–6; Year 6: 10–5 − 10–2 = 0–3; 6 + 5 + 3 = 14

14 months/3 = 5 months (to the nearest whole number)

**131**   Total number of pupils in the school: 16 + 18 + 22 + 17 + 19 + 25 + 19 = 136

Total number of pupils living in the school village: 7 + 10 + 12 + 13 + 11 + 18 + 14 = 85

Percentage: 85 out of 136 = 85/136 × 100% = 63% to the nearest whole %

**132**   Rather than work out all the percentages, make an estimate of the highest proportion. Look at the smallest differences between the two sets of numbers.

| Class | Proportion | % |
|-------|-----------|------|
| R | 7/16 | |
| 1 | 10/18 | |
| 2 | 12/22 | |
| 3 | 13/17 | 76.4 |
| 4 | 11/19 | |
| 5 | 18/25 | 72.0 |
| 6 | 14/19 | 73.6 |

Answer: (Year 3) 76.4%

**133**   2012: $\dfrac{4}{6+8+4} = \dfrac{4}{18} = 0.21$

2013: $\dfrac{6}{6+12+6} = \dfrac{6}{24} = 0.25$

2014: $\dfrac{6}{3+15+6} = \dfrac{6}{24} = 0.25$

0.25 > 0.24

Make sure only data for level 5 is used to arrive at the answer.

**134**   8 out of 6 + 8 + 4 = $\dfrac{8}{18}$

$\dfrac{8}{18} \times 100\% = 44.4\% = 44\%$ to the nearest whole number

**135**   Total number achieving level 4 and above = 12 + 13 + 16 + 8 + 2 + 4 + 0 + 0 + 1 = 56

Total number in year 6 = 56 + 2 + 4 + 0 + 7 + 7 + 6 = 82

56 out of 82 = $\dfrac{56}{82} \times 100\% = 68.29\% = 68\%$ (to the nearest whole number)

**136**   Class (1): Total number in class = 2 + 7 + 12 + 8 + 0 = 29

Level 3 percentage = $\dfrac{7}{29} \times 100\% = 24\%$

Class (2): Total number in class = 4 + 7 + 13 + 2 + 0 = 26

Level 3 percentage = $\dfrac{7}{26} \times 100\% = 27\%$

Class (3): Total number in class = 0 + 6 + 16 + 4 + 1 = 27

Level 3 percentage = $\dfrac{6}{27} \times 100\% = 22\%$

**137**   211 − 57 − 46 − 34 = 74

211 − 42 − 79 − 41 = 49

42 + 79 = 121; $\dfrac{121}{211} \times 100\% = 57\%$

45 + 88 + 56 = 189; $\dfrac{189}{211} \times 100\% = 89.57\% = 90\%$

211 − 40 = 171; $\dfrac{171}{211} \times 100\% = 81\%$

**138**   0.63 + 0.06 = 0.69

It's not an increase by 6% but an increase by 6 percentage points.

0.69 × 211 = 146 (to the nearest whole number)

Pupils who this year gained A*–C: 45 + 88 = 133

Number of additional pupils = 146 − 133 = 13

**139**

| Months | Diff. Autumn | Diff. Summer | Change |
|--------|--------------|--------------|--------|
| A | 18 | 20 | 2 |
| B | 0 | −2 | −2 |
| C | −2 | −2 | 0 |
| D | −2 | −7 | −5 |
| E | −2 | −8 | −6 |
| F | −8 | −10 | −2 |
| G | 1 | 0 | −1 |
| H | −11 | −11 | 0 |

**140**    Statement A: The highest total amount of money raised was at the school fete.

Sponsored activities total:

£89.45 + £93.87 + £145.35 = £328.67

School fete total:

£167.22 + £75.50 + £105.43 = £348.15

Sales total:

£67.50 + £35.20 + £68.30 = £171

£348.15 > £328.67 > £171

Statement A is true.

Statement B: Charity A will receive £509 to the nearest whole £.

£328.67 + £348.15 + £171 = £847.82

£847.82 × 3/5 = £508.692 = £509 to the nearest whole £

Statement B is true.

Statement C: The median amount raised of all the items listed is £89.45.

Nine items: median is the fifth when listed in order

£35.20; £67.50; £68.30; £75.50; £89.45

Statement C is true.

**141**    Boys: (76.4 + 79.6 + 75.8 + 78.5)/4 = 310.3/4 = 77.575

Girls: (75.3 + 78.7 + 78.3 + 78.7)/4 = 77.75

Difference: 77.75 − 77.575 = 0.175 = 0.2 (to 1 dp)

Keep all the decimal places until the last stage of the calculation.

**142** Statement A: The performance of the boys in the school is consistently below the national average.

The data for 2011 and 2012 contradict this statement.

Statement A is not true.

Statement B: The percentage of girls in the school achieving level 2 and above has increased every year.

The data for girls for 2011–2014 confirms this statement.

Statement B is true.

Statement C: The girls in the school consistently outperform the boys.

The data for girls, compared with that for the boys, confirms this statement.

Statement C is true.

Statement D: In 2013, the boys in the school were performing at 2.5% below the national average for that year.

2013 data for boys: 75.8 versus 78.3

78.3 − 75.8 = 2.5

Statement D is true.

**143** 78.5 + 0.6 = 79.1

78.7 + 0.2 = 78.9

89.2 + 0.6 = 89.8

87.4 + 0.2 = 87.6

**144** Improvement is the difference between the before and after scores. Pupil F has the highest improvement.

| | Before | After | Improvement |
|---|---|---|---|
| **A** | 15 | 22 | 7 |
| **B** | 20 | 25 | 5 |
| **C** | 32 | 34 | 2 |
| **D** | 16 | 19 | 3 |
| **E** | 25 | 21 | −4 |
| **F** | **20** | **32** | **12** |
| **G** | 16 | 19 | 3 |

|   | Before | After | Improvement |
|---|--------|-------|-------------|
| H | 17 | 28 | 11 |
| I | 29 | 33 | 4 |
| J | 31 | 38 | 7 |

**145**  Statement A: All the boys achieved improved scores after the additional support.

The scores in the second column of the boys' table are all higher.

Statement A is true.

Statement B: 20% of the girls achieved a lower score after the additional support.

There are 5 girls. 20% is one girl. Girl E did score lower after support.

Statement B is true.

Statement C: The mean difference in the boys' scores before and after the additional support was 7.4.

Mean 'before' = (20 + 16 + 17 + 29 + 31)/5 = 22.6

Mean 'after' = (32 + 19 + 28 + 33 + 38)/5 = 30

Difference 30 − 22.6 = 7.4

Statement C is true.

Statement D: The median girls' score after the additional support was 25 marks.

Marks in order are: 19, 21, 22, 25, 34. 5 scores. Median is third: 22

Statement D is not true.

Statement E: Pupil G scored 47.5% in the task after additional support.

19/40 × 100% = 47.5%

Statement E is true.

**146**  Statement A: Approximately $\frac{1}{10}$ of the pupils who took GCSE mathematics and GCSE music gained grades A* or A in both subjects.

Pupils who took GCSE mathematics and GCSE music and gained grades A* or A in both subjects = 5

Total number of students = 5 + 6 + 2 + 0 + 4 + 7 + 3 + 1 + 3 + 4 + 5 + 2 + 0 + 1 + 1 + 7 = 51

$$\frac{5}{51} \cong \frac{1}{10}$$

Statement A is true.

Statement B: More than $\frac{1}{6}$ of the pupils taking both GCSE mathematics and GCSE music gained grades F or G in mathematics.

Number gaining F/G in mathematics = 0 + 1 + 1 + 7 = 9

Number taking both = 51 as above

$$\frac{9}{51} = \frac{3}{17} > \frac{1}{6} = \frac{3}{18}$$

Statement B is true.

Statement C: 3/4 of the pupils who gained C and above in mathematics, gained A or A* in music.

Number who gained C or above in mathematics = 5 + 6 + 2 + 0 + 4 + 7 + 3 + 1 = 28

Of these, number who gained A*/A in music = 5 + 4 = 9

9 out of 28 = $\frac{9}{28} \neq \frac{3}{4}$

Statement C is not true.

**147**   From mathematics/French table, number gaining E and above:

5 + 8 + 1 + 2 + 11 + 5 + 3 + 9 + 11 = 55

Total number of pupils = 11 + 29 + 19 + 26 = 85

Fraction = $\frac{55}{85} = \frac{11}{17}$

Give answers in the lowest terms.

**148**   From mathematics/music table, number of pupils achieving C and above in both GCSE music and in GCSE mathematics = 3 + 2 + 1 + 9 = 15

Total number of pupils = 4 + 15 + 10 + 2 = 31

Proportion = 15/31 = 0.48 = 0.5 (to 1 dp)

**149**   Statement A: More than 40% of pupils in Years 7 and 8 have school dinners.

Total number of pupils = 54 + 114 + 102 = 270

40% of 270 = 108

114 > 108

Statement A is true.

Statement B: One-fifth of the pupils make other arrangements.

$$\frac{54}{270} = \frac{1}{5}$$

Statement B is true.

Statement C: Less than 1 in 3 pupils has a packed lunch.

⅓ of 270 = 90; 102 > 90

Statement C is not true.

**150**   Total number of pupils = 54 + 114 + 102 = 270

114 + 24 = 138

138 out of 270 = 138/270 × 100% = 51.1% =

51% (to nearest whole number)

**151**   100 − 15 − 26 − 36 − 22 = 1

1% spend more than 20 hours

1% of 74 = 0.01 × 74 = 0.74 = 1 (to the nearest whole person!)

**152**   26% of 74 pupils = 0.26 × 74 pupils = 19 pupils

Add 3 pupils: now 22 pupils playing 11–15 hours and 77 pupils in total.

% playing games for 11–15 hours per week is 22 ÷ 77 × 100 = 29 (A)

NB: not B because must still add up to 100%

**153**   In Year 7, 'None' occupies ¼ of the pie: 25%

In Year 7, 'Chess' occupies the same proportion as 'Music': 15%

In Year 7, 'Film' = 100 − 25 − 15 − 25 − 15 = 20

In Year 10, 'Film' = 100 − 30 − 10 − 35 − 5 = 20

**154**   School A: 45% of 103 = 0.45 × 103 = 46.35

School B: 25% of 95 = 0.25 × 95 = 23.75

46.35 + 23.75 = 70.1 = 70 (to the nearest whole number)

**155**   Statement A: A greater proportion of pupils are taking A levels at school B than at school A.

The sectors show percentages, so direct comparison of the sizes of the sectors can be made. The sector for A levels is larger in school A's pie.

Statement A is not true.

Statement B: One-quarter of the pupils at school A are planning on taking other vocational programmes.

School A's pie shows 'other vocational programmes as 25%'; 25% = $\frac{1}{4}$.

Statement B is true.

Statement C: More than half the pupils at school B are planning on doing an apprenticeship.

Apprenticeship sector in School B's pie chart shows 60%; 60% > 50% = $\frac{1}{2}$.

Statement C is true.

**156** Statement A: The proportion of pupils achieving A*–A improved in year two.

A*–A sector is smaller in year two chart.

Statement A is not true.

Statement B: The proportion of D–G grades remained the same.

The D–G sector is smaller in year two chart.

Statement 2 is not true.

Statement C: The proportion of pupils achieving A*–C grades improved in year 2.

The D–G sector is smaller in year two chart, so combined other grades increased in year two.

Statement C is true.

Statement D: We are not able to tell whether more pupils achieved a C and above in year two.

The pie charts show proportions only so it is not possible to say how many pupils achieved each grade.

Statement D is true.

**157** From the pie chart, in year one, half the pupils achieved grades D–G.

130 pupils/2 = 65 pupils

In year two, 30% of 120 gained grades D–G.

30% of 120 pupils = 0.3 × 120 pupils = 36 pupils

Comparing: 65 pupils − 36 pupils = 29 pupils

**158** Largest sector for level 5 is on the chart for 2011.

**159** Combining the sectors for level 4 and 5, in 2012 they form half of the circle.

**160** Data for level 4 and above:

A: 30 + 36 = 66; B: 50 + 20 = 70; C: 62 + 14 = 76; D = 70 + 5 = 75:

In order: 66, 70, 75, 76

Median = (70 + 75)/2 = 72.5

**161** 40/75 × 100% = 53%, ie A

**162**   Statement A: The mean percentage of GCSE grades A*–C for the first four years of the chart was 44% (to the nearest whole number).

Mean for years 2008–2011: (35% + 42% + 47% + 51%)/4 = 43.75% = 44% (to nearest whole number)

Statement A is true.

Statement B: The percentage of GCSE grades A*–C in 2008 was less than half of that is 2014.

2008 = 35%; 2014 = 75%

35 ÷ 75 = 0.46 < 0.5

Statement B is true.

Statement C: The percentage of grades A*–C increased each year.

2013 saw a decrease.

Statement C is not true.

Statement D: The median percentage of GCSE grades A*–C over the seven-year period was 51%.

The middlemost value if the columns are arranged in order of height is the data for 2011, so the median value was 51%.

Statement D is true.

**163**   Multiplying each value by its frequency, the total number of days of unauthorised absence

$= 15 \times 1 + 12 \times 2 + 8 \times 3 + 4 \times 4 + 18 \times 5 + 7 \times 6 + 5 \times 7 + 4 \times 8 + 7 \times 9 + 15 \times 10$

$= 15 + 24 + 24 + 16 + 90 + 42 + 35 + 32 + 63 + 150$

$= 491$

**164**   Statement A: The range of days of unauthorised absence is 10.

The highest number of days of consecutive unauthorised absence is 10; the lowest is 1.

Range = 10 – 1 = 9

Statement A is not true.

Statement B: The highest frequency (tallest bar) is for 5 consecutive days of unauthorised days of absence; the mode is 5.

Statement B is true.

Statement C: The median number of consecutive days of unauthorised absence is 5.5.

Accumulating the frequencies:

| | | |
|---|---|---|
| 1 | 15 | 15 |
| 2 | 12 | 27 |
| 3 | 8 | 35 |
| 4 | 4 | 39 |
| **5** | **18** | **57** |
| 6 | 7 | 64 |
| 7 | 5 | 69 |
| 8 | 4 | 73 |
| 9 | 7 | 80 |
| 10 | 15 | 95 |

95 recorded absences; median is the 48th

39 < 48 < 57 so median is 5

Statement C is not true.

**165**   Increases:

2008: 10 − 10 = 0

2009: 15 − 10 = 5

2010: 18 − 15 = 3

2011: 20 − 18 = 2

2012: 23 − 20 = 3

2013: 25 − 23 = 2

2014: 29 − 25 = 4

**166**   Average = (10 + 10 + 15 + 18 + 20 + 23 + 25 + 29)/8 = 150/8 = 18.758 years of data

**167**   Median = average of data items 4 and 5

2010: 18

2011: 20

(18 + 20)/2 = 38/2 = 19

**168**   Reading the column heights:

15 + 35 + 12 = 62

Proportion = 62/104 = 0.5961 … = 0.6 (to 1 dp)

**169**    Data from chart (first and third columns) = 15 + 12 = 27

Plus additional 25: 27 + 25 = 52

Proportion: 52 out of 104 = 52/104 × 100% = 50%

**170**    Statement A: The overall results in test 2 were higher than in test 1.

Test 2 shows generally higher marks: more achieved marks of between 61 and 80 for test 2. Fewer achieved marks of between 0 and 60 for test 2.

Statement A is true.

Statement B: The scores between 41 and 60 decreased in test 2 by one-third.

$$\frac{3}{9} = \frac{1}{3}$$

Statement B is true.

Statement C: 85% of pupils scored more than 40% in test 2.

6 + 15 + 3 = 24

$$\frac{24}{30} = 80\%$$

Statement C is not true.

**171**    Statement A: In all four years, the proportion of girls applying to university is greater than the proportion of boys applying for university.

| %     | 2011 | 2012 | 2013 | 2014 |
|-------|------|------|------|------|
| Girls | 30   | 40   | 24   | 30   |
| Boys  | 25   | 25   | 26   | 35   |

In 2013 and 2014, the percentage of girls is less than that of boys.

Statement A is not true.

Statement B: The highest proportion of boys applying for university was in 2012.

In 2014, 35% applied, which is greater than the 25% in 2012.

Statement B is not true.

Statement C: The highest proportion of all students applying for university was in 2012.

For both 2012 and 2014 the percentage is 65%.

Statement C is not true.

Statement D: In each year, more than 50% of the students applied for university.

Totals are:

| % | 2011 | 2012 | 2013 | 2014 |
|---|------|------|------|------|
| Girls | 30 | 40 | 24 | 30 |
| Boys | 25 | 25 | 26 | 35 |
| Total | 55 | 65 | 50 | 65 |

In 2013 only 50% applied.

Statement D is true.

**172** $\dfrac{19}{40} + \dfrac{29}{40} + \dfrac{27}{40} = \dfrac{75}{40}$

Mean = $\dfrac{75}{40} \div 3 = \dfrac{25}{40} = 0.625 \times 1005 = 62.5\% =$
63% (to nearest whole number)

**173** Statement A: The mean mark for test 1 is 25.

Test 1 results in order: 19, 25, 25, 27, 36.

Median is third value = 25.

Mode = 25 (frequency 2)

Mean = (25 + 36 + 27 + 25 + 19)/5 = 26.4

Statement A is not true.

Statement B: The range of marks in test 3 is 17.

Highest = 24; lowest = 15; range = 24 − 15 = 9

Statement B is true.

Statement C: The lowest marks were achieved in test 1.

The lowest mark was 15, pupil E in test 3.

Considering the total marks achieved:

Test 1: 25 + 36 + 27 + 25 + 19 = 132

Test 2: 28 + 31 + 29 + 27 + 18 = 133

Test 3: 16 + 24 + 19 + 22 + 15 = 96

Statement C is not true.

Statement D: The modal mark over all three tests was 25.

There are three modes: 19, 25 and 27.

Statement D is not true.

**174**  Data for 'Resistant materials' is

Year one: 35%

Year five: 10%

Drop in popularity = 35% − 10% = 25%

**175**  Data is: 40 30 50 35 25

In order: 25 30 35 40 50

Middle value is 35

**176**  Column 4 has the right data in the right order according to the legend.

**177**  55 + 20 + 35 = 110

Mean = 110/3 = 36.666 = 37% to the nearest whole percentage

**178**  Statement A: In school 3, 65% were graded as 'Needs improvement'.

Reading the school 3 column, 35% (values between 65% and 100%) were graded 'needs improvement'.

Statement A is not true.

Statement B: More than half the lessons in school 1 were graded 'Needs improvement'.

Reading the school 1 column, 55% were graded 'needs improvement' (between 45% and 100%).

$55\% > 50\% = \dfrac{1}{2}$

Statement B is true.

Statement C: In school 2, ⅘ of the lessons were graded 'good' or 'outstanding'.

Reading the school 2 column, 80% were graded 'good' or 'outstanding': $80\% = \dfrac{4}{5}$

Statement C is true.

**179**  School 2: 5 lessons are outstanding

On bar chart shown as 25%

1 lesson represents 25% ÷ 5 = 5%

100% ÷ 5% = 20%

**180**  The section within the bar needs to show the accumulation of the data:

15

15 + 75 = 90

90 + 10 = 100

**181**  Examine the points near the top right-hand corner.

**182**  The number of points in the top right-hand quadrant = 9

The total number of points = 20

9/20 = 0.45

**183** The school data exceeds the national data when the graph is higher, ie in 2011.

**184** Statement A: The school's highest percentage score was in 2011.

Statement A: The school's highest percentage score was in 2011.

The 2013 percentage score is higher than the 2011 percentage score.

Statement A is not true.

Statement B: 2010 was the year when the school made the greatest amount of improvement in percentage points.

Data is:

| Year | % score | Change |
|------|---------|--------|
| 2008 | 60 | |
| 2009 | 60 | 0 |
| 2010 | 73 | 13 |
| 2011 | 79 | 6 |
| 2012 | 73.5 | −4.5 |
| 2013 | 86 | 12.5 |

Statement B is true.

Statement C: The percentage of pupils gaining 5 A*–C grades in the school fell in 2012.

Data table above shows negative change in 2012.

Statement C is true.

Statement D: The school is performing consistently below the national average.

The school performs higher than the national average in 2011.

Statement D is not true.

**185** Cost = £300 + 100 × £1 = £400

**186** Reading the graph at 30 miles the values are:

Dashed: £150

Dotty: £275

Difference = £275 − £150 = £125

**187** Statement A: For a distance of 20 miles, the Dotty Company charges £125 more than the Dashed Company.

Distance of 20 miles:

Reading up from 20 miles on the horizontal axis, Dotty charges £250, Dashed charges £100

£250 − £100 = £150

Statement A is not true.

Statement B: Both companies charge the same amount for a distance of 80 miles.

At 80 miles, the lines meet, indicating the same price for the same distance.

Statement B is true.

Statement C: The cost of hiring the Dashed Company for a journey of 120 miles is £600.

Dashed charges are rising by £100 for every 20 miles.

For 100 miles, the charge is £500.

For 120 miles: £500 + £100 = £600

Statement C is true.

Statement D: The Dotty Company is cheaper for all journeys up to 60 miles.

The dashed line is below the dotty line for 0–60 miles, so the Dashed Company is cheaper for those distances.

Statement D is not true.

**188**   124 − 48 = 76

**189**   Statement A: Altogether, 126 pupils took part in the survey.

The grid divisions are 4 (20 ÷ 5) on the vertical scale. The highest point, which shows the total number of pupils, is at 124.

Statement A is not true.

Statement B: Half the pupils did less than 15 hours per week.

Half the pupils = 62

Reading across from 62 on the vertical axis, and down onto the horizontal axis, the reading is less than 15.

Statement B is true.

Statement C: Approximately 48 pupils did less than 10 hours per week.

Reading across from the vertical axis at 48, and then down to the horizontal axis, the reading is 10. This means 48 pupils did less than 10 hours homework.

Statement C is true.

Statement D: Exactly 12 pupils did more than 20 hours per week.

Read up from the horizontal axis at 20 hours, and across to the vertical axis, the reading is 115 pupils.

124 − 115 = 9

Statement D is not true.

**190**    Inspection of the boxplots to match the data

Data is:

|   | Low | LQ | M | UQ | High |
|---|-----|-----|-----|-----|------|
| **A** | 20 | 45 | 60 | 90 | 95 |
| **B** | 10 | 30 | 50 | 75 | 90 |
| **C** | 45 | 60 | 64 | 80 | 90 |
| **D** | 20 | 35 | 50 | 65 | 80 |

**191**    $\dfrac{1}{4}$ scored between 50 and 80

$\dfrac{1}{4}$ of 48 pupils = 12 pupils

**192**    Statement A: Many pupils found test 2 easier than test 1.

The marks for test 2 are generally lower, implying that it was more difficult.

Statement A is not true.

Statement B: The interquartile range of test 1 is more than twice that of the interquartile range of test 2.

Test 1 interquartile range 80 − 25 = 55

Test 2 interquartile range 45 − 20 = 25

55 > 25 × 2

Statement B is true.

Statement C: The range of marks for test 2 is 60.

Range for test 2 is 60 − 5 = 55

Statement C is not true.

Statement D: 25% of the pupils gained 80% or more in test 1.

Upper quartile for test 1 is 80%; above that 25% gained higher marks.

Statement D is true.

**193**    An increase by 13 percentage points increases all the marks, so the interquartile range is not changed.

45 − 20 = 25

**194**   Class 1: 80 − 20 = 60

Class 2: 85 − 30 = 55

Difference: 60 − 55 = 5

**195**   The interquartile range will remain the same, since all marks have been reduced: 70 − 45 = 25.

**196**   Statement A: The range of marks for class B is lower than for class A.

It is possible to decide on the size of the ranges by inspection. It can also be 'proved' mathematically:

Class A range: 98 − 44 = 54

Class B range: 75 − 45 = 30

Statement A is true.

Statement B: Fewer people in class A gained over 76% than in class B.

76% is the upper quartile for test A, and the highest mark for test B. 25% of pupils scored above 76 in test A and none scored higher in test B.

Statement B is not true.

Statement C: 21 pupils in class B scored 60 or more in the test.

60 is the lower quartile for test B.

75% of the pupils = $\dfrac{3}{4} \times 28 = 21$

Statement C is true.

Statement D: Seven pupils in class A gained more than 80%.

$\dfrac{7}{28} = 25$.

The upper quartile is marked at a score of less than 80%.

Statement D is not true.

**197**   By inspection, the values for boxplot 2 match.

|       | Low | LQ | M  | UQ | High |
|-------|-----|----|----|----|------|
| **1** | 30  | 45 | 60 | 75 | 80   |
| **2** | 30  | 50 | 70 | 80 | 85   |
| **3** | 30  | 38 | 50 | 70 | 90   |
| **4** | 30  | 40 | 65 | 75 | 85   |

**198**   Year four median = 42

Year five median = 48

Increase = 48 − 42 = 6

**199**   Year five: 59 − 35 = 24

Year four: 49 − 32 = 17

24 − 17 = 7

**200**   Statement A: The median has increased by 16 points over the three-year period.

Median in year three is 36; median in year five is 48

Increase is 12

Statement A is not true.

Statement B: There is a greater range of scores in year five than in either of the other two years.

Distance from top to bottom is greater for year five.

Statement B is true.

Statement C: The interquartile range in year four is 17.

Interquartile range in year three is 43 − 25 = 18

Statement C is true.

Statement D: All pupils have improved in reading over the three-year period.

It is not possible to tell whether all the pupils improved, as the boxplot only provides a summary of results.

Statement D is not true.

**201**   Look for the boxplot showing the highest top mark, and the highest bottom mark.

**202**   n = 104

$$\frac{n}{10} = \frac{104}{10} = 10.4$$

10.4 + 7 = 17.4 = 17 (to the nearest whole number)

**203**   F − 32 = 75 − 32 = 43

$$C = 5 \times \frac{43}{9} = 24$$

75°F = 24°C

**204**   65 × 0.6 + Part two mark × 0.4 = 70

39 + Part two mark × 0.4 = 70

Part two mark × 0.4 = 31

Part two mark = 31/0.4 = 78

**205**   $\frac{18}{45} \times 0.4 + \frac{28}{60} \times 0.6 = 0.16 + 0.28 = 0.44 = 0.44 \times 100\% = 44\%$

**206**    Paper 1:

30% of 63 out of 80 as a percentage = $0.3 \times 63/80 \times 100\% = 23.6\%$

Paper 2:

70% of 49 out of 65 as a percentage = $0.7 \times 49/65 \times 100\% = 52.8\%$

**207**    First paper: $\dfrac{16}{40} \times 100\% = 40\%$

20% of 40% = $\dfrac{20}{100} \times 40\% = 8\%$

Second paper: $\dfrac{45}{80} \times 100\% = 56.25\%$

80% of 56.25% = $\dfrac{80}{100} \times 56.25\% = 45\%$

Final score: 8% + 45% = 53%

**208**    $(0.3 \times 105 + 0.5 \times 96 + 0.2 \times 125)/2.5 = (31.5 + 48 + 25)/2.5 = 104.5/2.5 = 41.8 = 42$ (to the nearest whole number)

**209**    Time = distance ÷ speed

125 miles ÷ 50mph = 2.5 hours

11:00 − 2.5 hours = 8:30

**210**    Time taken to walk = 12km ÷ 5kph = 2.4 hours

0.4 of an hour is 24 minutes $(0.4 \times 60)$

$2 \times 15$ minutes = 30 minutes of breaks.

Total time = 2 hours 54 minutes

09:00 + 2:54 = 11:54

Finishing time = 11:54

**211**    11:15 + 0:30 = 11:45: time of leaving Calais: 11:45

48km $\times$ 5 ÷ 8 = 30 miles

30 miles ÷ 45mph = $\dfrac{2}{3}$ hour = 40 minutes

11:45 + 0:40 = 12:25

Time at hotel: 12:25

**212**    5 miles = 8km; 1km = $\dfrac{5}{8}$ miles

120km = $120 \times \dfrac{5}{8}$ miles = 75 miles

Time: 75 miles @ 50 mph takes 75/50 hours = 1.5 hours

16:30 − 1.5 hours = 15:00

Leave at 15:00

# Show me: solutions for numeracy practice papers

## Numeracy Practice Paper 1

### Mental questions

**1**  $20 \times 10$ minutes = 200 minutes

200 + 15 = 215

$215 \div 60 = 3$ hours and some left over!

$60 \times 3 = 180$

215 − 180 = 35

**2**  £253.05/3 = £84.35

**3**  $24 \times 2.5 =$ £60

**4**  1.2km $\times 4 = 4.8$km

**5**  $65/100 \times 80 = 13 \times 4 = 52$

**6**  €360 = $360 \times$ £0.8 = £288

**7**  $\dfrac{2}{3} \times 1074 = 2 \times 358 = 716$

716/10 = 72 (rounded up to the next whole number)

**8**  $3 \times 2$km = 6km

Time = distance/speed

6km/8kph = $\frac{3}{4}$ hr = 45 mins

**9**  $\dfrac{80}{100} \times 240 = 8 \times 24 = 192$

**10**  $0.4 \times 7.3 = (4 \times 73)/100 = 292/100 = 2.92$

**11**  $51/60 \times 100\% = 17 \times 5\% = 85\%$

**12**  $6 \times 25 = 150$

150/40 = 4 packs (rounded up to the nearest whole number)

## Onscreen questions

1  Number of siblings:

$(0 \times 5) + (1 \times 8) + (2 \times 7) + (3 \times 6) + (4 \times 3) + (5 \times 1) = 0 + 8 + 14 + 18 + 12 + 5 = 57$

Number of children surveyed:

$5 + 8 + 7 + 6 + 3 + 1 = 30$

Mean = 57/30 = 1.9

2  Number of staff = 6 + 9 + 5 + 8 + 7 + 1 = 36

Number who cycle = 5 + 1 = 6

Percentage who cycle = $6/36 \times 100\%$ = 16.6666% = 16.17% (to 2 dp)

3  Counting the number of points above the diagonal, there are 11 pupils who did better in the oral test.

11/28 = 0.3928 = 0.4 (to 1 dp)

4  Mon. wk 1

127 − 25 − 24 − 22 − 28 = 28

Tue. wk 5

126 − 26 − 26 − 27 − 24 = 23

Wed. wk 2

130 − 27 − 27 − 28 − 22 = 26

Fri. wk 2

121 − 25 − 21 − 26 − 25 = 24

5  Goals scored in six games:

$6 \times 4.8$ = 28.8; she scored 29 goals in 6 games

$7 \times 5$ = 35

35 − 29 = 6

She must score 6 goals in the seventh game

6  Statement A: Test 3 has the smallest range of marks.

Visual inspection shows Test three has smallest range.

Looking at data

| Test | High | Low | Range |
|------|------|-----|-------|
| 1 | 80 | 5 | 75 |
| 2 | 95 | 10 | 85 |
| 3 | 100 | 55 | 45 |
| 4 | 99 | 40 | 59 |

Statement A is true.

Statement B: Test 2 was found to be the most difficult.

Test 1's highest mark is lower than that of test 2, and test 1's lowest mark is lower than that of test 2, so test 2 is not the most difficult.

Statement B is not true.

Statement C: The interquartile range for test 1 was 40.

Test 1: LQ = 25; UQ = 65; IQR = 65 − 25 = 40

Statement C is true.

Statement D: Over half the pupils achieved over 65% in test 4.

The median value for test 4 is 65.

Statement D is true.

**7** 42 + 6 = 48

48/15 = 3 (rounded down to the nearest whole number)

This means there will be 3 free places

48 − 3 = 45

45 × £15.55 = £699.75

£699.75/48 = £14.58 (to the nearest penny)

£14.58 + £18 = £32.58

**8** Total number of students = 46 + 89 + 27 + 18 = 180

English A*–C:

46 + 89 = 135

135/180 = 75%

New target = 81%

0.81 × 180 = 146 (rounded up to nearest whole number)

146 − 135 = 11

**9** Total number of students = 46 + 89 + 27 + 18 = 180

% A*–A grades:

46/180 = 25.56%

37/180 = 20.56%

42/180 = 23.33%

51/180 = 28.33%

Mean percentage:

(25.55 + 20.55 + 23.33 + 28.33)%/4 = 97.76%/4 = 24.44% = 24% (to nearest whole number)

10    Statement A: There are more teachers under the age of 30 in the school in 2014 than in 2009.

The sector for 'Under 30' is smaller in the 2014 pie chart than in the 2009 pie chart.

Statement A is true.

Statement B: The age profile of the teachers in 2009 was generally younger than in 2014.

There were more under 30s and 30–39, but also more 50–59.

Statement B is not true.

Statement C: Approximately 75% of teachers in the school in 2009 were aged between 30 and 49 years.

In the 2009 chart, combining the 30–39 and 40–49 sectors creates a slice approximately 75% of the pie.

Statement C is true.

11

| Pupil | High | Low | Range |
|-------|------|-----|-------|
| 1 | 65 | 52 | 13 |
| 2 | 60 | 47 | 13 |
| 3 | 61 | 57 | 14 |
| **4** | **56** | **32** | **24** |

12    Statement A: The mode and the median are the same.

Data in order: 39, 62, 65, 65, 74, 87

Median = 65

65 appears twice so mode = 65 Statement A is true

Statement B: The mean is lower than the median.

Mean = (39 + 62 + 65 + 65 + 74 + 87)/6 = 392/6 = 65.3

65.3 > 65

Statement B is not true.

Statement C: The range is 48.

Range = 87 – 39 = 48

Statement C is true.

**13**   A: 14%; B: 6%; C: −14%; D: 1%; E: 12%. Pupil A made the most progress.

**14**   30 miles per hour means every mile takes 2 minutes

35 miles will take 70 minutes

Journey time = 1 hour 10 minutes

Play starts 19:30

Arrival time = 19:15

Departure time = 18:05

**15**   Car drivers: 8 + 6 = 14

Sample: 6 + 8 + 6 + 8 + 6 + 3 = 37

14/37 × 250 = 94.59 = 95 (to the next nearest whole number)

**16**   Median – there are 80 in the survey, so read across from 40 on the vertical axis, and then down to the horizontal axis.

18 hours.

# Numeracy Practice Paper 2

## Mental questions

**1**   $\dfrac{80}{200} = \dfrac{8}{20} = \dfrac{4}{10} = 0.4$

**2**   18/25 × 100% = 18 × 4% = 72%

16/20 × 100% = 16 × 5% = 80%

(72 + 80)%/2 = 76%

**3**   $\dfrac{33}{220} = \dfrac{3}{20}$

**4**   10% of £260 = £26

20% of £260 = £52

£260 + £52 = £312

**5**   $0.3 \times 5.7 = 3 \times \dfrac{57}{100} = \dfrac{171}{100} = 1.71$

**6**   $\dfrac{5m}{0.45m} = \dfrac{500}{45} = 11.11 = 11$ (rounded down to nearest whole number)

**7**   44.31% + 40.69% = 85% = $\dfrac{85}{100} = \dfrac{17}{20}$

**8**   20 + 22 + 17 + 19 + 18 = 96

96/5 = 19.2

**9**   70% of 60 = 0.7 × 60 = 42

**10**  £160.50 × 33 = £5296.50

**11**  1 yen = £0.005; £1 = 1/0.005 yen

£150 = 150/0.005 yen = 30,000 yen

**12**  47 mins + 15 mins = 62 mins = 1 hr 2 mins

Lesson ends 11:00

Start film at 9:58

## Onscreen questions

**1**  1 hr 30 mins + 1 hr 25 mins + 1 hr + 1 hr = 4 hrs 55 mins

5 × 4 hours = 20 hours

5 × 55 mins = 275 mins = 4 hrs 35 mins

20 hours + 4 hours + 35 mins = 24 hours 35 mins

**2**  Statement A: The average mark for test 5 was higher than any other test.

Total marks for each test are

259 (1), 257 (2), 260 (3), 277 (4) and 276 (5)

276 < 277

Statement A is not true.

Statement B: The greatest range of marks was achieved in test 2.

No need to calculate all the ranges.

Test 1 range = 94 − 38 = 56

Test 2 range = 89 − 34 = 55

56 > 55

Statement B is not true.

Statement C: The median mark for test 1 was 63.5.

Marks in order: 38, 43, 84, 94

Median: (43 + 84)/2 = 63.5 Statement C is true.

Statement D: Pupil A achieved the lowest mean score.

There is no need to calculate all the mean marks. Pupils B and C both achieved higher marks than A in every test, so their mean will be higher.

Pupil D mean = (38 + 45 + 52 + 61 + 67)/5 = 263/5 = 52.6

Pupil A mean = (43 + 34 + 52 + 49 + 63)/5 = 241/5 = 48.2

Statement D is true.

**3**   Mean = (49 + 87 + 80 + 61 + 58)/5 = 335/5 = 67

Median:

In order: 49, 58, 61, 80, 87

Median = 61

Difference = 67 − 61 = 6

**4**   Pupil A

$(45 + 2 \times 52 + 3 \times 75)/6$

= (45 + 104 + 225)/6

= 374/6 = 62.33

Pupil B

$(63 + 2 \times 61 + 3 \times 62)/6$

= (63 + 122 + 186)/6

= 371/6 = 61.83

Pupil C

$(82 + 2 \times 65 + 3 \times 61)/6$

= (82 + 130 + 183)/6

= 395/6 = 65.83

65.83 > 62.33 > 61.83

Pupil C scores highest

**5**   Statement A: The median mark for test 2 is higher than the median mark for test 1.

For median, compare score for 30th pupil.

Test 1 median < 60

Test 2 median = 60

Statement A is true.

Statement B: The interquartile range is higher in test 2 than in test 1.

IQR is between 15th and 45th pupils.

Test 1 IRQ = 64 − 44 = 20

Test 2 IRQ = 68 − 48 = 20

Statement B is not true.

Statement C: 25% of pupils in test 1 obtained less than 40 marks.

25% of 60 = 15

Test 1 for 40 marks: 12 pupils scored less than 40

Statement C is not true.

Statement D: The overall marks for test 2 are higher than for test 1.

The test 1 graph is above and left of the test 2 graph.

Statement D is true.

**6**  Total number of bikes checked = 12 + 15 + 22 + 14 + 9 + 2 + 1 = 75

Total number of faults =

$(0 \times 12) + (1 \times 15) + (2 \times 22) + (3 \times 14) + (4 \times 9) + (5 \times 2) + (6 \times 1)$

= 0 + 15 + 44 + 42 + 36 + 10 + 6

= 153

Mean = 153/75 = 2.04 = 2 (to the nearest whole number)

**7**  Statement A: The percentage of pupils achieving level 4 and above has steadily increased over the last five years.

The level 4 and above graph dips in 2013.

Statement A is not true.

Statement B: The best results of the last five years were achieved in 2014.

The high point for level 4 and above is 2014. For level 5 and above, 2014 is the same as 2010 but higher than any other year.

Statement B is true.

Statement C: In 2011, 57% of pupils at Key Stage 2 achieved scores below level 4.

Data for 2011 shows 84% achieved level 4 or above.

100% − 87% = 13%

Statement C is not true.

Statement D: In 2010 and in 2014, half of all pupils achieved level 5 and above.

Data for 2010: 50%

Data for 2015: 50%

Statement D is true.

**8**  Pets:

$(0 \times 5) + (1 \times 9) + (2 \times 8) + (3 \times 4) + (4 \times 3) + (5 \times 2) + (6 \times 1)$

= 0 + 9 + 16 + 12 + 12 + 10 + 6

= 65

Children:

$5 + 9 + 8 + 4 + 3 + 2 + 1 = 32$

Mean $= 65/32 = 2.03125 = 2.03$

**9**  $3 + 4 = 7$

£7054/7 = £1007.71

Retain decimal places (pence) until the final calculation.

£1007.71 $\times$ 4 = £4030.85 = £4031 (to the nearest whole £)

**10**  Imagine a line starting at (50, 0) and ending at (100, 50) and identify the point on that line: (85, 35).

**11**  Transport: £2352/30 = £78.40

Accommodation: 54,360 SEK/30 = 1812 SEK

£1 = 12.08 SEK

1 SEK = £1/12.08

1812 SEK = £1812/12.08 = £150

Food, etc: 1184 SEK = £1184/12.08 = £98.01

Total: £78.40 + £150 + £98.01 = £326.41

**12**  $101 - 84 = 17$

17/115 $\times$ 100% = 14.78% = 14.8% (1 dp)

**13**  The percentages given are for different quantities, so it would be incorrect to add the three percentages together and divide by 3.

Total number of girls = 113 + 52 + 79 = 244

Total number of pupils in the three schools = 210 + 108 + 152 = 470

Percentage = 244/470 $\times$ 100% = 51.9%

**14**  2012: 21% + 23% = 44%

2014: 25% + 27% = 52%

Difference = 8%

8% of 207 = 0.08 $\times$ 207 = 16.56 = 17 (to nearest whole person)

**15**  Class S interquartile range: $62 - 45 = 17$

Class W interquartile range: $69 - 40 = 29$

Difference = $29 - 17 = 12$

**16**  2012:

Level 4 and above = 51% + 5% = 56%

56% of 32 = 0.56 $\times$ 32 = 18

2014:

Level 4 and above = 63% + 6% = 69%

69% of 28 = 0.69 × 28 = 19

Difference = 19 − 18 = 1

# Numeracy Practice Paper 3

## Mental questions

1. 315:15 = 63:3 = 21:1

2. 0.005 ungraded

   1 − 0.005 = 0.995 achieved a grade

   0.995/0.005 = 995/5 = 199

3. 30 × €20 = €600

   €600 = 600 × £0.80 = £480

4. 40 × £8.50 = £340

   10% of £340 = £34

   £340 − £34 = £306

5. 3 + 4 = 7

   £1764/7 = £252

   £252 × 4 = £1008

6. 12% of 84 = 0.12 × 84 = 10.08 = 10 (to the nearest whole number)

   84 − 10 = 74

7. 5 × 1 hr 5 mins = 5 hrs + 25 mins

   Day is 7 hours long.

   7 hrs − 5 hrs 25 mins = 1 hr 35 mins

8. 38 × 6 = 228; 228 × £9 = £2052

9. Time taken (hrs) = distance (miles)/speed (mph)

   $$= \frac{60}{45} = \frac{4}{3} = 1\frac{1}{4}$$

   $1\frac{1}{3}$ hrs = 1 hr 20 mins

10. 4/9 are male; 5/9 are female

    5/9 of 63 = 5 × 7 = 35

**11** £425 out of £675 = $\dfrac{425}{675} = \dfrac{17}{27}$

**12** 52 × £5.50 = £286

## Onscreen questions

**1** Starting 15 mins earlier and ending 5 mins later adds 20 mins to each day. Reducing the break by 15 mins means net increase of 35 mins per day.

OR

Present school lesson time: 6 hrs 45 mins − 1 hr 30 mins = 5 hrs 15 mins

New time: 7 hrs 5 mins − 1 hr 15 mins = 5 hrs 50 mins

50 − 15 = 35

**2** 30 pupils achieved less than 40.

Total number taking the test = 108

108 − 30 = 78

**3** 0.5m$^2$ = 5000cm$^2$

5000/625 = 8

30/8 = 3.75 = 4 (rounded up to the next whole number)

**4** Cost of additional miles:

45 × 65p = £29.25

35/20 = 1 (rounded down)

Only 1 free entrance

35 − 1 = 34

34 × £4.50 = £153

Total cost:

£250 + £29.25 + £153 = £432.25

Cost per pupil = £432.25/35 = £12.35

**5** Mean score = sum of two scores/2

The pupil with the highest mean score is the pupil with the highest score total.

Look at the two pupils who scored the highest in each test, and whose points are nearest to (100, 100).

(96, 85) has mean score of 90.5

(83, 91) has mean score of 87

No one else scored higher than 87 on either test, so no more calculations required.

**6**  28/35 = 0.8

14/20 = 0.7

13/30 = 0.433 (3 dp)

23/30 = 0.767 (3 dp)

11/15 = 0.733 (3 dp)

The answer has to be correct to 2 dp, so retain third dp in the working.

Total = 3.433

3.433/5 = 0.6866 = 0.69 (2 dp)

**7**  $\dfrac{4}{11}$ of £5654 = 4/11 × £5654 = £2056

**8**  Length = 25m + 2 × 6m = 37m

Width = 16.5m + 2 × 6m = 28.5m

Area required: 37m × 28.5m = 1054.5m$^2$

**9**  Statement A: The total number of pupils in years 7 to 11 is 418.

Total number of pupils = 74 + 85 + 92 + 79 + 88 = 418

Statement A is true.

Statement B: The mean number of pupils per year group is 83 (to the nearest whole number).

418/5 = 83.6 = 84 (to the nearest whole number)

Statement B is not true.

Statement C: The median number of pupils per year group is 85.

In order: 74, 79, 85, 88, 92

Middlemost value = 85

Statement C is true.

Statement D: Approximately 21% of the pupils are in year 11.

88/418 × 100% = 21.05%

Statement D is true.

**10**  In school:

24 × 0.7 = 17

22 × 0.6 = 13

16 × 0.5 = 8

21 × 0.3 = 6

$28 \times 0.6 = 17$

$24 \times 0.25 = 6$

$17 \times 0.4 = 7$

Total number in school = $17 + 13 + 8 + 6 + 17 + 6 + 7 = 74$

**11**   Total number of minutes = $4 + 3 + 5 + 2 + 9 + 4 = 27$

Total number of secs = $26 + 52 + 25 + 55 + 29 + 17 = 204$

27 mins/6 = 4.5 mins = 4 mins 30 secs

204 secs/6 = 34 secs

4 mins 30 secs + 34 secs = 5 mins 4 secs

**12**   2014 interquartile range: $69 - 42 = 27$

2012 interquartile range: $65 - 35 = 30$

Difference = 3

**13**   Total number of laps:

$(1 \times 3) + (2 \times 26) + (3 \times 48) + (4 \times 36) + (5 \times 28) + (6 \times 10) + (7 \times 1) = 550$

Total distance:

$550 \times 400m = 220,000m = 220km$

**14**   Total number of pupils = $3 + 26 + 48 + 36 + 28 + 10 + 1 = 152$

Median is mean of pupils 76/77

Cumulative frequencies are

| Laps | Pupils | Cum Freq |
| --- | --- | --- |
| 1 | 3 | 3 |
| 2 | 26 | 29 |
| 3 | 48 | 77 |
| 4 | 36 | |
| 5 | 28 | |
| 6 | 10 | |
| 7 | 1 | |

Median pupils (76/77) fall into the category of 3 laps

**15**   59.4% of 2643 = $0.594 \times 2643 = 1569.942 = 1570$ (to the nearest whole number)

**16**  Statement A: Fewer Year 8 children spend more than three hours playing computer games per day than Year 7 children.

More than 3 hrs:

Year 7: $0.15 \times 28 = 4.2$

Year 8: $0.3 \times 35 = 10.5$

$10.5 > 4.2$

Statement A is not true.

Statement B: More than 50% of the Year 8 pupils surveyed play computer games for more than two hours per day.

More than 2 hours/Year 8:

$35\% + 30\% = 65\% > 50\%$

Statement B is true.

Statement C: Of the Year 7 children surveyed, only 4 play computer games for less than one hour per day.

Less than one hour/Year 7:

$15\%$ of $28 = 0.15 \times 28 = 4.2$

Statement C is true.

# Numeracy Practice Paper 4

## Mental questions

**1**  $58.5m \times 75m = 4387.5m^2$

**2**  £6525/60 = £108.75

**3**  $\dfrac{14}{322} = \dfrac{2}{46} = \dfrac{1}{23}$

**4**  $6.9m - 3.42m = 3.48m$

**5**  Ratio M:F = 7:13

Proportion of males = $7/(7 + 13) = 7/20 = 0.35$

**6**  $3 + 4.5 + 5.7 = 13.2$

$13.2km/3 = 4.4km = 4km + 400m$

**7**  $30 \times 20 \times 15 = 600 \times 15 = 9000$

**8**  $30 - 18 = 12$

12/30 arrived on time

12/30 × 100% = 40%

**9**  0.78 achieved

100 − 78 = 22

0.22 did not achieve

$0.22 = \dfrac{22}{100} = \dfrac{11}{50}$

**10**  12 stone = 12 × 6.35kg = 76.2kg

**11**  76% of 120 = 76/100 × 120 = 91.2 = 91 (to the nearest whole number)

**12**  16/20 × 100% = 80%

18/30 × 100% = 60%

(80 + 60)%/2 = 70%

## Onscreen questions

**1**  Substituting F = 79 in the formula:

5 × (79 − 32)/9 = 5 × 47/9 = 235/9 = 26.11 = 26 (to the nearest whole number)

**2**  4 and above:

6 + 1 + 8 + 3 = 18

Number of pupils:

2 + 4 + 9 + 6 + 1 + 1 + 3 + 5 + 8 + 3 = 42

Proportion:

$\dfrac{18}{42} = \dfrac{3}{7}$

**3**  Monday 15:30–17:30 = 2 hrs

2 hrs = 120 mins = 6 × 20 mins

Time for 6 appointments; 16 − 6 = 10 left to do.

Break 17:30–17:45

Monday 17:45–19:00 = 1 hr 15 min

1 hr 15 mins = 75 mins = 3 × 20 mins + 15 mins

Time for 3 appointments: 10 − 3 = 7 left to do.

Tuesday: 6 appointments before the break (same schedule as Monday) and final appointment at 17:45

Finish at 18:05

**4**    Test 3 has the lowest low mark and the lowest high mark.

**5**    Total number of observations = 10 + 8 + 14 + 9 = 41

Number graded as 'Good' = 5 + 3 + 5 + 2 = 15

15/41 × 100% = 36.6%

**6**    Cost of 45: 45 × £9.50 = £427.50

Cost of 50

15% discount means price is 0.85 × £9.50

50 × 0.85 × £9.50 = £403.75

Saving: £427.50 − £403.75 = £23.75

**7**    Pass score = 0.2A + 0.3B + 0.5C = 45

Substituting for parts A and B:

0.2 × 52 + 0.3 × 49 + 0.5C = 45

10.4 + 14.7 + 0.5C = 45

25.1 + 0.5C = 45

0.5C = 45 − 25.1 = 20.1

C = 40.2 = 40 (to the nearest whole number)

**8**    300 inches = 300 × 2.5cm = 750cm

290 inches = 290 × 2.5cm = 725cm

750cm × 725cm = 54,3750cm²

51m² = 510,000cm²

543,750 − 510,000 = 33,750cm²

**9**    $4\frac{3}{4}$ out of $21\frac{3}{4}$ = $\frac{4.75}{21.75}$ × 100% = 21.8 = 22 (to the nearest whole number)

**10**    Statement A: The card-making enterprise took the highest amount of money over the four weeks.

Card making: 32 + 56 + 65 + 43 = 196

Pot plants: 53 + 65 + 48 + 32 = 198

Badges: 44 + 35 + 69 + 65 = 213

196 < 198 < 213

Statement A is not true.

Statement B: The lowest sales were made by the pot-plant enterprise in week 4

Two lowest plotted points are card making (week 1) and pot plants (week 4)

Statement B is not true.

Statement C: The range of sales totals is £37.

Range = £69 − £32 = £37

Statement C is true.

Statement D: The mean sales total of the badge-making group is £50.58

£213/4 = £53.25

Statement D is not true.

**11**  210mm × 297mm = 21cm × 29.7cm = 623.7cm$^2$

**12**  Boys: (1.1 + 0.9 + −2.5 + − 0.2)/4 = −0.7/4 = −0.2 (1 dp)

Girls: (0.4 + 1.2 + 0.6 + 1.8)/4 = 4.0/4 = 1.0

**13**  2013: 77.8 + 76.4 + 81.5 + 75.5 = 311.2

311.2/4 = 77.8

2014: 78.7 + 79.9 + 83.4 + 79.2 = 321.2

321.2/4 = 80.3

Difference: 80.3 − 77.8 = 2.5

**14**  2013: 18% of 76 = 0.18 × 76 = 13.68 = 14 (1 dp)

2014: 23% of 85 = 0.23 × 85 = 19.55 = 20 (1 dp)

Difference: 20 − 14 = 6

**15**  Increase: 28.5 − 26.4 = 2.1

2.1/26.4 × 100% = 7.95% = 8.0%

**16**  £5 = €8; €1 = £$\frac{5}{8}$

Accommodation/meals:

€4400 = 4400 × £$\frac{5}{8}$ = £2750

£2750/20 = £137.50

Entry fees: £580/20 = £29

Sundries: £675/20 = £33.75

Spending money:

€50 = 50 × £$\frac{5}{8}$ = £31.25

Total cost per pupil = £137.50 + £75 + £29 + £33.75 + £31.25 = £306.50

# Literacy glossary

**Adjective:** adds a description for a noun: the *English* teacher. An adjectival phrase is an adverb with an adjective (eg *very clever*). An adjectival clause (a relative clause) contains a verb and begins with a relative adverb (when, why, where) or a relative pronoun (who, whom, whose, that or which); answers a question such as 'which one': Jane, *who came top in English*, was awarded the literature prize.

**Adverb:** often formed by adding -ly; modifies a verb, an adjective or another adverb. Adverbs describe how/where/when/for how long things are done. An adverbial phrase is a few words including an adverb: *as quickly as possible*. An adverbial clause (subordinate clause) contains a verb: *as soon as she saw sense*.

**Agreement:** rules of grammar dictate that agreement is required in terms of number (singular, plural), person (first, second, third), gender (male, female) and case (grammatical function of words such as pronouns).

**Ambiguity:** found in an expression that can be interpreted in more than one way; feature of unclear communication.

**Article:** there are three articles, the definite article (the) and two indefinite articles (a, an), which can be placed ahead of a noun. 'An' is used ahead of a noun which starts with a vowel.

**Audio:** using sound.

**Auxiliary verb:** see *verb*.

**Clause:** part of a sentence; it contains a noun or a pronoun and one finite verb (which can be 'understood').

**Closed syllable:** see *syllable*.

**Cohesion:** an underlying logic and consistency so as to allow the reader to follow the meaning; achieved through using grammatical features such as connectives to link information, or pronouns to refer back to a preceding noun.

**Colloquialism:** an everyday term which is unsuited to formal communications.

**Comparative:** an adjective ending in -er or preceded by 'more' which compares two people or things. See also *superlative*.

**Conjunction:** links two parts of a sentence together; see also *connective*. Coordinating conjunctions (and, but, or, so) link items of equal status; unequal items are linked by subordinating conjunctions (after, although, because, before, if, since, until, that, when, while).

**Connective:** a word that connects pairs of words, phrases, clauses and sentences; can be a conjunction (and) but adverbial phrases and clauses can also be connectives, eg finally, however, in other words, that is to say.

**Consistency:** maintaining eg the same tone throughout a letter, or styles regarding how words should be spelt (US/UK); see also *agreement*.

**Consonant:** letters and sounds that are not vowels.

**Contraction:** a shortened form created from two words: *we are* becomes *we're*.

**Contradiction:** a statement which contradicts; says the opposite of what has been suggested.

**Declarative sentence:** see *sentence*.

**Definite article:** 'the'; see *article*.

**Demonstrative pronoun:** see *pronoun*.

**Determiner:** limits or determines the reference of a noun which follows it (maybe later in the sentence).

| Determiner | Examples |
|---|---|
| articles | a, an, the |
| demonstratives | this, that, these, those |
| possessives | my, your, his, her, its, our, their |
| quantifiers | all, any, each, either, few, many, no, some |
| numbers | one, two, … |
| interrogatives | what, which, whose |

Closely linked to pronouns, and sometimes called 'adjectival pronouns', the determiner is often just the pronoun without a noun. The exception is our/ours.

|  | Pronoun | Determiner |
|---|---|---|
| **Demonstrative** | this | this (book) |
| **Indefinite** | some | some (pupils) |
| **Interrogative** | which | which (classroom) |
| **Personal** | we | we (teachers) |
| **Possessive** | ours | our (policy) |

**Dialect:** a version of a language which includes words and phrases particular to a region.

**Evaluate:** assess eg whether a statement is supported or implied by a test; make a judgement.

**Exclamative:** see *sentence*.

**Finite verb:** *see verb.*

**Grammar:** rules which determine how words are put together to form meaningful and unambiguous communications; includes syntax, the study of sentence structure.

**Homophones:** words that sound the same but are spelt differently.

**Imperative:** see *sentence*.

**Indefinite article:** 'a' or 'an'; see *article*.

**Infinitive verb:** base form of a verb; see *verb*.

**Interrogative pronoun:** see *pronoun*.

**Intransitive verb:** see *verb*.

**Mnemonic:** a device to help you to remember something, eg how to spell a word.

**Noun:** a word that names things such as people or places.

**Proper nouns** name people, places or institutions and always have a capital letter: Anne, London, Department for Education.

One test of a noun is: does 'a', 'an' or 'the' work in front of it?

A noun phrase is several words doing the work of a single noun, eg 'the head of humanities'.

**Number:** distinction used in the conjugation of verbs and in the spelling of nouns; either singular or plural.

**Object:** a noun (or pronoun) within a sentence, on the receiving end of some action: *Mr Jones read the lesson.* Not all sentences have objects.

**Open syllable:** see *syllable.*

**Paragraph:** one or more sentences grouped together to convey information about a single thought or topic, or a speaker's words; distinguished from previous and following paragraphs by a new line or spacing.

**Participle:** see *verb.*

**Person:** describes who is of concern in the sentence; can be first, second or third.

o  'I teach at the college' is written in the first person, from the writer's perspective. This is used in autobiographies and blogs.

o  'You should attend the art class' is written to the second person, and indicates only two people involved: the writer and the reader. This is commonly used in instruction manuals.

o  'He was absent too many times' is written about some other third person, from an outside perspective. This is used in most reporting in newspapers, and in the majority of novels where the writer is telling a story about a group of characters.

**Personal pronoun:** see *pronoun.*

**Phoneme:** a distinct unit of sound that distinguishes one word from another, eg 'b' and 'c' in bat and cat.

**Phonics:** a method of teaching reading in which people learn to associate letters with the speech sounds they represent, rather than learning to recognise the whole word as a unit.

**Phrase:** a group of words that act as a unit but do not include a verb, eg a noun phrase (he missed *almost every lesson*), an adjectival phrase (she is *fondly remembered*) or an adverbial phrase (he will arrive *in an hour*).

**Plural:** the form of a word that indicates more than one.

**Possessive pronoun:** see *pronoun.*

**Predicate:** part of a sentence which gives information about the subject, such as what the subject is, or is doing, or is like. (Mr Jones *taught Class B.*)

**Prefix:** a letter or letters added to the front of a word to make a new word.

**Preposition:** shows the position or relationship of one thing to another: *at* the chalkface, *over* the moon, *under* the table. NB: a prepositional phrase can work as an adverb or an adjective.

**Pronoun:** a word that stands in for a noun. Pronouns can be categorised according to their type (demonstrative, indefinite, interrogative, personal, possessive, reciprocal, reflexive and relative), where they appear in a sentence (subject/object), the person (first, second or third) and their number (singular/plural).

- **Demonstrative pronouns:** there are only four – this/that (singular) and these/those (plural).

- **Indefinite pronouns** provide a word for unspecified things or people. Examples are 'both', 'many', 'more' and 'most' plus any words starting with any-, every-, no- or some- and ending with -body, -one, -thing, such as 'nobody'.

- **Interrogative pronouns** are used in a question: which, what, who (subject), whom (object) and whose (possessive).

- **Personal pronouns** are a substitute for a noun, often a proper noun.

| Personal | Singular | | Plural | |
|---|---|---|---|---|
| | Subject | Object | Subject | Object |
| 1st person | I | me | we | us |
| 2nd person | you | you | you | you |
| 3rd person | he, she, it | him, her, it | they | them |

- **Possessive pronouns** indicate ownership or possession; see also *determiner*.

| Possessive | Singular | | Plural | |
|---|---|---|---|---|
| | Subject | Object | Subject | Object |
| 1st person | I | mine | we | ours |
| 2nd person | you | yours | you | yours |
| 3rd person | he, she, it | his, hers, its | they | theirs |

- **Reciprocal pronouns** show a reciprocal relationship: each other, one another.

- **Reflexive pronouns** end in -self or -selves and show something acting upon itself: myself, yourselves.

*Mary taught* herself *how to play the piano.*

- **Relative pronouns** can refer back to a previously mentioned noun and start a clause which adds information to the noun:

*Children* who do not attend regularly *tend to perform poorly in examinations.*

**Proper noun:** see *noun*.

**Punctuation:** marks used to separate words, sentences and parts of sentences, to clarify meaning.

**Sentence:** group of words starting with a capital letter and ending with a full stop or other closing punctuation (!, ?).

- **Declarative sentences** make a statement: *Mr Jones teaches Class B.*

- **Exclamative sentences** (an exclamation) express emotion: *Mr Jones teaches which class!*

- **Imperative sentences** (a command) give instruction: *Mr Jones, teach Class B.* Imperative sentences can also be exclamative: *Mr Jones, teach Class B!*

- **Interrogative sentences** (a question) ask for information: *Which class does Mr Jones teach?*

- **Sentence boundaries** – affected by capitalisation and appropriate punctuation – indicate the start and end of the sentence and the component parts of a sentence, eg a clause.

**Singular:** the form of a word that indicates only one.

**Standard English:** a version of English used in public communications, and expected in written texts.

**Statement:** a sentence which presents a fact or proposition.

**Style:** manner in which text is written; can reveal the writer's personality and voice, and perception of the audience; should match the needs of the communication (eg entertaining, informative).

**Subject:** the main noun (or pronoun) in a sentence: Mr Jones *read the lesson.* Every sentence needs a subject. Every sentence needs at least one finite verb.

**Suffix** (or **postfix**): a letter or letters added to the end of a word.

**Superlative:** an adjective ending in -est, or an adjective preceded by 'most', indicating the comparison of more than two people or things.

**Syllable:** a unit of spoken language; one uninterrupted sound. An **open syllable** ends on a vowel. A **closed syllable** ends on a consonant.

**Syntax:** see *grammar*.

**Tautology:** inclusion of superfluous words which repeat information already provided.

**Tense:** of a verb, indication of timeframe; see *verb*.

**Tone:** the attitude expressed through writing (eg formal/informal).

**Transitive verb:** see *verb*.

**Verb:** a 'doing' or 'being' word which describes some action or state. Every sentence has at least one finite verb within it.

The finite verb can consist of more than one word: the verb itself plus maybe an auxiliary verb. The finite always has a tense (past, present or future) and relates to a noun or pronoun which is the subject of the verb.

Writing out all the forms of a verb is called 'conjugating the verb'. It can help you to remember the different spellings of a verb, if you conjugate it and then look for patterns (see Table 1 for the conjugation of the verb 'to teach').

Finite verbs can be transitive (taking an object) and/or intransitive (not taking an object). See Table 2.

There are also non-finite verbs: the infinitive and the present and past participles, both of which can be used to create a finite version of the verb.

The infinitive form of the verb has the word 'to' in front of it: to buy, to teach, to think, to feel. A sentence is not grammatically correct if it just has an infinite verb; it needs a finite verb as well to complete the construction of the sentence.

In '*The headteacher decided to close the school early because of the adverse weather conditions*' the finite verb is 'decided' and 'to close' is an infinite verb.

The present participle of a verb is the -ing form of it, and a finite verb is created by using the appropriate form (right person, right tense) of the auxiliary verb 'to be'. It's called 'progressive' because it describes an action which continued to happen in the past or is continuing to happen in the present (see Table 3).

The past participle for regular verbs ends in -ed the same as the past tense form, but is used with the auxiliary verb 'to have' (see Table 4).

Many verbs are not regular! Then, the past tense differs from the past participle.

> *To write:   He <u>wrote</u> a letter.   He <u>had written</u> a letter.*

> *To be:   Mary <u>was</u> late.   Mary <u>has been</u> late many times.*

The perfect progressive tense involves using both auxiliary verbs: to be and to have.

| Past perfect progressive | Present perfect progressive |
|---|---|
| He <u>had been teaching</u> science. | She <u>has been teaching</u> art. |

**Voice:** active or passive, describes the form of verb used in a sentence. Active = *Mr Jones thanked the parents.* Passive = *The parents were thanked by Mr Jones.*

**Vowel:** a speech sound made with your mouth open and your tongue in the middle of your mouth not touching your teeth or lips. There are five vowels in the alphabet: a, e, i, o, u. All the other letters, apart from the vowels, are called consonants.

**Word class:** the role a word plays within a sentence; sometimes called 'part of speech'.

**Table 1** Conjugating the verb 'to teach'

| To teach | Subject | Past | Present | Future |
|----------|---------|------|---------|--------|
| first-person singular | I | taught | teach | will teach |
| first-person plural | We | | | |
| second-person singular/plural | You | | | |
| third-person singular | He, she, it | | teaches | |
| third-person plural | They | | teach | |

**Table 2** Transitive and intransitive verb form

| Subject | Transitive verb | Object | |
|---------|-----------------|--------|---|
| Proper noun | Past tense of 'to write' | Indefinite article | Noun |
| John | wrote | a | letter. |
| Subject | Intransitive verb | Adverb | |
| Pronoun | Present tense of 'to write' | | |
| He | writes | eloquently. | |

**Table 3** Progressive tenses

| To be teaching | Past progressive | Present progressive |
|----------------|------------------|---------------------|
| first-person singular | I was teaching | I am teaching |
| first-person plural | We were teaching | We are teaching |
| second person | You were teaching | You are teaching |
| third-person singular | He, she, it was teaching | He, she, it is teaching |
| third-person plural | They were teaching | They are teaching |

**Table 4** Perfect tenses

| To have worked | Past perfect | Present perfect |
|----------------|--------------|-----------------|
| first-person singular | I had worked | I have worked |
| first-person plural | We had worked | We have worked |
| second person | You had worked | You have worked |
| third-person singular | He, she, it had worked | He, she, it has worked |
| third-person plural | They had worked | They have worked |

# Numeracy glossary

**Accuracy:** the degree of precision required, eg to the nearest whole number; requires rounding of the result of the calculation.

**Age:** actual age and reading age are measured in years and months. This may be written as year. month (where the dot is not a decimal point!) or year-month.

**Algebra:** the part of mathematics where letters are used instead of numbers.

**Area:** a measure of the space occupied by a two-dimensional shape, calculated by multiplying two lengths.

**Average:** a single value chosen or calculated to represent a group of values. See also *mean*, *median* and *mode*.

**Bar chart:** presents data as vertical or horizontal bars; the length of the bar indicates frequency of a data value.

**Box and whisker** diagram/plot: the 'whiskers' show the complete range of the data; the 'box' shows where half of the data lies (also called the interquartile range), the extent of which is established by identifying the upper quartile and the lower quartile.

**Capacity:** a measure of how much can fill a volume of space, measured in millilitres (ml), centilitres (cl) or litres (l).

**Cohort:** a group, eg of pupils, who share some common characteristic, eg who are studying German.

**Consistently:** following a trend over time with little change.

**Conversion:** process of changing from one currency to another, or from one number form to another (fraction, decimal, percentage), or from one unit to another (cm to m).

**Correlation:** a measure of the strength of a relationship between two variables; can be positive (one increases as the other increases) or negative (one increases as the other decreases); see diagram on page 172.

**Cost:** money amount calculated using the formula: cost = quantity × price.

**Cumulative frequency:** the total number of data items up to a given data value; can be plotted on a cumulative frequency curve which shows the number/proportion/percentage who, for example, scored up to a given value.

**Decimal:** numbers based on the denary number system; can have a decimal point, which indicates where the whole number part ends and the fractional part starts.

**Denominator:** bottom of a fraction.

**Distance:** a measure of length, usually measured in millimetres (mm), centimetres (cm), metres (m) or kilometres (km).

**Distribution:** the shape of the spread of data; the 'normal' distribution is a bell shape.

**Exchange rate:** information needed in order to convert an amount of money in one currency to an amount of money in another currency; usually given as a ratio.

**Factor:** of a whole number is another whole number that divides into it without a remainder.

**Formula:** a statement in words, or an equation using letters, to describe the relationship between two or more variables.

**Fraction:** part of a whole, expressed as one number (numerator) divided by another (denominator).

**Frequency:** the number of times a data value occurs; see also *cumulative frequency*.

**Graph:** see *cumulative frequency curve*, *line graph* and *scatter graph*.

**Greater than:** symbolised by >, compares two quantities and identifies the bigger of the two.

**Interquartile range:** a measure of spread, representing the middle half of the data; the difference between the upper quartile and the lower quartile.

**Less than:** symbolised by <, compares two quantities and identifies the smaller of the two.

**Line graph:** a visual representation of the relationship between two sets of related data; axes are labelled with the data being measured (eg scores against years). Points are plotted and a line drawn to join these points.

**Lower quartile:** the middlemost value of the bottom half of the data; marks the first 25% when data is arranged in ascending order.

**Lowest terms:** form of a fraction that cannot be divided – there is no common factor in the numerator and denominator. Also applies to ratios; the form for which there is no common factor for the two numbers.

**Mean:** an average; calculated by adding up all the values and then dividing by the number of values.

**Measure:** applies to money, time, length (or distance), area and volume.

**Median:** an average; the middlemost value when the values are arranged in order; for an even number of data values, the mean of the two middlemost values is used as the median.

**Mode:** an average, the value that occurs most frequently, ie with the highest frequency; the most popular.

**Money:** currency measured in £ (pounds sterling) in the United Kingdom, in € (euros) in the eurozone.

**Numerator:** top of a fraction.

**Order of operations:** the order in which, in the absence of brackets, a calculation should be carried out: multiply and divide first, then add and subtract.

**Percentage:** an amount measured out of 100; 30/10 = 30%; /100 represented by the % sign.

**Percentage points:** the amount, expressed as percentage, by which two percentages differ.

**Percentile:** when a data set is arranged in order and then divided into 100 parts, each part is a percentile; the first percentile is the value of the data item which marks the first $\frac{1}{100}$ of the data set.

**Perimeter:** the distance around a shape.

**Pie chart:** a method of presenting data; a circle cut into slices (from the centre to the circumference) with each sector of the circle representing a share of the total population.

**Place value:** the value of a digit, determined by its position within a number.

**Population:** in a survey, the group that is included in the data collection process.

**Prediction:** an estimate of future performance based on data from past event.

**Proportion:** the relationship between some part of a whole with the whole; usually expressed as a fraction, but can also be given as a percentage or as a decimal.

**Quartiles:** identify the quarter marks when the data is arranged in ascending order; see *lower quartile* and *upper quartile*.

**Range:** the difference between the highest and lowest values; gives a measure of the spread of the data.

**Ratio:** describes the relationship between two parts of a whole; expressed using the : sign.

**Raw data:** values as collected, prior to any production of statistics or presentation of the data in tabular form or using charts or other diagrams.

**Rounding:** adjusting the answer to a calculation to fit whatever level of accuracy is required; involves looking at the next digit and rounding up/down according to that digit. Depending on the context, it may be appropriate to round up or down, regardless of the place value of the digit to be rounded.

**Scatter graph:** compares two paired sets of data by recording, as a single point, each pair; each point represents, for example, one person.

**Sector:** part of a circle (a slice) created by two radii and the circumference between them.

**Simplest form:** see *lowest terms*.

**Speed:** the rate of change of position, measured for example in kilometres per hour.

**Spread:** a measure of how stretched or squeezed the data is in a distribution; also called dispersion.

**Statistics:** information derived from raw data.

**Table:** arrangements of rows and columns to present raw data in a concise fashion.

**Time:** measure involving seconds, minutes, hours, days, weeks and years.

**Trend:** when a line graph continues in a particular direction (upwards/downwards), this indicates a trend, eg of increasing scores, of decreasing numbers.

**Two-way table:** method of displaying raw data so as to compare two sets of data within a tabular format.

**Upper quartile:** the middlemost value of the top half of the data; marks position of 75% when data is arranged in ascending order.

**Variable:** data which varies, for example, over time or between people or tests or schools; examples include test scores or ages.

**Volume:** a measure of the space occupied by a three-dimensional shape, calculated by multiplying three lengths.

**Weighting:** a method of giving more credit to one test result than to another; usually expressed as a formula.

**Whole number:** a number with no fractional part.

# Abbreviations and acronyms

| | | | |
|---|---|---|---|
| **ALIS** | Advanced Level Information System | **LSCB** | Local Safeguarding Children Board |
| **AO** | assessment only | **m** | metre |
| **cl** | centilitre | **mm** | millimetre |
| **cm** | centimetre | **NCTL** | National College for Teaching and Leadership |
| **CME** | children missing education | **NEET** | not in education, employment or training |
| **CPD** | continuing professional development | **NSPCC** | National Society for the Prevention of Cruelty to Children |
| **DfE** | Department for Education | | |
| **dp** | decimal place(s) | **NVQ** | National Vocational Qualification |
| **EYFS** | Early Years Foundation Stage | **Ofsted** | Office for Standards in Education |
| **FAQ** | frequently asked question | **PC** | personal computer |
| **GCSE** | General Certificate of Secondary Education | **PGCE** | post-graduate certificate of education |
| **HM** | Her Majesty's | **QTS** | qualified teacher status |
| **HSE** | Health and Safety Executive | **RIS** | Researchers in Schools |
| **ITT** | initial teacher training | **RoSPA** | Royal Society for the Prevention of Accidents |
| **km** | kilometre | | |
| **KS** | key stage | **SCITT** | school-led training |
| **l** | litre | **SEN** | special educational needs |
| | | **SEP** | School Experience Programme |
| **LA** | local authority | **SKE** | subject knowledge enhancement |

# Index

Terms in **bold** are main topics from the Professional Skills Test specification.